CU00839372

Empire's First Soldiers

*To, Paddy
With Love
Ram
Sep 2015*

Empire's First Soldiers

D P Ramachandran

Lancer * New Delhi * Olympia Fields IL
www.lancerpublishers.com

Published in the United States

by Lancer Publishers,
a division of Lancer Inter Consult, Inc.
19900 Governors Drive, Suite 104
Olympia Fields IL 60461

Published in India

by Lancer Publishers & Distributors
2/42 (B), Sarvapriya Vihar,
New Delhi-110016

© DP Ramachandran 2008

All rights reserved. No part of this publication
may be reproduced, stored in a retrieval system or transmitted,
in any form or by any means, electronic, mechanical, photocopying,
recording or otherwise, without the prior permission of the publishers.
For additional information, contact Lancer Publishers

Printed at Sona Printers, New Delhi.
Printed and bound in India.

ISBN: 0-9796174-7-2   978-0-9796174-7-8

Online Military Bookshop
www.lancerpublishers.com

To

The Indian Soldier
Who demands so little, but gives so much

If indulging in self-conceit, though thinkest "I will not fight",
vain is this, thy resolve. Nature will compel thee.

The Bhagavadgita, XVIII, 59.

Contents

Book III
India at War

ACKNOWLEDGEMENTS

This book wouldn't have happened but for Mr. S. Muthiah, the well-known historian, entrusting me with the task of doing an article on the military history of Madras for the Association of British Scholars. I am therefore absolutely indebted to Mr. Muthiah, not only for acquainting me with the subject, but also for his guidance and encouragement while I worked on it.

I can't find words strong enough to thank Lt. Col. VM Mahendran, SM (Retd) of the Madras Regiment, whose collection of rare books on the history of his regiment – so generously made available to me – was my primary source of research to a large extent. A truly affectionate friend one could always count on, I cannot forget his readiness to help whenever needed, whether it's arranging for me to visit the Madras Regimental Centre at Wellington or filling me in with bits of information which I had difficulty in finding otherwise.

I am equally thankful to Brig. KP Chandrasekaran (Retd) of the Madras Engineers, for very kindly sharing his memories with me – being a very senior officer – of his days in service; and making his copy of the 'History of the Corps of Engineers' available to me, which was of invaluable help in comprehending the overall nature of the Sappers' war.

I owe a very special thanks to Col. SS Rajan (Retd) of the Bombay Engineers who, being a resident of Bangalore (and having had only e-mail acquaintance with me earlier), so kindly arranged for my visit to the Madras Engineer Group and Centre there, besides having been of constant help whenever I needed a technical clarification. I am indeed grateful to his entire family for their wonderful hospitality.

I am indebted to Lt. Col. CV Prathap, VSM (Retd) of the 16th Light

Cavalry, for helping me obtain the post-Independence history of his Regiment, and for recounting for me, his own experience as a young officer during the Indo-Pak War 1965.

I owe my gratitude to Brig. PV Sahadevan, AVSM, VrC, VSM (Retd) of the Madras Regiment, for granting me an interview, and recounting his experience – in as much details as possible after so many years – during the Battle of Basantar in 1971, wherein, as a major, he commanded one of the leading companies in the Indian attack.

Lastly, but most respectfully, I thank the oldest officer and the only World War II veteran I had had the honour to interact with on this project, Lt. Col. GT Thampi of the Gorkha Rifles, who had originally been commissioned in the Travancore State Forces. He patiently went through my initial draft with age-defying energy, and with great clarity of memory, was able to corroborate or correct the parts dealing with the turbulent period of 1940s. (Many personalities who appear in the text, but are no more, were personally known to him.) I remain grateful for his encouragement and blessing.

There are a number of other officers from all three wings of the Indian Armed Forces, both retired and serving, who have rendered help and support to me in the overall effort one way or the other. I am grateful to all of them.

Thank you; I hope to do you proud.

PREFACE

The 'Empire' intended in the title is the British one; but this book is neither an attempt to glorify that institution, nor one to vilify it. My story is about soldiering in India, and the British Empire just happens to be part of it. Behind this work is my firm conviction that the creation and evolution of the Indian Army has been one of the best things that happened to this country in the last three hundred years or so, no matter how and what the circumstances were. It may not sound fashionable in the current intellectual climate to talk of anything related to the empire even in remotely favourable terms. But then one cannot tell a story honestly without ridding oneself of the biases and baggage. Like millions of Indians of my generation born around the time of independence, I too grew up hating the 'wicked Englishman' who had enslaved the nation for almost two hundred years. However, having read a fair bit of history, and turned somewhat worldly-wise, I am inclined to view the British adventurism in India from an unbiased, and comparatively fairer, angle.

Without doubt, the British Empire in India was an accident of history. To start with, the British had no political ambitions when they established trade with the subcontinent in the 17th Century. They were content with their meek role as traders for nearly a hundred years of their presence in India initially. Even afterwards they were reluctant participants to begin with, in the politico-military struggle that ensued, and that too, primarily to counter the French militarism, consequent to the extension of the rivalry between the two European neighbours to the subcontinent. In fact, but for the penny-pinching policy of the French Government, it could very well have been a French Empire that resulted in India instead of a British one. Then again, French or British, no European empire would ever have been possible in India, but for the internecine quarrels of the native rulers of the land, which presented the ideal environment for a foreign power to exploit the situation. The British, at best, were just about as much in the game as so many other players were—they just turned out to be the smartest. If anything, the native rulers, the Rajahs and Nawabs and others of their ilk, who with their indulgence and criminal stupidity gave away their sovereignty in a platter to the foreigners, were the ones guilty of inflicting the shame of the British Empire on the country, than the British themselves, who after all, only took what was up for grabs, notwithstanding the utterly unscrupulous manner in which they went about it.

It is not even as if the empire was a crowning achievement of the British arms; essentially, India was conquered for the British by Indians. That's the subject of my story, at least part of it. As it turned out, the British who began their military enterprise in India in the mid-1700s by raising an army of the natives along the Coromandel Coast, ended up, by the end of the Second World War, with the largest voluntary army the world had ever known, a highly competent fighting force called the Indian Army, which had by then proved itself second to none in battlefields all across the world. The very survival of Britain's Indian Empire had by then, come to depend solely on the loyalty of this army. It had, in the British perspective of the day, assumed Frankenstein proportions.

Britain, weakened as she was after the war, and the dreadful experience of 1857 still haunting her, was in no shape to take on the might of the Indian Army, should it become rebellious. And there was every indication that it might, with small-scale mutinies, scattered though, being reported; the great army was getting restive. (The situation had turned so alarming, that some in the establishment had even begun working on a contingency plan, Operation 'Bedlam', for a possible scenario of the army turning hostile.) No wonder the British found themselves on thin ice as they were being hemmed in by the tumultuous events in the subcontinent at that juncture (the naval mutiny, the sudden volatility the nationalist movement had gained with the trial of the Indian National Army Prisoners, and the threat of an impending civil war due to communal tensions, to name the most notable of these), and meekly gave into the Indian demand for independence. There can be no doubt that they had very much been hastened in that decision by concerns of their grip weakening on the powerful sword that was the Indian Army. Historically parallel to this is the fact that, though suppressed, it was the Sepoy Rising of 1857 – a watershed like no other in India's British Experience – that put an end to the crude hegemony of East India Company and placed India directly under the British Crown; a step which, whether the British intended it so or not, was to put India on her inexorable march to freedom.

Thus, in a strange way, the Indian soldier, without whom Britain couldn't have created her empire, had himself proven inherently instrumental in dismantling it. Few political pundits – who espouse the theory of the independence having been solely won through the satyagraha movement – would want to admit though, that the impact of the armed forces in propelling the country towards her freedom was so profound.

I am neither a historian nor a political commentator. I am a mere enthusiast of military history, who likes reading about battles and wars, and enjoys, as a pastime, narrating a good story when I come across one. The argument put forth in the preceding paragraphs is intended only to make the point that in spite of the colonial aura of its beginnings, the Indian Army is one of the best things that could have happened to this country. This book is about its soldiers, who made the empire and broke it as well, in a manner of speaking. Not all of them are in it though; the story I have here is essentially that of the Southern Indian soldier, or the 'Madras soldier', as he is popularly identified. To begin with however, it is also the story of the entire Indian soldiery that we see today, since the Indian Army had its origins in South India, where the British first began raising a native army of 'Sepoys' in mid 18th Century. Towards the ending too, it once again evolves into a tale of the whole

xvi   Empire's First Soldiers

Indian Army, the modern day edifice that integrates troops from all over the country.

I was drawn to this subject while I was doing some research on the military history of the Madras City, to prepare a paper for the Association of British Scholars, which is compiling a record of the city. Southern India witnessed almost continuous warfare during the second half of the 18th Century, with two raging contests that came to be known as the 'Carnatic' and the 'Mysore' wars, culminating with the fall of Tipu Sultan, and the establishment of British supremacy over the entire region. In this cauldron of fire was born the Madras Army (closely followed by the raising of the other two Presidency Armies, the Bengal and the Bombay ones), mostly comprising natives recruited and trained in modern warfare by the British, along with a fair complement of European troops. Having evolved itself into a superb fighting force by the dawn of the 19th Century, it went on to win the Maratha Wars for the British during the first two decades of it, before reaping glory overseas by almost single-handedly winning three hard fought campaigns, the 1st and 2nd Burma Wars and the 1st China War, during the next thirty years or so.

By now Southern India had become somewhat of a backwater militarily, with the focus of the subcontinental operations shifting north and northwestward. This led to the stagnation and downsizing of the Madras Army (vis-à-vis the rapid expansion of the Bengal Army), with the British preferring to recruit troops from areas nearer to the theatre of operations; except for those with engineering skills, for whom they continued to be dependent on Southern India – the famed Madras Sappers and Miners – for the most part. Although a contingent of the Madras Infantry took part in the 3rd Burma War towards the end of the 19th Century, when all the three Presidency Armies were amalgamated to form the Indian Army in 1895, the Madras troops were the lowest represented in it. The situation continued to be so with the infantry and cavalry troops from the South going virtually extinct for a period, despite certain amount of mobilization and some units of the Madras

Infantry being engaged in action during the 1st World War. Finally it was the large-scale recruitment and operations during the 2nd World War which saw the Madras troops regain their former glory, so much so that by the end of the war, nearly one third of the Indian Army was constituted of troops from the South.

The Madras Regiment, re-raised during the war, has since expanded to take its rightful place amongst the finest regiments of Indian infantry, and also the pride of place of being the oldest among them. The Madras Sappers and Miners, formed into the Madras Engineer Group (MEG) in 1933 itself, carries its legacy of unhindered glory, having expanded multifold, enjoying the precedence of seniority over the other two engineer groups of the army, the Bombay and Bengal ones. Of the many regiments of the old Madras Native Cavalry which had their troop composition changed, one, the 16th Light Cavalry, had been restored to its former composition in 1946 to make it a fully South Indian Unit; the only cavalry regiment of the kind in the Indian Army now, which too enjoys precedence of being the senior most regiment of the Armoured Corps (as the cavalry as a whole has been designated after World War II). Apart from these exclusively South Indian segments of the army, we also have men from the South serving in large numbers in all arms and services, the army having since adopted a policy of mixed class composition in its ranks, with only old regiments as exception.

That, briefly, is the history of the Madras Army and its descendents who form part of the Indian Army today. This book however is not an elaboration of that history. Instead it merely attempts at the narration of all the major battles that were fought during the course of that history. Many of those battles were magnificent pieces of action that form the rich legacy of the Southern Soldier, tucked away in the folds of history. My endeavour is to recreate those battles in a reader friendly fashion. The historical background is touched upon only inasmuch as to maintain the storyline. Admittedly, towards the end of the book it becomes a story of the whole Indian Army, rather than that of the Madras troops as such (particularly the chapters on Siachen, Sri Lanka and Kargil), due to the composite manner of troops being engaged and lack of information on participation of individual units. These chapters as well as the ones on counter-insurgency operations and UN missions, all of which deal with contemporary subjects, merely outlines the story, since any attempt beyond that would have been unrealistic, given the limited information available. If I sound critical at times about the role of the political or military leadership involved (especially in the post-independence operations), it is only because I found it difficult to write on events that occurred in my own lifetime without mentioning the obvious.

This book is about battles, about men who fought them and about those who led them. The heroes on each occasion are the soldiers who fought well, irrespective where they came from or which side they fought on. From the perspective of my story, Robert Clive, who with barely 200 sepoys and 100 Europeans under him successfully defended the fort at Arcot against a 15,000-strong Mughal Army, was as much a hero as Haider Ali who, riding at the head of his swashbuckling cavalry, outwitted the British and terrorized them into submission at Madras. Kerala Varma Pazhassi Raja, who fought the British forces to a standstill with his guerilla army in the jungles of Wayanad, is one of the heroes in the book; and so is David Baird, who led the assault of the Madras Army on the fortifications of Seringapatam. Then there is the galaxy of Indian officers – from RS Noronha of the Madras Regiment who won his first Military Cross at Sita Ridge in Burma during the 2nd World War, to Rupesh Pradhan of the Madras Engineers who won his Vir Chakra at Kargil – who, in little over half a century, convincingly rebuffed the arrogant British notion that Indians cannot make good officers. The greatest heroes all throughout are of course, the men whom they all led, the doughty soldiers of the South.

This book in no way can be considered to contain a comprehensive history of the Madras Regiment, the Madras Engineer Group or the 16th Light Cavalry, except that the outline histories of these esteemed institutions form an integral part of my story. While all efforts have been made to ensure accuracy of information on this score, I render an unqualified apology for any errors that may have unwittingly crept in. I also regret that the names of many more gallant officers and men who were involved in the battles that I narrate, which eminently merit to appear in the pages of this book, do not do so due to constraints of space.

The underlying theme of my story, as the opening paragraphs of this preface suggest, is how India has stood to benefit from professional soldiering. But in the current scenario, it is ironical that a country like ours with the inherent advantage of possessing the finest fighting force in Asia should be seen by the world as a soft state, cowering in front of all and sundry. At the eve of the millennium when the country's External Affairs Minister escorted a bunch of thugs to Kandahar to be handed over to their cronies, our national honour stood defiled as never before. Then our parliament itself was attacked. One humiliation after another is heaped on us as the terrorists kill with absolute immunity – women and children are massacred in shopping malls, academics are attacked at institutions of excellence.

It is far too obvious that the parameters of national security and the rules of war have changed. The enemy, who no more wears a uniform, has far easier options to get where he wants to without getting into trouble with our soldier guarding the border from his pillbox. A busy market place or a crowded train offers a far favoured target for him than an army outpost. And no amount of vigilance can stop a crafty professional from creating mayhem. Mere commonsense should tell us that our current anti-terrorist operations, apart from being a hugely wasteful exercise, are proving counter-productive, fatally detrimental to the morale of the troops as the recent fratricidal killings within the forces show, and with the unfortunate consequence of alienating the soldiers from our own people.

It might very well be time that we made a stand, come what may, to defend the lives of our people and the nation's honour, even if it meant calling the enemy's bluff and taking the fight to him. But that certainly calls for a change in our collective mindset. We need to change from being a nation of moaners and whiners – as we so convincingly displayed to the whole world through television images of grown up men beating their breasts like nannies in front of the Prime Minister's house during the Kandahar crisis – to that of a resilient people who could, if called up on, live with 'blood, sweat and tears'.

A state founded on Gandhian ideals, it is only proper that we follow non-aggression on other countries of the world as a national policy. But that doesn't mean we forfeit the right to defend ourselves. We have been victims of aggression all through the history, because we always lacked military power. Now that we have it (thanks to the 'Empire', whether we want to admit it or not), we might as well use it, at least to a deterrent effect. Or else, we will be wasting a unique potential the country is bestowed with. The Indian soldier, given the benefit of proper training, has always won against formidable odds; he did that more than two hundred and fifty years ago on the banks of Adyar down south, and he did that so very recently on the heights of Kargil up north. That's the story I have.

June, 2007   DPR

GLOSSARY OF PLACE NAMES

(This glossary lists the names of places and countries spelt in the text as they were in the pre-independence days, against the original – uncorrupted – or changed form in which they are currently known)

Names as they appear in the text	Current name
Ahmednagar	Ahmadnagar
Alleppey	Alappuzha
Arni	Arani
Bombay	Mumbai
Burma	Myanmar
Calcutta	Kolkota
Calicut	Kozhikode
Canara	Kannad
Cannanore	Kannur
Cawnpore	Kanpur
Ceylon	Sri Lanka
Chingleput	Chengalpattu
Cochin	Kochi
Conjeeveram	kanchipuram
Coorg	Kodagu
Madras	Chennai
Madura	Madurai
Masulipatam	Machilipatnam
Nagapatam	Nagapattinam
Nagpore	Nagpur
Peking	Beijing
Poona	Pune
Pudukotta	Pudukkottai

Quilon	Kollam
Ramnad	Ramanathapuram
Seringapatam	Srirangapatna
Sholapore	Solapur
Tanjore	Thanjavur
Tellicherry	Thalassery
Tinnevelly	Tirunelveli
Tranquebar	Tarangambadi
Trichinopoly	Tiruchchirappalli
Trivandrum	Thiruvananthapuram
Vizagapatam	Vishakhapatnam
Wandiwash	Vandavasi
Ypres	Leper

LIST OF MAPS

BOOK I

WARS OF THE SOUTH

1

BATTLE OF ADYAR

A piece of action that charted the course of history

I t was a pleasant morning, going by the weather conditions round the year along the Coromandel Coast. The year was 1746, the month, that of October, and the date, the 24th. Little else but the weather has probably remained unchanged in over 250 years since. It's the time of the year when the Northeast Monsoon sets in, bringing relief to that parched stretch of India's eastern seaboard after six months of gruelling summer. With the rains, Adyar, the river that flows along the southern districts of the Madras Metropolis, Chennai if you will, often breaches the sandbar at its mouth to join the Bay of Bengal. For most part of the year otherwise, the bar contains the river as more or less a backwater, polluted with the urban filth now, but not so then when the city hadn't yet reached the river. Madras was no more than a township about four miles to the north, separated from the river itself by the old Portuguese settlement of San Thome, which eventually was to become a part of the city. If you stood overlooking the river's mouth even today, it's not difficult to visualize the scene. Towards the sandbar, that season, the river formed two channels, embracing an island in between. Here, across the expanse of the river, on that October morning, two armies faced each other, to fight a battle, the outcome of which, in the years to come, was to conceptualize the greatest military enterprise the Indian Subcontinent had known in all its history – the creation of the Indian Army.

Occupying the northern bank of the river, was the Army of the Nawab of Carnatic, 10,000-strong, commanded by the reigning Nawab's eldest son, Mahfuz Khan; the most powerful military force engaged in Southern India at that time. Facing them, on the southern bank, was a puny force, one tenth of its adversary in size, put together by *Compagnie des Indes Orientales*, the French East India Company, consisting of 300 Europeans and 700 sepoys, the French-trained Indian soldiers, under a Swiss engineer officer, Captain Louis Paradis. The Nawab's Army, with San Thome to its rear, stretched right up to the sea on the left, planting its artillery along the river bank, to contest the French force crossing; a quintessential David-versus-Goliath show. But cross the French did, the troops fording the river braving artillery fire, following the classic European technique of the musketry salvo; drawn up in three ranks and advancing, while firing successive volleys of shot. Then they fell on the enemy with the bayonets. The Nawab's line broke, and after a brief resistance at San Thome, his whole army fled westward. The French had made a point – numbers didn't matter; training and discipline did. The large ill-trained armies of the East could easily be defeated by much smaller forces, disciplined and well-trained in modern warfare as had been evolved in the West. And more significant was the assertion that so trained, the Indian soldiers could fight as good as or better than the Europeans, as the sepoys demonstrated, steady under fire with their musketry and drill, alongside the Europeans, in the Battle of Adyar. The lesson was not lost on the British, though they were only bystanders.

Brief though, the engagement had its background and causes dating back to an event which took place some two and a half centuries earlier, on the opposite side of the Peninsular India. On 27 May 1498, the Portuguese mariner, Vasco da Gama, landed at the port of Calicut on the Malabar Coast, after his historic voyage round the Cape of Good Hope, which opened the sea route to India for the Europeans for the first time. It marked the beginning of an era of trade and conquest in Asia by the European nations, intertwined with treachery and cunning, traitorously complemented by the inept native rulers and their internecine quarrels, which left most of the South and Southeast Asia colonized before the end of the 19th Century. Ironically, the Portuguese themselves were to perform in the final act of the colonial chapter of the Indian Subcontinent, when on 19 December 1961, four hundred and sixty-three years, six months, and twenty-two days, to the date after Vasco da Gama set foot at Calicut, the pitiful Portuguese garrison at Goa capitulated before the might of the free India's army, which marched in to wipe out that last bit of colonial shame from the country's soil.

In the beginning, it was all about trade; but imperialism soon raised its ugly head, and the rivalry between the European competitors readily found a parallel in the ongoing wars in the subcontinent between the indigenous forces, the two merging eventually to shape the history of the land. As pioneers in the game, the Portuguese managed to monopolize the Indian Ocean trade for over a hundred years, right through the 16th Century, while greedily pursuing their imperialistic designs with territorial acquisitions and the infamous Inquisition. And then came the Dutch, who appeared on the scene by the end of the 1500s. The Portuguese power was on the decline by the beginning of the 17th Century, and the Dutch started emerging the dominant maritime power, occupying one Portuguese possession after the other, to crown themselves as the most successful trading nation of that century. Britain was at it too, modest though, from early 17th Century itself. The English East India Company – John Company then – made its first foray into the mainland trade with the setting up of a factory at Surat, 150 miles north of Bombay on the West Coast, in 1612. They followed it up by gaining a toehold at Madras on the Coromandel Coast by the middle of the century, and erecting there the first ever English fort in the east, Fort St. George, named after England's patron saint.

About a mile to the south of the fort lay the Portuguese settlement of San Thome, established more than a century earlier. And 23 miles to the north, at a place called Pulicat, was a Dutch fort, erected in 1610. The Danes had formed a settlement too, at Tranquebar, 200 miles down south along the coast. The least successful in the race, they were destined to content themselves with that solitary possession. The French, though the last to arrive (the French East India Company having been formed only in 1664), launched themselves with great vigour. Commencing with a factory each at Surat on the West Coast and Masulipatam on the East Coast, they soon raised a settlement at Pondicherry, ninety miles south of Madras, which became the headquarters of all French activities in India. Before the end of the century, they were entrenched in Bengal too, with a settlement at Chandranagar. Thus, at the dawn of the 18th Century, the French and the British were emerging the new maritime powers to reckon with in the east, more or less overshadowing the Dutch, as they did the Portuguese, early the past century.

This was the period in Indian history when the once-powerful Mughal Empire was tottering. Aurangzeb Alamgir, the last of the Mughals who mattered, died in 1707, leaving behind a grossly ill-administered empire, on the verge of economic and military collapse; resultant of his disastrous military campaigns and religious intolerance. Zahir-ud-Din Babur, the first Mughal, had laid the foundations of that empire in Northern India early in 16th Century, even as the advent of the Portuguese was telling on the shores to the South. In about 200 years since, it had grown to encompass most of India.

Until the Mughal times, South India had remained more or less a Hindu domain under the Vijayanagar Empire, although the Muslim invasions had been ravaging the North for more than three centuries prior to Babur. Then in 1565, even before the Mughals had turned their full attention southward, the combined forces of two independent Muslim kingdoms of the Deccan, Bijapur and Golconda, defeated Sree Ranga Rayal, the Rajah of Vijayanagar, in the Battle of Talikota. Although his dynasty survived for almost a hundred years thereafter, moving its capital to Chandragiri further south, it ultimately collapsed under external aggression and internal dissent.

The Deccan kingdoms themselves were eventually annexed by Aurangzeb, but he was totally outwitted by a third – and a Hindu – power on the rise in the Deccan, the Marathas. Organized into a superb fighting force by *Chatrapathi* Shivaji, probably the finest military genius the subcontinent ever produced, they posed the biggest challenge to the Mughal power. They had also ventured southward into the Carnatic, occupying places as far as Tanjore, Gingee and Vellore, before the death of Shivaji in 1680. In the years to follow they were to grow into the most formidable military power in the subcontinent, well into building a Hindu Empire, until at last they were dealt a crushing blow by the defeat at the hands of Ahmed Shah Abdali, the King of Afghanistan, in the Third Battle of Panipat in 1761. Nevertheless, for almost a century, 1707 to 1805, Maratha power held sway over greater part of India, their fiery horsemen proving the scourge of many a territory (Their light cavalry was rated one of the best in the world). This added a new dimension to the military balance in the Carnatic, as it did almost everywhere across the land.

Six years after the death of Aurangzeb, Farrukh Siyar, the third emperor to succeed, appointed one of his generals, Asaf Jah, as the provincial ruler for the entire Deccan with the title, Nizam-ul-Mulk. Little over a decade from then, as the empire started breaking up; the Nizam became an independent sovereign, with Hyderabad as his capital. Towards 1740s, Dost Ali, the Nawab who ruled the Carnatic under the Nizam's writ, in a bid for independence, launched his own expansionist schemes, occupying the principalities of Trichinopoly and Madura, two of the last few remaining Hindu pockets in the South. But his attacks on the Maratha-held Tanjore boomeranged, and the Marathas, sweeping down from the north in 1740-41, took Trichinopoly. Dost Ali was killed and his son-in-law, Chanda Sahib, taken prisoner. The deceased Nawab's son, Safdar Ali, succeeded him but was murdered by his cousin, Murtaza Ali, in about a year's time. The Nizam intervened at this point, retook Trichinopoly, and replaced Murtaza by an officer of his own, Anwar-ud-Din Khan, early in 1743.

The new Nawab's seat was one insecure polity, with the partisans of the displaced family vying to stage a comeback; and to compound matters, there were also speculations adrift on the succession of the ageing Nizam. Southern India was soon to turn into a crucible of internal strife, with rival Nizams, Nawabs and Rajahs staking their claims, and the populace owing allegiance to none of them. Into this was added another element, as the Anglo-French rivalry – which had come to the fore with other Europeans out of the picture – spilled over into the politics of the land. Eventually, a bloody power struggle was to unfold in the Carnatic, between two main warring sections of the rulers, wherein the two European nations found themselves pitted against each other, supporting the opposite sides.

The declaration of war in Europe, between France and England in 1744, provided the catalyst for the drama to take shape. The French Governor in India at that time was a man of exceptional brilliance, evenly matched by his cunning, General Joseph Francois Dupleix. He had a vision that he was willing to stake his last penny to realize, a French Empire in India. Opportunity presented itself for him with the war, and he went for the jugular; to grab the prime possession of Britain in India, Madras. The township, by then more than a century since its founding, had grown into a prosperous trading post. Fort St. George, a small square structure of about 100 yards by 100 yards at the time of its inception, designed for a garrison of 100 soldiers, had been developed into a much bigger affair with a garrison of about 400 men; half of them Europeans, and the rest native Indians and *topass*-es, Eurasians of Indo-Portuguese lineage. But these were just for appearances. Madras, militarily, was a disaster waiting to happen. The Army of the English East India Company those days, if it could be called one, was merely a watch-and-ward outfit, comprising at best, soldiers or mercenaries well past their prime and untrained civilians recruited as peons and factory watchmen. Trade, and not warfare, was the priority of the Company even after 150 years of its presence in the Indian Ocean Zone.

The French, on the other hand, had pioneered the concept of sepoy levies[1], enrolment and training of Indian soldiers to fight under their colours. The sepoys – derived from '*sipahi*' in Persian, meaning 'soldier' – were recruited from footloose mercenaries, of whom Southern India seem to have had an abundance. They went where the money was good; warriors for hire. Not that the profession lacked social respect; on the contrary, to be a fighting man was considered a matter of honour. Neither did it make a difference under whose flag one fought, since the Indian nationhood, in a political and military sense, was a notion yet unborn. The French too found it an excellent proposition that gave them the much-needed military clout, without too much dependence on the European soldiery, who were hard to get and far more expensive to maintain. No wonder they felt bold enough to seize the initiative when the time came, with a plan of action.

All that the British had done by way of defence – with their traditional faith in naval strength – was to get the Admiralty at London to dispatch a naval squadron for the protection of the English interests in the Indian Ocean. In the event, when the French made their move in September 1746, the squadron under its cowardly commander, Commodore Edward Peyton, deserted the coast, leaving Madras to its fate. (The squadron had lost its original commander, Commodore Curtis Barnett, a brave and capable officer, to illness earlier.) The French force with nine ships and two bomb vessels, carrying some 3000 men, sailed from Pondicherry after nightfall on 1 September to appear before Madras at daybreak on the 3rd. It was commanded by Admiral Bernard la Bourdonnais, the Governor of Mauritius and Reunion (*isle de France* and *isle Bourbon* then, in French possession), an immensely capable man whose doggedness had done wonders in the development of those islands. Responding enthusiastically to a call for reinforcements from Dupleix, he had put together a squadron by fitting out country craft round a nucleus of one vessel of war and four merchantmen, and set sail in May 1746 with his 3000-men force

1. Dupleix is often credited with this innovation, which is factually incorrect. The term *sipahi* – for an Indian soldier in European service – was used by the French first at Mahe on the West Coast in 1721, when they were involved in hostilities with the neighbouring British settlement of Tellicherry. Later in North Africa they shortened it to sound *spahi*. The British made it to 'sepoy'. The Mahe sepoys were first brought to the East Coast by Dupleix's predecessor Dumas, and later more of them were inducted when war broke out with England.

on board, which comprised Europeans and the sepoys, as well as some Africans.

The British capitulated at Madras without much ado once the French troops landed and invested Fort St. George, and subjected it to bombardment from land as well as sea for a couple of days. The French commander in a hurry to occupy the fort, lest he be interrupted by the return of the British squadron, offered a 'treaty of ransom' under which the town would be returned to the British after the surrender on payment of a ransom. Accepting it, the Governor, Nicholas Morse, surrendered the fort on 10 September. The French had become the masters of Madras.

The Nawab of Carnatic, Anwar-ud-Din Khan, ever since he heard about the declaration of war in Europe, had been cautioning both the French at Pondicherry and the British at Madras, not to bring in their hostilities on to his shores. But for all the right noises, he didn't really back up the injunction militarily. (In fact it proved to be a British undoing to take him too seriously and blow the one chance they had, by not attacking Pondicherry while they could, when the naval squadron was in readiness with Commodore Barnett in command.) And when it became apparent that there was no stopping the French anyway, he extracted an assurance of sorts from Dupleix that Madras would be handed over to him if and when they took it. That however did not happen after they took possession of the township, and an indignant Nawab sought to settle the score. He waited until la Bourdonnais left with his fleet on 12 October after formalization of the treaty with the English; and then assembled an army under his son, Mahfuz Khan, at San Thome and St. Thomas Mount[2]. The French garrison of Madras, now commanded by M. Barthelemy, prepared for defence.

The native army moved in, and copying the French offensive, besieged the town from the west. The French, their water supply cut,

---

2. A small hill feature on the southwestern outskirts of Madras named after St. Thomas the Apostle, who is believed to have been martyred there.

made a sally on the 22nd and dislodged some of the enemy. Mahfuz Khan retired westward to Egmore and then to San Thome. The 1000-man force under Paradis, sent from Pondicherry to reinforce the beleaguered French, landed on the south bank of Adyar on the 24th morning, while a force of equal strength under another officer, De la Tour, marched southward from Madras to join the former. It wasn't a day for De la Tour to see action; Paradis and his men had already won the day before the former could get to the scene. The Nawab's army of 10,000 was routed in the Battle of Adyar (or Battle of San Thome, as chronicled at times), that one swift piece of action which turned out to be the genesis of a new soldiering culture to evolve in India down the years. Geoffrey Parker, one of the most eminent military historians of modern times, was to call it a 'turning point in Indian history'.

The immediate consequence of the battle was that San Thome, which was a Nawab's possession, became a French one. The place had always been a military hotspot, changing hands quite often between the various foreign and Indian powers, ever since its formation as a settlement by the Portuguese in early 1500s. But this time around for Dupleix the defeat of the Nawab meant much more than the possession of the place. With the native power held in check, he was the master of the situation. Rather unscrupulously, he went on to annul the treaty of ransom with the British. The British at Madras naturally resented this; and many soldiers and civilians held prisoner there escaped from the town and found their way to Fort St. David, an English possession near Cuddalore, 100 miles to the south, an old fort bought off the Marathas – and renamed – more than fifty years earlier. Among the escapees was young Robert Clive, who had joined the East India Company in Madras as a writer in 1744, when he was only 19. Following the fall of Madras the English activities in the peninsula came to be headquartered at Fort St. David, which became the target of repeated French attacks.

The British held on, somehow repulsing the attacks. Initially the Nawab kept his army in the neighbourhood in support, but later he made terms with the French and withdrew. Reprieve for the British came when a naval squadron of theirs under Commodore Thomas Griffin arrived at a most opportune moment, to repulse the severest French attack till then, in March 1747. Subsequent French attempts during the year too failed to take the fort. The English were finding the nerve to fight. The East India Company was also initiating measures to strengthen its army. Early 1748, Major Stringer Lawrence, a veteran of many wars, arrived from England and took over command of the garrison. A professional to the boot, he got straight down to business building a proper fighting outfit with whatever manpower he could find; a process that was to result in the creation of the Madras Army, the finest fighting force the subcontinent had known till then. The men of the Madras European Regiment[3] – which had been in existence for nearly a century by then, but had never seen a major battle – began to earn their keep for the first time. The artillery was beefed up too. But Lawrence carved a niche for himself in the annals of Indian military history by adopting a simple measure which his commonsense dictated – raising sepoy levies after the French model, and that heralded the beginnings of the native infantry. In time it was to become the mainstay of the army, and emerge as the forerunner of the Indian Army, since the British, tasting success with their experiment in the South, copied it in their other two presidencies, Bengal and Bombay, too.

Lawrence's skill and capability were soon on display when he repulsed a French attack in force at Cuddalore, timed when the English naval squadron was temporarily away in June that year. But even with a field commander of his calibre the British could do no more than hold off the French, until the arrival of Admiral Edward Boscawen from

---

3. The 1st Battalion of the European Regiment of the East India Company was raised at Madras in 1668, mostly with men recruited from London. In the years that followed the fighting at Fort St. David, it was to mould itself into a great regiment, which saw glorious service. Renamed, first the Royal Madras Fusiliers, and later when taken over by the British Government, the 102nd Foot, it finally became the Royal Dublin Fusiliers; and was again serving in Madras in 1922 when disbanded, after Southern Ireland became an independent republic. A brass tablet, close to the pulpit at the St. Mary's Church at Fort St. George, commemorates this British regiment born in Madras, with its unique history.

England in July with a large flotilla carrying twelve companies of troops. The garrison now with some 4000 Europeans and 20,000 Indians found itself in a dominant position for the first time. The admiral went on the offensive almost immediately, attacking Pondicherry, with Lawrence joining by land. An ill-conceived move, it ended in a fiasco with Lawrence being taken prisoner, and the admiral having had to lift the siege he had laid with the onset of monsoon in October. The French continued to have the upper hand. However before the end of the year, hostilities were called off following the peace agreement of Aix-la-Chapelle between France and England. Lawrence was released, and Madras was to be restored to the British. The first chapter of the Anglo-French rivalry in India was over, and by then the sepoy force had become a common military feature of both the sides.

The officers and men of the Madras garrison, as well as many civilians with them, distinguished themselves in the actions at Fort St. David. Of the civilian volunteers, the greatest acclaim went to Robert Clive, who was granted an ensign's commission. Lawrence had instinctively recognized the outstanding soldierly traits in the young ensign, and taken him under his wings. Promoted a lieutenant, Clive accompanied Lawrence on a brief expedition to Tanjore to restore the throne of the deposed Raja there, and later as his quartermaster to Madras when it was restored to the British in August 1749. The close association of these two remarkable men was to lead to far reaching consequences; one would be remembered as the creator of the British Empire in India, and the other, as the 'father of the Indian Army'.

2

ARCOT

The making of a legend

On the dusty plains inland, seventy miles to the west of Madras, lay the town of Arcot, the capital of the Nawab of Carnatic. Even as the French and British guns fell silent in 1748, trouble was brewing in the Carnatic, which would in three years' time, draw every warring faction to this historic township, for their rendezvous with destiny. Asaf Jah, the old Nizam, died that year, and the succession by his son, Nazir Jang, was contested by a grandson, Musaffar Jang. Chanda Sahib, released by the Marathas and reappearing in the Carnatic with their support at this juncture, pledged his support to Musaffar Jang. Dupleix, with his own axe to grind, supported the duo. A master of political intrigue, who possessed a great insight of the weaknesses inherent in India's political system, he was waiting for just such an opportunity to exploit those to meet his own ends. He had contrived the effective use of his limited military strength to tilt the balance of forces as it suited him, until the very sovereignty of the Indian rulers became dependent on his support – the classical ruse the British were to employ to build their empire in India in later years.

In August 1749, just about the time Madras was being restored to

---

1   Admiral Boscawen formally took possession of Fort St. George from the French in August 1749 as per the terms of the peace treaty, and subsequently, learning of Dupleix's designs to keep San Thome in French possession, annexed the town in October that year, hoisting the British colours there uncontested, finally making it a part of the city. Madras continued to remain a subordinate station to Fort St. David until April 1752, when it again became the capital of the Presidency.

the British[1], the two Indian princes and their French allies attacked and defeated the reigning Nawab of Carnatic, Anwar-ud-Din. The Nawab was slain in battle, his elder son, Mahfuz Khan, captured, and his capital, Arcot, taken. His younger son, Muhammed Ali, escaped to Trichinopoly, 200 miles south, with a small force, and set himself up as the Nawab with the blessings of Nazir Jang, the Nizam, and some help from the British. In the ultimate lineup, on one side were Musaffar Jang and Chanda Sahib, actively supported by the French, and on the other, Nazir Jang and Muhammed Ali, with a rather halfhearted British support. It was an undeclared war between the two European nations who were otherwise supposed to be at peace with each other.

In May 1750, Nazir Jang descended on the Carnatic with a massive army, and defeated his French-sponsored rivals; but in December that year, he was assassinated. Muhammed Ali again took refuge in Trichinopoly, with a British garrison for protection. Musaffar Jang, who was elevated the Nizam by the French, was promptly ambushed and murdered by some remnant forces loyal to his murdered predecessor. The French set up Salabat Jang, the brother of Nazir Jang, as the new Nizam. Even as the military environment in the Carnatic turned so explosive, the East India Company chose to adopt the bizarre measure of cutting down the salary of Stringer Lawrence substantially, prompting him to quit the job in a huff and go home early in 1751. The British, still headquartered at Fort St. David, were once again left with no competent field commander to handle a crisis. An attempt to recover Madura which had been occupied by Chanda Sahib by a British force, dispatched from Trichinopoly under Captain James Cope, was soundly beaten back. Another force under a grossly incompetent Swiss mercenary, Captain Rudolph de Guingins, dispatched from Fort St. David to stem the enemy advance on Trichinopoly, abandoned the field and fled, without even putting up a fight when confronted by the enemy at a place called Volconda.

De Guingins ended up taking refuge in Trchinopoly himself, cooped up with Muhammed Ali. The French and their allies laid siege to the place.

Robert Clive who had reverted to civilian life, but had accompanied the expedition of De Guingins in his capacity as the Commissary, witnessed this humiliating turn of events with growing frustration. Fiercely determined to salvage the honour of the British arms, he rode back to Fort St. David and offered to join the army without pay, provided he was given a captain's commission. He wanted his own command, and a captain's rank would ensure that. The Governor, Thomas Saunders, desperately short of officers, agreed. Lawrence's absence was to propel Clive into fame, and a place in history that would engross posterity.

After being engaged in a couple of supply and reinforcement missions to Trichinopoly initially, Clive volunteered to lead an expedition to Arcot for an attack on the town, the thinly held capital of Chanda Sahib, as a diversionary tactics to relieve the pressure on Trichinopoly. It was an audacious plan, originally put forward by the young Nawab, Muhammed Ali, and Clive persuaded Saunders to approve it. Gathering whatever troops that could be spared, he proceeded to Madras where he was reinforced by troops of the Fort St. George garrison. He marched out of Madras at the head of a column of 200 Europeans and 500 sepoys with three field guns between them, late in August 1751. He had eight officers; all of them civilian volunteers. After a week-long march through the scorching sun and drenching rain at a mile-eating pace, which tested the endurance of the troops to the extreme, the column entered Arcot on 1 September uncontested.

The swiftness of the move stumped the enemy's chance to reinforce their fort, and the 1000-strong garrison had fled without a fight. But Clive's small force was far from secure holding the town. The enemy garrison was camped within striking distance, and a force of 2000 horsemen was on the way from Trichinopoly to reinforce them. And the fort that there was, was hardly a defensible one. Situated right in the middle of the town, the closely built up areas surrounding it gave excellent cover for the enemy, and its mile-long walls were far too extensive to be defended by 700 men. The crumbling bastions couldn't support cannons, and the moat had been filled in at many places. Attempts to do up the defences and burn down the surrounding buildings for better field of fire met with no success. Clive decided to take the fight to the enemy, and took out a sally to their camp; but they pulled away. Yet another raid, a surprise one at night, after about a fortnight, met with better luck and caused some casualties and disarray in the enemy ranks.

The enemy made the first move after about a fortnight, with a night attack, when the British force was depleted considerably, having sent out a large detachment to Conjeeveram, almost half the way to Madras, to escort two guns arriving to bolster the defences of the fort. The defenders however fought it off successfully. But they were in deep trouble soon with the arrival of some 4000 enemy troops, including some French ones, commanded by Raza Sahib, Chanda Sahib's younger son. And there was news of more reinforcements to follow. Now to add to the defenders' woes, they were forced to depart with 250 men, who were sent back to Madras, which was under threat of being attacked. Clive was left with just 120 Europeans and 200 sepoys, not counting the sick and the wounded.

During the night on 23 September, the enemy army moved in and occupied the town. In a desperate bid to surprise them Clive's men pushed their artillery pieces out of the fort and opened up, even attempting to seize the French guns which were abandoned for a while. It only resulted in disaster when the enemy snipers took them on from the built-up area around, and the men had to withdraw in a hurry, hauling their guns back into the fort under intense fire. The casualty toll was heavy; fifteen killed and as many wounded. Engaging the enemy outside the fort was no more an option; Clive resolved to make a stand within the fort. The siege of Arcot was on, a saga of endurance and courage that was to last fifty long days.

The besieging army of Raza Sahib had at least 10,000 men in its ranks, against Clive's 300 holding the fort. The defenders faced a formidable challenge. They were fairly well off on provisions, with stocks enough to sustain them for at least three months. And, brackish though, water was available in a reservoir, thanks to the ingenuity of a local mason who blocked the channel through which it could be drained from outside. But the manpower was sheerly inadequate to man the battlements and patrol the walls constantly. The sniper fire was so intense that the sentries could hardly raise their heads above the parapet, and the fear of a surprise attack loomed large perpetually. The enemy fire took its toll; casualties were mounting, and that, added with sickness and fatigue, was telling on the morale of the men. Clive and his officers plodded on, tenacious and determined, trying to cheer up their men; always assuring them that relief was at hand. To break the monotony they attempted a sortie once and exchanged some artillery fire with the besiegers, but all of it came to nothing.

The enemy didn't attack either, playing the waiting game to wear the men down. Clive desperately hoped for some reinforcements to arrive. He had somehow kept his communication open with Saunders at Fort St. David, through Indian horse couriers who were pretty fast, and news arrived ultimately that a relief column of 130 Europeans and 100 sepoys was on its way. It was too small a force for the task; nevertheless, the news helped lift the spirits of the men immensely. Then came the shattering bit; the tiny force had been intercepted by a large enemy force, and had had to return to Madras.

The siege went on without let up, through October and into November, intense musketry raking the fort walls constantly. To add to the enemy's clout, some French heavy guns arrived from Pondicherry, and started pounding the fort mercilessly. One of the two British 18-pounders was disabled. The fort walls were reduced to rubble at many points. The defenders desperately struggled to throw up improvised works. The situation was getting out of hand. The garrison had by now been reduced to a pitiful 200; 80 Europeans and 120 sepoys still on their feet. Doggedly, they persevered.

Early in November there was news that some 6000 Marathas

hired by Nawab Muhammed Ali were closing in on Arcot to help the British; a morale booster for the battle weary troops. There was more to cheer about, as news arrived that a new relief force under Captain James Kilpatrick was on its way from Madras. These were disconcerting developments for the besieging army. Raza Sahib resolved to put pressure on the British before it was too late. He served an ultimatum to Clive, to surrender on fair terms or be annihilated. Clive rejected it with scorn. Raza Sahib's army of almost 15,000 moved for the offensive. The valiant 200 at the fort braced themselves for the assault.

The attack came at the predawn hour on 14 November. The leading attackers rushed forward with ladders to scale the walls screaming battle cries, while elephants, their foreheads protected by iron shields, charged at the gates to batter them down. A horde of attacking infantry milled around behind with muskets and spears. The elephants were taken care of easily enough, as the defenders opened fire from the fort, aiming for their unprotected flanks. The beasts reared up in pain, and stampeded the troops behind. By then, attacks were being mounted on two major breaches caused by the French guns. Clive had his men concentrating their fire on these breaches, the frontline musketeers backed up by loaders, who handed them a loaded weapon as soon as they had fired one and handed it back. This rapid fire blunted the attacks. Men at the ramparts hurled down grenades on the second line of attackers to stem their rush.

On one of the breaches the commander of the attacking forces, Abdul Khader Khan, was shot down as he led his men from the front in a ferocious charge. On the other breach where the moat was deep, a raft on which a number of attacking troops tried crossing over capsized as the defenders brought down gunfire on it. Wave after wave of brave but disorganized attacks were being driven off by the defenders who kept their cool. The attack, extremely gallant if reckless, was wavering. And the French allies of Raza Sahib refused to join the battle; their commander, Goupil, having earlier disapproved the storming of the fort. Raza Sahib realized that the battle was lost, and disengaged. The attack had lasted only one hour. 300 men of the attacking army lay dead scattered around the fort. The defenders' losses were just four dead and two wounded.

Within the fort the exhausted garrison picked itself up for the next assault, as the enemy kept up relentless cannon fire and musketry. By noon they called off firing, and under a flag of truce, sought permission to carry their dead, which was granted. Once the bodies were carried off, the pounding commenced again. It went on for twelve hours, until it ceased at two in the morning. Clive and his men waited tensely for the next predawn assault, which they had no doubt would be coming. But it didn't – when the day broke, they found the enemy gone; the bombardment was merely to cover the retreat. The siege had been lifted.

Raza Sahib, it turned out, had no more had the option to stage another attack. He had information that was yet to reach Clive; Kilpatrick with his relief column was less than a day away. They entered Arcot that afternoon. And the Marathas under their fearsome leader, Morari Rao, weren't very far either. After 75 days of entering Arcot and 50 days of closed siege, Clive and his men had won a victory, the like of which comes along but rarely in military history anywhere. Robert Harvey, the author of a recently written biography of Clive, laments the relative obscurity of this feat in the history of the British arms, in these eloquent words:

There were to be few greater expeditions in the history of British arms. The 600 who rode down the valley of death in the Crimea a hundred years later went down in posterity as an example of bravery – and bungling. Clive's 700 – reduced to 300 in the actual defence of Arcot – are much less popularly celebrated, but their feat was achieved against far greater odds. It was an example of staggering boldness, resolution and, above all, endurance. Perhaps it was only their success that was to diminish their achievement in the eyes of their fellow countrymen. The British – like the Japanese – respect the nobility of failure.

Even in the best of accounts written on the saga of Arcot, and the many more battles which the Britons and Indians fought together that were to take place during the era that followed, of almost two centuries until the end of the Second World War, a fact which is seldom highlighted in adequate measure is that, more than half the men who fought these battles were Indians; and many more were fought by them alone, officered by the British though. But then, the sepoys only made history; they didn't write them – the westerners did.

Arcot, after Adyar, displayed once again, that given the benefit of proper training, the sepoy could turn out to be a formidably staunch fighter. While Adyar was a one-stroke affair, when Louis Paradis combined surprise with the dash and discipline of his troops, Arcot proved to be a testing ground of grit and determination, not only for Robert Clive, but for his sepoys and the Madras Europeans as well. Although they all had seen a fair amount of action at Fort St. David, they had nothing concrete to show by way of a laudable victory. The French in fact, had turned out by far the stronger side. It was the first occasion when the mettle of the sepoys was tested under such duress, and they came out with flying colours.

The Arcot lore even has a mythical tale praising the sepoys' sacrificial trait, when they gave away their rice rations to their European comrades who were more susceptible to hunger, and sustained themselves on the water in which the rice was cooked. Of course this sounds rather improbable; knowing as we do that the garrison was fairly well provisioned during the siege. However the siege did generate a lot of camaraderie between the two, as it often happens between men who stand by each other when the chips are down. And the sad fact that no official recognition was accorded to the sepoys' contribution – unlike that of the Madras European Regiment, which was awarded the Battle Honour, ARCOT, the oldest battle honour to be awarded by Britain for operations in India – could only be attributed to the reason that the sepoys were yet to be organized into identifiable regiments or units. Nevertheless, they proved themselves fine fighting men, who only needed the right leadership. The raw courage of the sepoys was never in question, as the ones in Raza Sahib's army demonstrated when they stormed the fort. In fact, the winning sides at Adyar and Arcot, one French and the other British, had one factor in common; both had leaders who were brave and competent. The watchword of warfare couldn't have been amplified better – There are no good soldiers and bad soldiers; there are only good officers and bad officers.

The British victory at Arcot altered the course of conflict going on in the Carnatic almost irrevocably. The aura of invincibility that the French had built up about themselves had been effectively challenged for the first time, when a native army supported by them was foiled in its bid to take the fort by a tiny but determined British garrison. Clive, the hero of the hour, more than anyone else, was to exploit the situation to the hilt, to the advantage of the British. After a fortnight of rest and recuperation, he set out in pursuit of the defeated army of Raza Sahib, to destroy it if he could, before the French had time to reinforce it and stabilize the situation. He had a force of over 1000 – 200 Europeans, 300 sepoys and 600 Maratha horsemen – for the mission. But as it turned out the hunter became the hunted, and he found himself drawn up in defence on 3 December with his force holding a hillock near the town of Arni, 17 miles south of Arcot, against a French-led force, superior in numbers and well-organized.

The attackers had to traverse a flooded rice field to access the position frontally, and were restricted to move along a narrow causeway. Clive skillfully brought down his artillery fire down the slope to break up the advance guard and pin the enemy down. Meanwhile a flanking column of the enemy had come up against the Maratha cavalry holding the left, and the repeated charges the horsemen made were being beaten back. Clive ordered two guns to go to the support of the Marathas. A confusion created by the gunners when they forgot to carry the ammunition and had to retract was misinterpreted by the French, as an attempt to snatch their guns that were exposed and undefended on the causeway. They pulled out part of the force on the left flank to go to the defence of the guns. This gave the Marathas the break they needed, and supported by British guns, they launched an attack, driving the enemy back.

Simultaneously, the sepoys deployed to the right of the position launched an attack on the French reinforcements sent to protect the guns, hemmed in as they were by the musket fire from the hillock. Clive now sent his remaining troops sweeping down the hill to push the enemy back from the causeway. The French and their sepoys fought back furiously, but in the end lost ground under relentless pressure. Meanwhile the Marathas too were forcing the enemy back on the left flank. They continued the attack through the night, even as Clive broke off from the fight. By the next morning the enemy was gone, leaving behind their dead and the wounded, about 200, 50 of them French. Clive had a dozen sepoy casualties, and none British or Maratha. For the first time, he had won a major field battle, and that, against a well-trained enemy. His military reputation was on the rise.

The British had taken a leaf out of the French book and gone for the sepoy levies. At Arni, the British sepoys had got the better of the French ones. And soon many were deserting the French and joining up with Clive. The sepoys, British or French, admired the winners, and had no time for a side that won't join the battle, as the French did at Arcot; no matter what. It remains doubtful whether Clive could have withstood the final enemy assault at Arcot, had Raza Sahib's sepoys not been denied the French support at the crucial hour. It was the history's moment, when M. Goupil, the French commander at Arcot, could, in all probability, have prevented the British Empire in India from happening, or even helped create one of France.

Clive followed up his victory at Arni with an attack on Conjeeveram, where a small enemy force under a Portuguese mercenary was holding two British officers as hostages. A one-sided affair where the enemy had no artillery and the Indian governor of the township had colluded with Clive, it was over in two days with the enemy force fleeing at night, leaving behind the hostages; but not before Clive had lost one of his best officers and close friend, John Bulkley, cut down by enemy fire.

Sending half his troops to Arcot, Clive now returned to Fort St. David to a hero's welcome. But there wasn't to be any rest, as early in 1752 Madras came under attack by Raza Sahib's army, still showing plenty of teeth, though depleted.

Clive rushed to the rescue with some 500 sepoys; and reinforced by troops sent by Kilpatrick from Arcot and some British soldiers arriving from Bengal by coincidence, stalemated Raza Sahib with a force almost equal to his. Raza Sahib pulled out with his force, and in a smart move, headed for Arcot to attack the poorly defended township. Clive's forces rushed after them, and walked straight into an ambush at Kaveripak, ten miles short of Arcot, late in the evening on 28 February. It was brilliantly planned and executed by Raza Sahib, proving himself for once equal in stature to any of the European commanders in the field. The British found themselves in a precarious situation, with enemy cannons blasting them from all around in the darkness. Then luck and treachery intervened in Clive's favour, as was to happen again in his military career at a future date, at the historic battle of Plassey; a stigma that will haunt him to the end of his days, and a legacy of shame that Indians as a people would carry for ever. Through a *topass* acting as his spy, he succeeded in bribing off an Indian commander, who turned traitor to pull out his troops holding one of the flanks, enabling the British force to get behind the position unnoticed, and stage a surprise attack. Caught unawares, the ambush broke, and Clive was able to extricate himself and his men to safety, having lost some 40 Europeans and 30 sepoys.

It was a decisive defeat for Raza Sahib, whose forces melted away. But the war was far from over. The French and their allies still held the cards, as Trichinopoly was under their siege, with Nawab Muhammed Ali trapped in the town in the company of the cowardly British commander, de Guingins, and his troops. Clive's victories had in no way persuaded Chanda Sahib, the French protégé, to give up his advantage. In the event, it would take a lot more of battling before the British could accomplish that. The day of the sepoy had just begun.

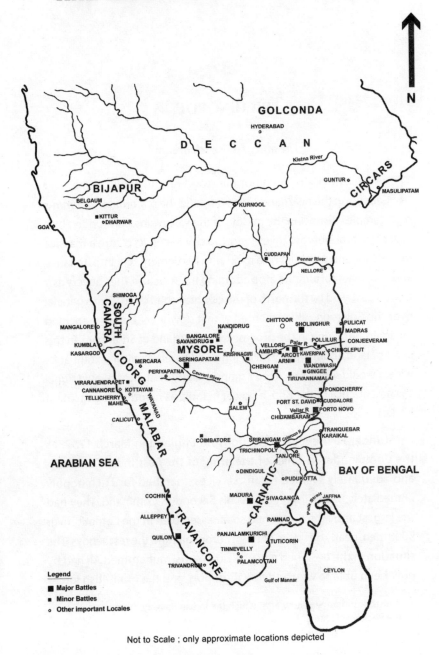

CARNATIC & MYSORE WARS AND REBELLIONS OF THE SOUTH

N

GOLCONDA

HYDERABAD

D E C C A N

Kistna River

CIRCARS

BIJAPUR

BELGAUM

GUNTUR

MASULIPATAM

KITTUR
DHARWAR

GOA

KURNOOL

CUDDAPAH

Pennar River

NELLORE

SHIMOGA

SOUTH CANARA

MANGALORE

NANDIDRUG

CHITTOOR

SHOLINGHUR

PULICAT
MADRAS

KUMBLA

BANGALORE
SAVANDRUG

POLLILUR

CONJEEVERAM

KASARGOD

MYSORE

VELLORE

Palar R.

KRISHNAGIRI

AMBUR

ARCOT

KAVERIPAK

CHINGLEPUT

COORG

MERCARA

SERINGAPATAM

CHENGAM

ARNI

WANDIWASH

PERIYAPATNA

Cauveri River

GINGEE

TIRUVANNAMALAI

VIRARAJENDRAPET

CANNANORE

KOTTAYAM

WAYNAD

PONDICHERRY

TELLICHERRY

MAHE

SALEM

FORT ST. DAVID

CUDDALORE

MALABAR

Vellar R.

PORTO NOVO

CALICUT

CHIDAMBARAM

COIMBATORE

SRIRANGAM

Coleroon R.

TRANQUEBAR

KARAIKAL

TRICHINOPOLY

TANJORE

ARABIAN SEA

DINDIGUL

PUDUKOTTA

CARNATIC

BAY OF BENGAL

COCHIN

MADURA

SIVAGANGA

Palk Strait

JAFFNA

ALLEPPEY

RAMNAD

TRAVANCORE

QUILON

PANJALAMKURICHI

TUTICORIN

TINNEVELLY

TRIVANDRUM

PALAMCOTTAH

CEYLON

Gulf of Mannar

Legend
■ Major Battles
■ Minor Battles
○ Other important Locales

Not to Scale ; only approximate locations depicted

3

TRICHINOPOLY

The end of a French dream

The ancient city of Trichinopoly stood on the banks of the river Cauvery in the heartland of the Carnatic, the tall, ornate *gopuram*-s of its temples distinct in the middle of the vast plains. Surrounded by a wall of sorts about four miles long, the city had in its centre a massive fortress, ingeniously built on a rock[1] with battlements cut into its flanks, and two beautiful temples atop adorning the structure. The Cauvery as it flowed eastward by the north of the city, branched off to form a parallel river, the Coleroon, which merged with it downriver before branching off again, enclosing in the process the river island of Srirangam. In this sliver of land about twenty miles long and barely a mile in extent at its widest, would soon be enacted a grand military drama, that would signal the ascendancy of the British power in India as no other engagement hitherto did.

Stringer Lawrence, returning from England in March 1752, as the Commander-in-Chief of the army of the East India Company, and adequately salaried for his services, marched for Trichinopoly immediately, with Clive in tow as his Second-in-Command. They had the largest army the British had so far assembled in the Carnatic, over 3000 men, nearly one third of them Europeans and the rest sepoys. The situation in the besieged city was ridiculous. Muhammed Ali had by now been able to woo additional support, and the pro-British forces

---

1. A historic monument now, after which the Indian Railways have named a train, the Rock Fort Express.

in the city, which included those of his own and his allies, the Prince of Mysore and the Regent of Tanjore, as well as Morari Rao's Marathas, numbered about 40,000 men, outnumbering the besieging army of 30,000 or so. Still, de Guingins, distrusting the loyalty of his Indian allies, refused to attack. The besieging armies of Chanda Sahib and the French commander, Jacques Law, were camped to the east of the city.

Arriving on the plains outside Trichinopoly on the morning of 29 March, Lawrence's force was met by Captain John Dalton, a Fort St. David veteran, with a force of some 200 Europeans and 400 sepoys. They had come out of the fort un-intercepted by the besiegers. Even as the two forces halted for breakfast, they were attacked by a huge enemy force. Lawrence rallied his forces to counter the threat, and the two armies faced each other across the vast plain. A thundering cannonade followed, when the two sides matched each other's firepower. The British scored an advantage by positioning their guns under the cover of a village nearby. The enemy guns, caught out in the open, were forced to withdraw in the end, and their infantry, and finally the cavalry, followed suit after holding on their own for quite some time. It was a successful start for the British, which helped lift the spirits of the besieged army. Lawrence however could not go on the offensive, since his Indian allies chose to wait for an astrologically suitable day. In frustration, he attempted a raid of the enemy camp at night; but the party sent on the mission missed the camp altogether in the dark, and was spotted by the French while it returned to the city at dawn. The French commander, now unnerved by the possibility of being attacked in the open, withdrew his force across the river to Srirangam.

The towering structure of a Vishnu temple at the middle of the island – a marvel of Indian architecture, it is one of Southern India's main pilgrim centres and a great tourist attraction now – dominated the landscape, with a similar but smaller temple nearby. Both were multi-walled and well-fortified, offering the French a safe haven. Lawrence reacted swiftly, by dispatching a force under Clive across the two rivers to cut off Law's line of communication with Pondicherry northward.

The force consisted of nearly half the troops the British had; some 400 Europeans, 1200 sepoys, 700 Marathas, and most of the Tanjore Army. Lawrence was left with 500 Europeans, 1000 sepoys, the remaining Marathas and a large contingent of Mysore. Clive's force forded the rivers during the night of 4 April, and took up position in two strongly walled temples at the village of Samayapuram in the neighbourhood of Srirangam to the north, effectively isolating Law. In a strange reversal of roles, the besiegers had become the besieged, before they had even seriously engaged each other.

News arrived within a few days that French reinforcements under an old general, Monsieur d' Auteuil, were on its way. Clive, intending to ambush the column at Utatur, a narrow pass a few miles from his position, requested Lawrence for additional troops to hold Samayapuram while he moved out on the mission. Lawrence, not prepared to split his forces anymore, refused to oblige. Clive went for a gamble, marching out with his entire force by nightfall to lay the ambush, leaving Samayapuram virtually unguarded. Law got the wind of it in no time, and had had a force of some 80 Frenchmen and 500 sepoys dispatched forthwith to seize the temples at Samayapuram.

Clive, when he had force marched his men to Utatur, found that the French general had called a halt, well-protected within a fort there; and rushed back to Samayapuram, to arrive at the temple complex by eleven o' clock. Just about the same time, the French force, making its way to Samayapuram in the dark, captured a British sepoy, who told them about Clive's return. But Calquier, the French commander, didn't quite believe it, and had the prisoner lead his troops to the British camp at gunpoint. An English deserter and a former sergeant, Kelsey, now a French officer with Calquier, bluffed his way through into the British camp with his troops, and to Clive's quarters itself, posing as a British officer bringing in reinforcements from Trichinopoly. The cover was blown when he failed to give the password when challenged by the sentry at the entrance to Clive's quarters, and fighting broke out.

In the melee that ensued with furious hand to hand fighting in the dark, Clive himself was slashed on the face and some men cut down on either side. At the end of it the French found themselves holding the smaller of the two temples, while Clive rallied his men at the bigger temple. After intense exchange of fire throughout the night the British tried to storm the enemy position at dawn, but were beaten back. So were the French when they tried to break out, their commander impaled to death in the process. Clive tried to negotiate as the stand-off continued, but Kelsey, now in command of the French, won't surrender, aware that being a deserter he faced certain execution. However at length, outnumbered and isolated, and many of his soldiers deserting, he surrendered, and was promptly hanged to death, along with the unfortunate British sepoy who had led the French into the camp.

Fresh information arriving told Clive of Law and Chanda Sahib preparing to attack his position, by transporting the troops across the rivers on rafts; the water levels being on the rise. Finding himself in the dire predicament of getting trapped in a pincer movement if d'Auteuil chose to move against him from Utatur, he asked for reinforcements once again; but Lawrence refused this time too. Determined to have his way, Clive crossed the river on horseback to plead his case. Lawrence remained adamant, apprehensive that any weakening of his strength at Trichinopoly might lead to the French slipping out of the trap and making it to their coastal settlement of Karaikal, less than a hundred miles away, from where they could be shipped off to Pondicherry. Finally however he relented, and sent Dalton across with a couple of hundred troops to attack d'Atueuil.

Dalton staged an assault on Utatur, which served to deter d'Atueuil from moving out of the fort; but on return, found the river no more fordable, and joined Clive at Samayapuram. Jointly, they attacked a French pocket on the river bank to their side at a place called Pitchanda. Once their guns were in position at a temple there, Chanda Sahib's sprawling camp across the river on the island fell in range. They promptly opened up on the camp early morning, creating widespread panic among the large number of civilian camp followers who began fleeing to safety, out of range of the guns. The guns now turned on Pitchanda itself, where the French were holding fast, their snipers firing away at the gunners in the temple. After a few hours of intense bombardment they raised a white flag. But the British sepoys mistook the French drummers starting up for a call to arms, and stormed a breach in the wall. Some of the French tried to break out across the river, and fifteen of them drowned; the rest surrendered.

The British continued with the cannonade across the river at Chanda Sahib's camp. Caught in the open under the heavy fire and the French guns not retaliating, the huge army of the Indian prince started wilting away demoralized. There were large-scale desertions, until at last he was left with some 2000 cavalry and 3000 infantry, with which he took refuge in the larger temple on the island. Law withdrew with his force into the smaller temple. He too had suffered from desertions, about 1500 of his Europeans and most of the sepoys joining the British ranks. While Lawrence crossed over to Srirangam with the bulk of his army, Clive went over to mop up the remainder of the enemy at Utatur. D'Auteuil soon surrendered his weakened garrison, and Clive joined Lawrence back at Srirangam on 30 May.

On the 31st, Lawrence opened up with a massive cannonade, to batter Law into submission. Law refused to surrender, unless his troops were guaranteed safe passage to Pondicherry. The British, pretending to be under Muhammed Ali's command, warned that the Nawab planned to slaughter the whole garrison. Realising the hopelessness of the situation, the French commander capitulated on 3 June. He and his officers were given parole, while his men were sent off to prison. Chanda Sahib wasn't so lucky. He was beheaded on orders of the Tanjore general, Mankoji, to whom he surrendered. No doubt the Tanjoreans had a score to settle with him, but it had the touch of a divine retribution, as he met his end in the *Dalawai Mandapam,* the very premises in which, nearly thirty years before, he had sworn on the Holy Koran not to cause trouble to Queen Minakshi of Madura; an oath he broke when he sacked Madura, which led to the dowager queen's tragic end.

Thus ended one of the bloodiest power struggles the Carnatic ever witnessed. Nawab Muhammed Ali of Arcot was now the undisputed ruler of the Carnatic, albeit militarily dependent on the British for his continuance on the throne. It was also the end of Dupleix's grand dream of a French Empire in India. Although the war lingered on for another two years, the French once inflicting a defeat on the British at Gingee, and even attempting yet another siege of Trichinopoly, the power and prestige of France in India had been discredited beyond redemption in the temples of Srirangam in that Carnatic summer. The French would of course make another bid, at Madras, before the end of the decade, but Trichinopoly, more or less, was the end of the road for them. More so for Dupleix, the Frenchman who authored the concept of a European empire in India, which the British eventually were to find success with. Replaced by Godeheu in 1754 and recalled home, he was to die in disgrace ten years later.

In the crucible of Trichinopoly and its aftermath, the sepoy army was undergoing a great transformation. Lawrence brought about significant reorganization. The sepoys were formed into companies for the first time under their own officers called subedars. More and more of them were learning the use of firearms, although only some of them carried any still, that too the clumsy matchlocks, guns in which power was ignited by a match. Most sepoys were armed with only spears, swords or whatever weapons they could lay their hands on. This early Madras Army on the march would have struck an interesting contrast to a marching contingent of the Indian Army today; of well-trimmed and smartly attired soldiers carrying compact rifles. There were the European soldiers, burly ruffians mostly, sun-tanned and stuffed up in their red coats and heavy boots, shouldering their awfully long muskets, accompanied by the agile if thinly built sepoys, brown or black, and barelegged, lightly clad in cotton shirts and shorts, displaying an array of weaponry, matchlocks to machetes and battleaxes; all marching to the beat of tom-toms, in a cloud of dust along the torrid South Indian plain, as cheerful as any army could be.

Lawrence soon added some artillery and cavalry elements to it. Instead of a mere gun crew available so far, two companies of foot artillery were formed; so was a squadron of European cavalry raised. Cannon-fodder as they might very well have been considered to an extent, there is every reason to believe that the sepoys were often the cutting edge of the army in battle, undeterred as long as the European firepower was there to support them. Dalton, writing in his memoirs about the action beyond the river prior to Clive and he joining Lawrence at Srirangam, narrated their daredevilry thus:

Eight hundred of these sepoys were the very same who had made the resolute attempt to storm the breaches at Arcot when Clive commanded there and since deserted to him. They were a parcel of resolute fellows, and the continued series of success which for a considerable time had attended our arms made 'em look upon themselves as sure of victory when supported by an English battalion. These people being in the van never waited for the form of drawing up, but each company pressing for the honour of advancing their colours first, they set up a shout and ran at the French in the most daring manner, who had formed themselves in the front of their camp and had begun to fire briskly upon them with their artillery, but they seemed to give very little attention to it, still running on in the same intrepid manner, and the Marathas charging at the same time, they fairly drove the French from their ground.

Undismayed by the debacle at Srirangam, Dupleix soon found the ploy to keep the heat on, as the alliances were soon shifting, with the Mysoreans falling out with the Nawab for going back on his word to hand over Trichinopoly to them in return for their help, and the Marathas being always there for the highest bidder. The battle was lost, but the war wasn't. Lawrence, concerned about the security of Trichinopoly, was forced to maintain a garrison there, precariously sustained against the French disrupting his supply routes. Into this confused war scenario of the Carnatic, burst out an Indian hero, Muhammed Yusuf Khan, better known as Nellore Subedar, one of the finest soldiers the Carnatic has produced. Believed to have been born a Hindu in the southern district of Ramnad with the original name of Maruthanayagam Pillai, and converted to Islam later, he seems to have had a chequered career to begin with, before enlisting[2] under Clive in 1752. A natural with the ways of soldiering and leadership, it wasn't long before his outstanding talents were noticed by all. With his intimate knowledge of the country and a penchant for fast manoeuvres, he soon became the scourge of the French in open country warfare. The survival of the British garrison at Trichinopoly during the two years from 1752 to 1754 virtually became dependant on his skills in protecting the supply convoys from the French. Grateful for his services, the British made him the Commandant of all the Company's Sepoys in 1754, and presented him a gold medal the following year. Stringer Lawrence, in his journal, used almost similar words in praising the soldierly attributes of Yusuf Khan and Robert Clive. Clive reverted to his civilian occupation by the end of 1752, and the following year, having got married at Madras, sailed to England on leave. Both Yusuf Khan and Robert Clive were to figure prominently in the script of wars to be fought during the rest of the decade and after, not with the same consequences though.

In September 1754, the British clout was enhanced with the arrival of a naval squadron from England under Admiral Charles Watson, carrying an infantry regiment, the 39th Foot[3], commanded by Colonel John Adlercron. This display of force prompted the French to make peace with the British expeditiously. An ailing Lawrence was relieved of the field command by Lieutenant Colonel Alexander Heron, and Lawrence himself, commissioned a lieutenant colonel earlier, was presented with the Company's Sword of Honour; but was superceded as the Commander-in-Chief by Adlercron who was senior to him. Appointed a member of the Madras Council, he was to lead a civilian life for a

2. Having received his military training from the French initially, he commanded the Nellore sepoys and cavalry against the British at Arcot. At the end of the siege, he offered the services of his force to the victorious British.

3. The first British Regiment to serve in India, it later became the 1st Battalion, the Dorsetshire Regiment, with its proud motto, *Primus in Indis,* the First in India.

while, until trouble loomed over the Carnatic once again and was called back to arms.

Clive, commissioned a lieutenant colonel by the Company, was back on the scene by May 1756. It was the time when Calcutta was turning a hotspot for the British. Fort William there fell to the Nawab, Siraj-ud-Dulla, in June. An expeditionary force of the Company's troops under Clive sailed aboard Watson's fleet in October. He won the historic battle of Plassey on 23 June 1757, with the greater proportion of his troops from Madras. Apart from 250 men of the 39th Foot; 528 men of the Madras European Regiment, 109 men of the Madras Artillery, 160 Madras Lascars and 940 Madras Sepoys, took the field that day. Clive's reputation soared after Plassey, and he was to blaze newer trails, to be crowned by an accomplishment no Briton could match. But for all its publicized glory, Plassey was no big military victory, the least so, when compared with Arcot. At Arcot, Clive the soldier had won; at Plassey, Clive the manipulator. He was no more to appear on the Carnatic scene. The Clive House, a building in Fort St. George that now houses the offices and library of the Archeological Survey of India, where he once lived, and some portraits and other memorabilia reminds us of this early hero of the sepoys. Far less are memorials for him in his home country, which was to benefit from his achievements as it would from that of no other progeny of its; and there, he met his tragic end in ignominy, and lies buried in an anonymous grave.

4

SIEGE OF MADRAS

The birth of a regiment under fire

Even as the British power was on the ascent in Bengal, the war in Carnatic was far from over, and on the Coromandel Coast, the French, under Brigadier General Marquis de Bussy, ruled the roost from Vizagapatam to Masulipatam. And war had again broken out in Europe between the two rivals. In April 1758, a French fleet delivered reinforcements to Pondicherry under an impetuous new Governor General, Lieutenant General Count Thomas Arthur Lally; an Irish born soldier who had risen to fame in the French Army. The very next day of his arriving he attacked the British at Cuddalore, who surrendered meekly in less than a week's time. He let the garrison withdraw into Fort St. David, and besieged it with 3500 Europeans. After holding out for about a month, with no strong commander and troops deserting, the demoralized garrison capitulated. Lally went on to reduce the fort to ruins. Fort St. David was never restored, and militarily, passed into oblivion. After an expedition to Tanjore to replenish his treasury, Lally turned his attention to Madras.

If the French commander had imagined anything remotely comparable to la Bourdannais's walkover at Madras twelve years earlier, he was in for a rude surprise. Fort St. George had been turned fairly impregnable by a massive extension of the fortifications undertaken after the war ended in 1754. And instead of an inept garrison under an ineffective commander, well-trained troops under Lawrence's capable command were waiting to take on the French threat. The preparations for defence of Madras started in earnest, once Lally landed on the coast. Provisions were stocked, and water supply organized, to cater for a six months' siege. Lawrence positioned himself with a field force at St. Thomas Mount to form a screen. The enemy was reported at Vandalur to his south on 6 December. On 10 December the field force fell back to position itself in front of Harris Bridge on the main thoroughfare, Mount Road. On 12th the French drove in detachments to San Thome and Egmore, and Lawrence retreated to the fort, leaving pickets to guard the Black Town, the part of the township occupied by Indians – later named George Town to remove the racial connotation – which fell outside the fort to its northwest.

The French force comprising some 3000 Europeans and an equal number of sepoys, with 500-strong native cavalry, encamped to the south and west of the fort. The defending British garrison comprised 1758 Europeans and 2220 sepoys. Captain Achilles Preston, commanding a force at Chingleput, and Major John Caillaud joining him with his troops from Tanjore, were engaged to strike at the enemy's lines of communication. And there was Yusuf Khan, the daring Indian ally of the British, coming to their aid, which often made the difference, as his forces went ravaging the countryside up to the gates of Pondicherry, cutting across the French supply routes, and caused havoc around Conjeeveram, from where the French drew fair amount of supplies.

The French crossed the Cooum at daybreak on the 14th, and marching through Vepery, entered the Black Town unopposed, as the British pickets pulled back to the fort. The French flag was hoisted on the Armenian Church. An immediate sortie undertaken by Colonel William Draper with 600 men resulted in stiff fighting, which ended with the British backtracking to the fort. Both sides lost upwards of 200 men in this action. A French brigadier-general, Count d' Easting, was taken prisoner. Lally dug in with his army outside, while Lawrence settled down with his garrison within the fort for a long haul. Thus began the siege of Madras, which was to last sixty-seven days. It saw heavy shelling throughout by both sides, and occasional forays by the British to no avail, as well as a brave stand at the Mount, first by Preston and then by Caillaud, along with Yusuf Khan. The garrison church, St. Mary's, being bombproof, was the only building within the fort to escape serious damage. But the garrison held on, with no sign of relenting. A despairing Lally, lifted the siege on 17 February 1759, hastened in the act by the arrival of a British naval squadron bringing more troops.

While the siege was on, the 100-men strong companies of the sepoys were grouped into battalions for better command and control. Few great occurrences in India's history has had so less fanfare, but had so big an impact. Because this event, amidst the heat of the battle, while Madras faced the biggest military crisis in all its 350-year old history, signifies itself for being the birth of the Madras Regiment, the oldest regiment of the Indian Army. Then called the Coast Sepoys, it began with two battalions, the 1st and the 2nd, of over a 1000 men each, commanded by a British officer of the rank of captain, and an Indian Commandant. The companies were commanded by Indian officers of the rank of subedar. They now wore uniforms[1], and were finally issued with regular muskets. The sepoy force performed both as infantry and pioneers, and suffered a due proportion of the casualties, 107 killed and 217 wounded. Interestingly, almost two centuries later, in 1946, a tattoo held outside Fort St. George reenacted this historic siege, bringing in French sepoys from Pondicherry as well.

Five months after the siege was raised, Stringer Lawrence left for England. Although the 'Old Cock' – a soldiers' soldier, his men called him so affectionately – was to return to India once again as the Commander-in-Chief with the rank of a major general, his days in the battlefield were clearly over. He bid farewell to India in 1766, to die peacefully in London nine years later, and was buried at Dunchideock, in Devon. The East India

---

1. From 1756, the East India Company started providing uniforms made of broadcloth to its sepoys, partly to make use of that material, of which they had a surplus of stock; however the sepoys still went barefoot, until 1811 when they were issued with sandals.

Company erected a monument for him at Westminster Abbey, which bears the inscription:

> Discipline established, fortresses protected, settlements extended, French and Indian Armies defeated, and peace concluded in the Carnatic.

But peace, in no way, was to be concluded in the Carnatic for almost a quarter of a century after Lawrence died. On the heels of the reverse at Madras, the French suffered another setback when Colonel Francis Forde, commanding a force from Bengal, defeated Bussy and took Masulipatam. It was followed by a British setback, when a few months later Major Cholmondeley Brereton, who was officiating as the commander of the army at Madras after Lawrence's departure, made an attempt to take Wandiwash, but was repulsed with heavy casualties; 200 killed or wounded. Then in October 1759, Lieutenant Colonel Eyre Coote, a veteran of the battle of Plassey, arrived at Madras with his Regiment, the 84th Foot, and took over command. He launched an offensive, and in a decisive battle fought on 22 January 1760, defeated Lally at Wandiwash, taking Bussy prisoner. The French strongholds then fell in rapid succession, until only Pondicherry and the hill forts of Gingee and Thiagar remained.

By the end of 1760, the British laid siege to Pondicherry by a land-and-sea operation in which two naval squadrons also chipped in, bringing about the surrender of the garrison in less than a month's time. Count Lally was sent off to France. Impeached for the loss of the French possessions in India and tried for treason, he was executed after incarceration at the Bastille for three years. The demolition of the buildings and fortifications went on at Pondicherry, until the settlement was reduced to ruins by the end of the year 1761. Although the place was restored to them at a later stage, the French were finished in India.

Eyre Coote's campaign was more or less a European affair, unlike what had by then become a common practice of the sepoys forming the frontline troops in any assault; although they did take some 70 casualties; and fought a couple of sharp engagements at Devicottah, Perumalcoil and Villanoor. The Madras Army was now to enter the most unpleasant phase of its history, marring its unblemished record of chivalry so far. It went after the weak rulers of the Carnatic, bullying them into submission one after the other. The real villain of the piece was the weak-kneed Nawab of Arcot who, unable to pay off the enormous debt he had run up with the East India Company for military hardware and troops to sustain the war, consented to the British enforcing the collection of taxes, said to be due from these subsidiary states; just the right ploy the British needed to consolidate their gains. A four-battalion force, assembled at Arcot in September 1761, commenced the operations by an attack on Vellore nearby. The fort there fell in December. Nellore soon followed suit. The Poligars[2] of Kalahasti and Venkatagiri were reduced to acquiescence thereafter, and with the Rajah of Tanjore agreeing to pay up, the operations came to an unholy end.

While the role of the sepoys in these operations smacks of rank mercenariness, it has to be viewed from the perspective of the military culture of the times. Entire armies were made up of mercenaries, including the European ones; and it wasn't uncommon to find Europeans in the service of Indian rulers too, although not in such large numbers as were the sepoys with the European powers. Both had no specific loyalties, except that of assured payments (and the booty as well), and a winning chance in a set battle. That the loyalty of the Europeans to anyone side was not above suspect was obvious from the frequent desertions prevalent in their armies; contained to an extent though, by the strict practice of deserters being executed if caught.

The primary attraction for the sepoys to flock under the European powers was the opportunity of getting superior training, besides the prospects of regular pay, proper uniforms and necessary weaponry. (Such motives couldn't be considered far different from those of

2. A legacy of the Vijayanagar Empire, the Poligars were local chieftains, empowered to collect taxes from the inhabitants of their areas. 'Poligar' is the anglicized form of 'Palaikkaran', meaning 'holder of an armed camp' in Tamil, which aptly indicates how they drew power.

the modern day Non-Resident Indians, who seek greener pastures abroad.) They were men of honour who refused to live off the fat of the land, and chose to live dangerously, probably finding it fun. And as far as they were concerned, the French and the British were just two new players in the *tamasha* that the power politics of the Carnatic had become. Also, once the situation stabilized, with the French out of picture, the British sepoys were invariably 'true to their salt'. Of course, it goes to the credit of the British officers, who were by and large endowed with admirable qualities of leadership, to have been able to win the loyalty of the sepoys to a very high degree, and successfully harness the great military potential available in the subcontinent. But this was purely a comrades-in-arms relation, and that the sepoys had no great sense of allegiance to the British Crown became evident when a mutiny broke out in Vellore early the following century, and almost the entire British garrison was massacred. That, as well as the much larger rising in Northern and Central India in1857, were clear indicators of the delicate nature of the sepoy-officer relation. As long as an officer was sensitive to the pride and prejudices – often cast-or-religion-based – of his men and learned not to offend them (and always led from the front), he was the master of the game. It was no easy job. No wonder, the success of the British officers in commanding the Indian troops remains quite a marvel; one that could be a classic piece of study for the human resources managers today.

Britain declared war with Spain in 1762, and the Madras Army was off to its first stint of overseas operations. A naval force moved against the Spanish settlement of Manila in the Philippines, carrying troops under General William Draper, in August. 650 of them were sepoy-volunteers. The force took Manila by storm early in October. Except for being an act of war against an enemy, it served the British no big purpose, and the place was restored to the Spanish at the end of the war in a couple of years, as was Pondicherry to the French.

The English East India Company had by now come of age as a

claimant for political authority in the subcontinent, shedding any pretensions of being a trading organization. If realization dawned on the princely class of India of the enormity of their blunder, it was too late in the day to salvage the situation. The British had the most formidable military machine in the subcontinent at their disposal to assert their will – the three Presidency Armies of Madras, Bengal and Bombay. The juggernaut was about to crush the Carnatic. Yet there were enough proud men south of the Vindhyas prepared to take on the British might; not one of them the original lame duck rulers who had pawned off the country to the foreigners. They were ordinary men with obscure backgrounds, who shot into prominence sheerly on the weight of their courage to stand up and fight. Each one of them was to give the British a run for their money; some would even have succeeded in stopping them on their tracks, if only their countrymen had rallied behind them. That never happened, and the way was open for the foreigner. For the British, the era of conquest was just beginning; and for the Indians, the day of the icons and martyrs.

5

WAR OF THE KHAN SAHIB

The death of an Indian hero

The veiled imposition of the British authority, that the Nawab's inglorious tax collection drive was, went unimpeded until it hit the southern provinces of Madura and Tinnevelly. Beyond and adjacent to these was the Marava country, comprising Ramnad and Sivaganga. The Maravas – who assumed the name of Thevars later – were a brave, free-spirited people who paid obeisance[1] to no one. Traditional warriors, their ancestors had conquered and held the greater part of Ceylon for several centuries. They formed the main military muscle of the southern provinces.

Mainly armed with pikes twelve to eighteen feet long, they were adept at constructing crude but effective barriers of mud walls and thorn hedges, and repairing breaches with readily available stuff like

---

1. S. C. Hill, in his biography of Yusuf Khan, refers to an interesting quote from an unpublished manuscript of the times, which summarizes what the Kallars (mentioned as *Kallans* in the book) – a sub-caste of the Maravas who lived in the hilly and woody parts of the country, and proved an exceptionally tough and cunning lot with their intimate knowledge of secret paths and ambush sites – thought of the payment of taxes in general: 'The Heaven supplies the earth with rain, cattle plough for us, and we labour to improve and cultivate the land. Whilst such is the case we alone ought to enjoy the fruit thereof. What reason is there to be obedient and pay tribute to a person like ourselves?' And much to the consternation of the animal rights activists and moralists, the men of the Marava territory continue to be passionate about holding their robust if highly dangerous game of 'Jallikat', in which participants, like gladiators, try to take on a powerfully built bull let loose amongst them and tame it, many of them invariably getting gored in the act.

the trunks of the palm trees that withstood fair amount of battering by the artillery. With these primitive devices, they had given the British a bloody nose while defending Madura under Chanda Sahib's flag, when James Cope tried to storm the place, losing ninety of his men in the attempt. Even after the victory at Trichinopoly, the British or the Nawab's authority was hardly recognized by the defiant Maravas, and at least one British officer, Colonel Alexander Heron, had his military career ending in disgrace when he miserably failed to bring them round. And the Nawab's worthless brother, Mahfuz Khan, who accompanied the colonel, only added to his infamy from the Battle of Adyar when he not only failed, but betrayed his own brother by joining hands with the rebels.

Finally in 1759 when the British chose a man to discipline the southern districts, it was not one of their own, but the Indian who by then had become their most trusted ally, and whom almost every Briton in India at that time thought of as the bravest Indian soldier they had known – Muhammed Yusuf Khan, popularly known as Khan Sahib. That he indeed had no equals among his compatriots had been too well established, when he soundly thrashed the celebrated soldier of the South, Haider Ali, when they took the field against each other at the Nattam Pass near Solavandan, less than two years earlier. The Mysorean general was in fact holding a subordinate command in his army during the siege of Trichinopoly when, fighting for the same side, Yusuf Khan was making a name for himself.

The Company's choice of Yusuf Khan as the renter[2] for Madura and Tinnevelly was not favoured by the Nawab at all. He didn't trust the man. The Nawab's distrust arose essentially from the inherent weakness the Indian rulers suffered as a class – the fear of their sovereignty being usurped when ever one of their own vassals grew too powerful

---

2. A renter was empowered to collect taxes from the people and administer the province, while having to pay a fixed amount to the government. Later the job seems to have gone to the 'collector', a colonial apparition that still haunts the Indian administrative system, the district administrators to date being designated so, implying that he is there solely to *collect*, and not to *deliver*.

(as it often did happen indeed). Added to that might have been the prejudice due to Yusuf Khan's humble origins. He chose to convert to Islam, in all probability, to break out of the confines of a cast-ridden society he had born into as a Hindu. Belonging to the Vellala Caste, which wasn't considered a princely one, he could never have pursued his true aspirations, as the casteless Islam would permit. But that didn't either impress the Nawab, or he merely played the cast card with the British to denigrate Yusuf Khan, and cash in on their own prejudices on similar lines. Whatever it was, the hatred was too intense. But for the time being, he had not much of an option but to go along with the British decision.

Arriving at Madura in May 1759, Yusuf Khan found the entire southern provinces in a state of rebellion. He had brought along a body of troops with him; some six companies of sepoys, sixty horse, and six European gunners. Another 3000 men, sent by the Tondaiman rulers of Pudukotta and two Marava Poligars who were friendly, joined him soon. But he was handicapped by the shortage of armament and stores to undertake any serious operation. Nevertheless, making his own gunpowder and procuring firearms and guns from the Dutch at Nagapatam and the Danes at Tranquebar, he took on the most troublesome Poligars and reduced them to submission in less than two months. And during the next couple of years, combining firmness with fairness and prudence, he not only brought peace to the provinces, but won over the inhabitants by providing them an excellent administration; so much so that the ranks of his army were being joined by the hardened fighters of the area. His writ now ran unquestioned in the southern districts.

Meanwhile the insinuations of the Nawab, who was feeling increasingly insecure with the rising popularity of Yusuf Khan, were telling on the British. Yusuf Khan too, sensing a change of mood in the British camp (many a Briton who was his comrade-in-arms had left, and he could rely on very few to back him up), began planning for a possible showdown with them. Besides inducting more native troops, he enlisted some 200 French ones under a gallant officer, Claude Flamicourt; and began strengthening the fortifications at Madura and other strongholds. Hostilities which broke out between Yusuf Khan and the British ally on the West Coast, the King of Travancore, by the end of 1762 (which was actually started by the latter, to end in his own defeat and a treaty of alliance between the two), precipitated an open rebellion. Incensed by the perceived defiance of Yusuf Khan in acting on his own without reference to the Company, as well as his other suspicious actions like raising of fresh troops, the Company called him back to Madras to render an explanation. Distrustful of the Nawab and his influence on the British, he didn't go, but sent a letter complaining of the Nawab's treachery, which fell on deaf ears. The Company's interest lay with the Nawab, and Yusuf Khan's soldierly contributions were conveniently forgotten. That his discontent was with the Nawab, and not with the Company, who was his employer, didn't make a difference; the British prepared for war, and Yusuf Khan threw off his allegiance with them.

Early in 1763, declaring his independence as the Governor of Madura and Tinnevelly, Yusuf Khan raised the French colours in his camp and at the various forts in his possession. The British assembled a force of nearly 10,000 men in Trichinopoly under Colonel George Monson; half of them sepoys in some five battalions, over 1500 Europeans including two troops of their cavalry (Dragoons – the German hussars), 2000 of the Nawab's native cavalry, and the rest the Nawab's infantry and irregulars recruited locally. Their vanguard, under Achilles Preston, now a major, reached Tirupuvanum, fifteen miles southeast of Madura early in August. Yusuf Khan, true to his style, went into the offensive, skirmishing with the advancing column. Then on the 11th he attacked one of their reconnaissance parties and created mayhem, leaving over 150 of their sepoys killed or wounded. (He even contemplated attacking Trichinopoly, but was dissuaded from it by the French officers.) The British force came up in front of Madura early in September, and laid a siege.

Yusuf Khan had in his garrison some 3000 sepoys, 1000 horse, one troop of European hussars, 200 French and about 5000 irregulars (mostly Kallars). He was also estimated to have had an equal number of sepoys and irregulars distributed in his other forts. The first probe of the defences Colonel Monson conducted met with a drubbing. He had taken a battalion of the sepoys, along with the hussars, some 300 native cavalry, a section of the Europeans and two guns. At the southwest angle of the fort, they came up against an embankment with a parallel one behind, and plain ground spanning in between. The second embankment was held by some 300 troopers of Yusuf Khan's cavalry. Monson ordered his cavalry to cross over into the plain, with the sepoys covering them from behind the first embankment. The hussars crossed, and charged on without forming up, while the native cavalry hesitated. Yusuf Khan's horsemen grabbed the chance and charged down into the small body of hussars, driving them back to the first bank in confusion. Although most of them managed to cross over under the steady covering fire from the sepoys, about seventeen of them were killed or wounded. One officer, Lieutenant Samuel Stephenson, was killed, and another, Captain Donald Campbell, was wounded and taken prisoner. (The officer was looked after well and sent back to the British camp by Yusuf Khan, who was personally in command at the engagement.)

As the ineffectual siege continued with the besieged moving in and out of the fort with total impunity, the moral of the British troops sagged. The Europeans began deserting, and sickness was taking its toll on the troops. After a fortnight or so, the British commenced work on trenches in preparation for an assault, and opened fire on the fort on the 24th; but it hardly made any impact against the far superior firepower of the defenders. Peppered by heavy musketry and gunfire, the besiegers took a number of casualties. Early the following month, a sortie out of the fort by a mixed force of Indians and Europeans under a French officer, Monsieur Marchand, caused the British further casualties. Finding the situation hopeless, Monson lifted the siege and retreated with his troops to Tirupuvanum by 12 November. The inglorious operation had cost the British heavy casualties and a terrible loss of face. They had been squarely beaten back by an enemy whose potential they had grossly underrated, and were left licking their wounds. Yusuf Khan's own losses were minimal, and the victory, having broken the British invincibility, was a shot in the arm for his forces. The garrison's only significant loss was that of its gallant French commander, Flamicourt, who was killed a day or two before the siege was lifted; forcing Yusuf Khan to give the command of his European troops to Marchand, a brave but unscrupulous man, whom he didn't trust instinctively.

It was celebration time for Yusuf Khan and his garrison. And he felicitated his troops generously, offering away gifts (even a promissory note of 50,000 rupees to Marchand). But he knew better than to keep his guard down. Repairing and strengthening of the fortifications took priority, and he began enlisting more and more men into his army; in anticipation of the next British offensive he knew would be coming. He certainly was in contact with Haider Ali, who had come to power in Mysore by now. The latter did help by encouraging his own men to enlist under Yusuf Khan; so did the Rajah of Tanjore, who sent over the French in his service to boost the garrison at Madura. But a full-blooded united effort that could have toppled the British was not forthcoming. It was the same old story of fence sitters that India was familiar with. Haider probably had his own misgivings of Yusuf Khan posing a future challenge, while the Tanjore Rajah just took the wait-and-watch attitude, to see which way the wind blew. In a strange move, Yusuf Khan also made overtures to the British at Madras early in 1764, to make amends (Some considered it a ploy to get a spy inside Madras in the person of his courier). But the latter demanded the surrender of all the forts and places in his possession, which he refused. The British laid another siege.

After the first siege Monson had been relieved of his command for ill-health. Preston commanded the field army briefly until February 1764, when Major Charles Campbell, senior to him in service, took over. Campbell spent the first couple of months of his command preparing for an assault on Madura by erecting batteries, with the eminently capable Chief Engineer of the Company, Major John Call, to take care of the job. Meanwhile a field force commanded by Preston was engaged in cutting off Yusuf Khan's lines of communication with Tinnevelly and the neighbouring provinces to the south, east and west, as well as Dindigul to the north; all the places he could be reinforced or supplied from. The operation was only partly successful, since there was no stopping the Kallars who kept opening new routes. The prolonged standoff found both besiegers and the besieged racked by sickness and desertion. While Yusuf Khan was somewhat better off than the British inasmuch as the sickness among his troops went, he certainly suffered on account of desertions. In a flagrant betrayal, a German officer, Monsieur Riquet, went over to the enemy with his hussars. On 29 April, with their batteries in place, the British stormed the garrison's outposts. It was a lightning strike brilliantly executed by Campbell, with Call handling the artillery, and Preston leading the combined assault by the Europeans and the sepoys, with both native and the European cavalry charging alongside. Yusuf Khan lost five redoubts in one stroke, and his casualties were heavy – 400 sepoys, along with 8 Europeans and some 20 topass-es killed or wounded, and 16 Europeans and topass-es taken prisoner.

It nearly took another two months for the British to get set, and make up their mind for the assault on the fort itself. A trench was dug about 400 yards from the fort, and breaching operations put under way. Towards the middle of June, breaching batteries opened up, and shortly thereafter mines were sprung. The fortifications of Madura were old, at least five hundred yards of the rampart in a state of total ruin. Some of the bastions collapsed under the gunfire, one from the concussion of a defenders' gun itself. Mines caused considerable damage too, although the surrounding ditch wasn't filled in by the falling debris as Call had intended. However the pioneers who ventured into the ditch reported that it could be crossed (They didn't detect the deep holes the defenders had dug in the ditch while scouring it out to raise the glacis – a piece of information the British had from a spy, but ignored. These holes and the water from the seasonal rains were to somewhat hamper the assault). Yusuf Khan couldn't match the firepower of the enemy; but at close quarters, he kept up intense fire on the breaching parties, and casualties mounted on the British side. He attempted a sally once, early when the breaching work started, which was repulsed with the loss of some fifty men, while on the British side two officers and four Europeans were killed and one officer wounded.

After some hesitation for the need to ascertain the enemy strong points, while the war council met more than once, the British resolved to attack the fort on 26 June. There were some six practicable breaches and the assault was to be launched on a wide front, with about 4000 sepoys and 800 Europeans, including their cavalrymen in a dismounted role. Preston was to command on the right, and Major John Wood on the left. The defending garrison had about 4000 men in all, more than half of them sepoys, 800 or so cavalrymen, about an equal number of irregulars who were mostly Kallars, with a spattering of *topass*-es and Africans who were known as *coffre*-es, and only about 100 Europeans, half of them gunners. When the British had hoisted the Nawab's flag at their camp while opening up with the breaching batteries, Yusuf Khan had responded by hoisting a yellow flag at the fort – the customary Indian signal of the times to declare that there shall be no surrender. It was going to be a fight to the finish.

The British had planned a dawn attack. The assaulting troops formed up in time by 3 a.m.; but the artillerymen blundered with their disposition in the dark and there was delay. Consequently, it was broad day light by the time the signal was given for the assault. The defenders were of course, ready. The attackers rushed into the ditch and into the misery of the knee-deep water, many falling into the deep holes. Nevertheless, they struggled across and stormed the breaches. A bloody hand-to-hand fight ensued, and the attackers had the upper hand in the end, breaking through the first line of defenders. Then they came up against the pike-men. It was as if they had run into a wall of steel; a deadly form of defence that their swords and muskets were of no use against. The pike-men, under cover on either side of the breach, kept pushing their long weapons at each other, creating an unbreakable barricade, while their friends on towers above brought merry hell down on the attackers with musket fire and hand grenades, added with the shower of stones. And many of the attackers, to their dismay, found that their cartridges, wet from crossing the ditch, won't fire. The situation was desperate. Yet the stubborn ones pushed on, some even making it to the summit of the walls, only to be cut down. Preston, the gallant leader he was, urged his men on, and climbed a tower, with three sepoy officers for company. He went down with a bullet in the groin. With one of his companions also shot, the other two managed to recover their two friends to safety. The struggle continued for an hour or so more, only to end in retreat. The British had been beaten back a second time by Yusuf Khan.

The British losses were nearly 200 killed or wounded, two-thirds of them Europeans including twelve officers, and the rest sepoys. The Europeans obviously had a lead role up front. No loss was as hurting as that of Preston, who succumbed to his wound after a couple of weeks. He was one of those fine officers, like Clive and Dalton before him, who had endeared himself to his sepoys, and they looked up to. Ironically in the end, he took his life in his hands in a fight he had reservations about (He had advised a blockade to wear the enemy out instead of the assault, which he considered foolhardy); and fell fighting an enemy who was once his comrade in arms. That enemy, Yusuf Khan, was right then quite elated about the victory, although he had lost some 250 men. He assured his troops that the British would give up the siege now, hoping desperately that he would prove right, since his lack of provisions had him in a spot. And as it turned out, the British, instead of packing up and leaving, practically marshalled the entire forces of the Presidency in the field, and converted the siege into a blockade, isolating Madura completely. Preston lived long enough to see his advice being accepted.

A crisis was building up within the fort. The prolonged privations had ground the morale of the troops down to a miserably low state. (Commendably, Yusuf Khan's sepoys, by and large stuck with him, the only notable case of desertion having been that of a subedar switching sides with just about fifty of his men; as against the Europeans and *topass*-es who proved turncoats of the worst order.) The garrison had plenty of ammunition, but very little food. Of the families of the men, Yusuf Khan had managed to evacuate some to safety, but many including his own family were trapped within the fort. Virtually choked for provisions as the blockade became more and more effective, the conditions within the fort worsened. The Indian occupants had come to subsist on the meager ration of old rice; the Europeans had started eating horses or other animals they could find. Scarcity bred discontent. Compounding the problem was the disloyalty within the garrison.

The chief miscreant was the French commander Marchand. A man of dubious background and reputation, he could never get along with Yusuf Khan. They had been associated with each other for long, from the time they fought the Rajah of Travancore together; but their chemistry never matched. Both were men of violent temper, and Marchand had even been thrown into the prison once by an exasperated Yusuf Khan, only to be rescued by the intervention of Flamicourt. When the blockade had gone on for more than two months, Yusuf Khan, realizing the hopelessness of his situation, sought terms from the British. He was willing to surrender the fort, if he would be permitted go free with some troops and his family. The British refused any such terms, insisting on an unconditional surrender. Marchand, who had been acting as the intermediary, had suggested to Yusuf Khan that the best option for him was to cut his way through the blockade and run with a small body of troops; an idea the latter ruled out immediately, since it would have warranted of him to leave behind his family and most of his men at the mercy of the Nawab.

By now Yusuf Khan had been reduced to an acute state of despair, which often found him in his worst moods; and his strained relationship with Marchand gave way to frequent quarrels. In a spurt of anger one day, Yusuf Khan struck Marchand with his riding whip; an insult the Frenchman would have found difficult to live down. That proved to be the last straw anyway, for to Marchand, already seeking some selfish means to save his skin, revenge came as a powerful motivator, and he went on to hatch a conspiracy within the fort. The situation couldn't have been more ideal for such a ploy to succeed, with a prevailing rumour that Yusuf Khan might attempt to cut and run with his confidants, which made the entire garrison feel insecure. Marchand glibly used the rumour – which had its origin in his own suggestion to adopt such a course – to fan the flames of discontent. Instigated thoroughly, the native officers joined Marchand, and cornered Yusuf Khan in his quarters on the afternoon of 13 October. He was overpowered as he drew his sword, and bound by his own turban. Mudali, a brave young man loyal to Yusuf Khan, who raised an alarm and attempted to rescue his master with some five or six hundred men, was swiftly cut down; and his group, left leaderless, soon dissuaded in the attempt by two field guns placed in front of the quarters.

Yusuf Khan begged to be put to sword, rather than being delivered to the Nawab. A desperate plea by Yusuf Khan's wife (she was believed to have been of Portuguese lineage), offering the fort and all the treasure within it to Marchand, bore no fruit either. The following day Campbell rode in with his cavalry and took the surrender of the fort from Marchand. Yusuf Khan was handed over to the Nawab's officers, who bound him down in a palanquin and carried him to a temple, where he was confined for the night. His wife and family were dispatched to Trichinopoly at the same time. Yusuf Khan himself accepted his fate with dignity, and made no appeal whatever to spare his life. The next day, 15 October 1764, at five o'clock in the evening, he was hanged as a rebel in front of the British camp before Madura, by order of the Nawab of Arcot. And with him went the rank of the Indian Commandant of the Sepoys, one which no one else ever held. The British abolished it once and for all, relegating the Indian officers of the future to subordinate positions.

While on all accounts, the Nawab had taken an uncompromising stand in the case of Yusuf Khan, there is enough evidence to show that the British were very much in connivance to perpetrate so cruel an end to their staunchest ally in arms, whom Lawrence himself had described as 'a born soldier' and 'better of his colour I never saw in the country'. And little did Yusuf Khan, the lion-hearted fighter he was, realize that his own countrymen, whom he considered friends and wrote to proudly about his victories, had hardly a thought for him. Haider Ali, for whatever reasons, positively wrote to the British, offering his allegiance to them; and the Rajah of Tanjore even supplied them with some troops, while the King of Travancore, who was treaty-bound to help Yusuf Khan, didn't even raise a finger.

In the lexicon of Indian military heroes, the name of Yusuf Khan seldom finds a mention. Yet here was a man, who matched the British in the field on every count, and stood his ground as few in the subcontinent ever did. Nothing could better summarize the life of Yusuf Khan as did the words of S.C. Hill, in the introductory chapter to his book, 'Yusuf Khan the Rebel Commandant'. It seemed to him, he wrote, 'well worthwhile, in the absence of any professedly authoritative account of the life of Yusuf Khan, to attempt a sketch of the career of this extraordinary personage, who, beginning life as a humble peasant, raised himself to high rank in the East India Company's service; then by his administrative ability, reduced to order the two most turbulent provinces of Southern India; and finally when compelled, as James Mill says, to rebel against the Nawab in self-defence, managed to maintain against that Prince assisted by the whole available power of the English, for a period of nearly two years, falling at last only by the treachery of his own troops and not by the force of his enemies.' He adds:

Yusuf Khan was, in fact, of the same type as Haider Ali – one of those men of genius who naturally came to the front in times of great political or social unrest. Had he been left without outside interference to settle his quarrel with his native suzerain, like Haider Ali with the Rajas of Mysore, there is absolutely no doubt that he would have succeeded in establishing his independence. As it was, the same Power in whose service he had risen to distinction was fated to be the effective agency of his ruin; still, in spite of his failure, in spite even of his execution as a rebel, it must be remembered that for many years, and those some of the darkest, Yusuf Khan had served the English faithfully; that in his last struggle he fought chivalrously and died gallantly; that amongst the people whom he had governed he left a reputation for ability, firmness, and justice; that, though he could win no pity from his mortal enemy the Nawab, his courage was admired and his fate lamented by the British soldiers who fought against him, whilst long after his death his administration of Madura and Tinnevelly was spoken of in high terms by the British officials who held charge of those provinces.

The dead body of Muhammed Yusuf Khan, decapitated and dismembered, as was the barbaric system of the times, was buried in the village of his birth, Samattipuram, two miles west of Madura. A small square mosque, built over the spot later, still exists, and is known by its half-Hindu-half-Muslim name, Khan Sahib's *Pallivasal;* a sad, rather inconspicuous memorial for a man who single-handedly stalled the British onslaught for nearly two years.

(The title of this chapter is an adaptation of that of a Tamil ballad on the life and times of Yusuf Khan.)

6

THE DAY OF THE MYSORE HORSEMEN

Two great generals and their glorious battles

B arely three years after Yusuf Khan was hanged, Haider Ali exploded into the Carnatic scene. The *Killedar,* fort keeper, of Dindigul to begin with politically, he had usurped the sovereignty of Mysore during the previous decade, and had become a power to be reckoned with by early 1760s. Allied with the Nizam of Hyderabad he invaded the Carnatic towards the end of August 1767, which brought him into confrontation with the British. The cutting edge of the Mysore Army was its cavalry, an element the Madras Army and the British could hardly boast of any. In the next three decades or so till the dawn of the 19th Century, in the period marked by what came to be known as the Mysore Wars, four of them one after the other, these horsemen of Mysore would set the plains of Carnatic ablaze; and to meet the challenge, the Madras Army would grow into a formidable fighting machine, fully complemented by all arms – the cavalry[1], artillery[2]

---

1. The Madras Native Cavalry was formed in 1784, by transferring four of the Nawab's cavalry regiments to the East India Company, along with the Governor's Bodyguard Madras which had been raised in 1778; and some new raisings were added during the next couple of years. Some of the Indian Army's present cavalry – since named the Armoured Corps – units are the descendants of these regiments; one among them, the 16th Light Cavalry, still maintains an exclusively South Indian troop composition.

2. The first native company of the Madras Foot Artillery was formed in 1784, and many were raised later. All of them however were disbanded along with the native artillery all over India after the rebellion of 1857. No Indian Artillery was formed by the British afterwards (except for the 1st Field Regiment raised in 1935 under the Royal Artillery); and the present Regiment of Artillery, which came into being after independence, have many units constituted of South Indian Gunners.

and the engineers[3]. The infantry itself – some 19 battalions by the time of Haider Ali's invasion – would undergo various reorganizations[4], and massive expansion. But all those were to happen in the future. When Haider's invasion came, the British were hardly in any shape to take it on.

Colonel Joseph Smith took the field with 800 Europeans and 5000 sepoys, supported by some 30 European cavalrymen and 16 guns, against a vastly superior army of Haider. Aiming to strengthen the frontier, he commenced with an attempt to take the fortress at Krishnagiri in the northern Carnatic, occupied by the enemy. It ended in a fiasco, with almost the entire lot of European Grenadiers who stormed the fort getting wiped out. He then set out for Tiruvannamalai, 70 miles to the southeast, for replenishment and to link up with reinforcements under Colonel John Wood. En route, the enemy intercepted him in a defile between the hills near Chengam on 2 September.

The sepoy battalion leading the March reacted with lightning alacrity, and swept the Nizam's troops off a feature they were holding at the point of bayonet. Haider's main army, converging to the site for the kill, found itself confronted by the sepoys holding the vantage point, by now reinforced by Smith with more men. Haider, as was his wont, attacked right away, and was promptly repulsed. Undeterred, he threw

---

3. The Engineers began as Pioneers who were troops employed as manual labour, for digging trenches, building fortifications, making roads, and so on; but were to turn to reliable combatants soon. Their separate identity from the infantry was recognized in 1780, when the first two regular companies of theirs with 100 men each were raised. Over the next few years, as the requirement increased, the number rose to eight companies, first named from 'A' to 'H', then '1' to '8', and finally '9' to '16', the status at which they remained close to 150 years. They were to expand and evolve themselves into the celebrated Madras Sappers and Miners (MEG, the Madras Engineer Group, now), one of the finest combat engineers in the history of warfare the world over.
4. The Coast Sepoy Battalions distributed to various garrisons all across the peninsula were all first renamed and renumbered, those based in the south assuming the title Carnatic Battalions, and those in the north Circar Battalions. Subsequently from 1784 however the distinction was dissolved and all came to be known as Madras Battalions.

in more troops in attack after attack, with he himself dismounted and leading. But it wasn't his day, and he gave up after one last attempt at a breakthrough from the flank with woods for cover. Haider himself had been wounded, and he had lost about 2000 men. Meanwhile the British rearguard, bringing up the field guns, came under attack. The Grenadier Battalion[5] of the sepoys, guarding the guns, rallied to their rescue, and trounced the enemy in a powerful counterattack. Haider's troops, pursued till sunset, left behind two of their guns. For the sepoy battalions, this one-day battle at Chengam was a trendsetter – they had manoeuvred like true professionals in a tight situation, and fought and won a stiff field battle all on their own. More of those were to follow.

Smith linked up with Wood at Tiruvannamalai, and their combined forces now numbered some 9000 sepoys, 1400 Europeans and 34 guns. Haider attacked the force at Tiruvannamalai itself. He opened up with a cannonade on 26 September, aiming to force Smith to move forward against him and into a swamp which lay in between. But Smith chose to outflank, and occupy the vantage point of a hill to Haider's left. Haider took it for an attempt by the British to withdraw to Arcot, and rushed to attack their flank and rear. The two forces, to their mutual surprise, ran into each other round the hill. Once again the sepoys seized the initiative swiftly in a testing moment, and charged forward in a rage. The enemy, unnerved by the ferocity of the charge, gave ground, but soon occupied a strong position among some rocks. Without losing the momentum, the sepoys pushed on. It was an impossible situation. The sepoys were clearly outnumbered, their miniscule force almost engulfed by Haider's army forming a huge semicircle in front. But that, as Smith himself wrote, 'did not prevent our men from marching on with a firmness that will ever do them honour, for notwithstanding all efforts from cannon, musketry, rockets and horse, they could not decompose our lines'.

In the end, discipline and courage prevailed over the numbers, and even firepower. Haider had to give in, and by the time the sepoys were

---

5. The grenadier battalions were formed usually by taking out the flank companies of the other battalions.

obliged to halt with the nightfall, they had driven the enemy off the ground and captured nine cannon. They took up the pursuit early next morning, and the enemy's retreat became a rout; giving them a haul of another 55 guns or more. Eventually, Smith, his line of communication stretched, called them to a halt. It was a thumbing victory, with the enemy losses amounting to some 4000 men and 64 guns with a large quantity of stores. Comparatively, the Madras Army's casualties were negligible; only 150 killed or wounded. The British were immensely benefited at least on one score – it forced Haider's daredevil son, Tipu, to turn back in aid of his father from Madras, where he had them on tenterhooks with his cavalry rampaging at the outskirts.

These initial victories were poor consolation to the British, since Haider with his fast moving cavalry totally outclassed them in mobile warfare and continued to dominate the field. And the East India Company with its penny-pinching policy still stuck to the infantry which was cheaper. Even as Smith took a breather after Tiruvannamalai, Haider went on the offensive once again taking Tirupattur and Vaniambadi to the north in a blitz, and came up against the rock fort at Ambur in the area on 10 November. The garrison of the fort made up of some 600 sepoys and 15 Europeans, commanded by Captain Calvert, refused to surrender. Pounded by gunfire constantly, and striking out with sallies every now and then to deter the enemy from storming the fort, they held out for nearly a month, until at last Haider retired on 6 December, with the approach of the Smith's army from Vellore. The resolute defence of the fort by those handful of men came to be recognized as the bravest action of the campaign, and the battalion involved, the 10 Madras Infantry, was awarded a badge depicting a rock fort, with 'Amboor' inscribed on it. It was the first of the many distinctions the Madras sepoys were to win in battles over the years.

By the end of 1767, Haider's ally, the Nizam, got cold feet, when he heard of a British advance from Bengal on Hyderabad, and backed out of the fight, making separate peace with the British. Haider continued with the campaign; and for the next year and a quarter, the Madras Army found itself engaged in a series of battles from one end of the northern Carnatic to the other, with changing fortunes; none of them decisive. The terror of the Mysore horsemen continued to hold sway over the Carnatic. Then in a brilliant stroke in March 1769, Haider lured Smith's main army away from Madras to Cuddalore by a feint, and making a surprise display at St. Thomas Mount with a 6000-strong force of cavalry, forced the Governor, Charles Bourchier, to sign a treaty of alliance. So ended the 1st Mysore War; and very definitely, it was Advantage Haider Ali. The British however did not honour the treaty when Haider called for aid against the Marathas the next year, partly influenced by the Nawab of Arcot, there having been no love lost between the two. This was a grudge he was to nurse when things came to a flash point in another eleven years, and the 2nd Mysore War broke out.

In Europe, Britain and France were at war with each other again by early 1778. In India the British opened the account by taking Pondicherry, which had been restored to the French earlier. Then in March 1779, they went for Mahe on the West Coast which, although a French possession, happened to have been a protectorate of Haider. Rubbed up the wrong way, he forged an alliance with the Marathas and the Nizam, and invaded the Carnatic in July 1780; and that triggered off the 2nd Mysore War. Although Governor Thomas Rumbold attempted a secret conciliatory mission, things came to a head when Haider's cavalry raided the suburbs of Madras, and his forces besieged Arcot.

What followed was a British nightmare. Aiming to relieve Arcot, Major General Sir Hector Munro, the Commander-in-Chief, marched with a force of 4500 men to Conjeeveram, where a 2700-strong force of Colonel William Baillie, marching from Guntur, was expected to join him. Baillie, delayed by a flooded river, was intercepted by a Mysore force under Tipu near Perambakkam on 6 September. The two forces only skirmished for the next three days, while both awaited reinforcements. On the 9th, a 1000-strong detachment from Conjeeveram under Colonel Fletcher succeeded in eluding the enemy, and joined Baillie. By then Haider's main force, deployed on the route to Conjeeveram, converged on Perambakkam. Baillie, on encountering this force as he set out for Conjeeveram on the 9th evening, pulled back to stay put for the night at a place called Pollilur. By the time he took up the march again early morning, it was too late – he had been surrounded.

Caught out in the open and exposed to the crossfire of some fifty guns, the sepoys made a brave stand forming a square, managing to hold off the enemy for a while, only to be mercilessly cut down by the charging horsemen in the end. The force of nearly 4000 was virtually annihilated, its commander himself wounded and taken prisoner. Meanwhile finding Haider's force out of the way, Munro advanced towards Perambakkam; but beat a hasty retreat as soon as he heard of the debacle, abandoning his heavy guns and stores, and didn't stop until he got to Chingleput, more than 20 miles away. With Haider's cavalry hot on his tail, he lost upwards of 500 killed or wounded, mostly Baillie's gallant sepoys, who had broken through the cordon and formed the rearguard of the retreat. If it was a most infamous reverse for the British, it was also a grand opportunity lost for Haider – had he had only followed up the rout by attacking Munro at Chingleput, it was curtains for the British, at least for the time being.

As it turned out, Lieutenant General Sir Eyer Coote, Commander-in-Chief, India, landed at Madras with reinforcements from Bengal in November and took over the direction of the war; to fight what was to be the second and last campaign of his illustrious career in the Carnatic. Although the field force he could put together was no match for Haider's massive army, he chose to go on the offensive. However, Haider, holding almost all the cards strategically, with almost every British fort under siege by his forces and some taken, was in no hurry for a field battle. And more than six months passed before Coote could engage him. Then on 1 July 1781, their forces met each other among the sand dunes beside the seaside village of Porto Novo, 20 miles south of Cuddalore.

Coote had made an abortive attempt during the previous month to take Haider's fortification at Chidambaram further south, and was marching back to Cuddalore where he was camped for replenishment by sea from Madras. Haider, to pursue his advantage after the British repulse, overtook them by a 100-mile detour and interposed his force at Porto Novo. The force, estimated to have been comprising some 40,000 cavalry and an equal number of infantry, including 600 Europeans, was deployed among the sand dunes with the batteries covering the road to Cuddalore. Coote, with some 60-odd guns, easily outmatched the enemy's artillery, but had only about 8000 men in his ranks in ten sepoy and three European battalions.

On sighting the enemy, Coote swung right to advance close to sea under cover of sand dunes, and then positioning the guns on some sand hills, wheeled west to face the enemy in a two-line formation. Meanwhile Haider manoeuvred his artillery expertly – hauled by the special breed of bullocks the Mysore Army was famous for – to block the British advance. Even as Coote's first line advanced under a tremendous cannonade, the second line came under a furious infantry attack with the cavalry and the guns in close support. With own artillery right at hand for back up, the second line, consisting solely of the sepoys, fought back fiercely to repulse three successive attacks. Running out of patience, Haider ordered a cavalry charge on both the lines simultaneously; but the sepoys won't give ground. Frustrated at the outcome, he disengaged from the fight. The Madras Army, exhausted, with no cavalry to exploit the situation, could only watch the enemy go. Indecisive though, it was a brilliant victory for the sepoys; their small force had outwitted a much larger force; and Haider's casualties were considerably heavy; almost 4000 killed or wounded, with the Madras Army losing less than half that number.

The contest was to be taken up again within a couple of months. Coote, marching to relieve Vellore, ran into Haider at Sholinghur, about 25 miles short of his destination on 27 September, to fight, by all accounts, the most spectacular battle of the campaign. The Madras Army had been reinforced and had 10,000 sepoys and 1500 Europeans in its ranks, besides more than 50 guns and a detachment of the Nawab's cavalry. The Mysoreans had a force bigger than any assembled before, over 100,000 men of cavalry and infantry and 70 guns.

The two forces sighted each other early morning near the foot of a hill. The Mysoreans had their forward troops in a rocky ridge. The Madras Army gained an initial advantage by rushing the ridge and occupying it. The enemy could now be seen some three miles to the south. Coote went for an outflanking manoeuvre by the enemy's left, whereat the broken terrain caused some gaps in the formation. It was too good an opportunity for Haider's cavalry to miss. They came charging through the gaps in a murderous frenzy, as their gunners pounded the advancing troops in an incessant barrage. For the sepoys, it was a moment of trial, the like of which they had never been through before; and they stood their ground magnificently well, pouring down a massed volley of steady fire. Their front rankers mowed down, the horsemen were forced to swing away. And the moment of glory came, when Haider's household cavalry made a thrust. Even while it was resolutely fought off, the sepoys of the 21st Carnatic Battalion seized the leading cavalry standard. His cavalry charge fizzling out, Haider sensed the futility of further contest and quietly pulled out his guns to safety. The British now had the mastery of the field, but once again with very little cavalry for pursuit, failed to exploit the advantage.

Still, it was a glorious battle, which saw the sepoys withstand a full-blooded cavalry charge, and foil it by their sheer courage and grit. The enemy losses were believed to have been in the range of 5000 men, and their own, though lesser, would have been considerable too. 14 battalions of the Madras Infantry, as well as the 3rd Madras Native Cavalry Regiment (the Nawab's) and the Madras Pioneers distinguished themselves in the battle, and all of them were later awarded the Battle Honour, SHOLINGHUR. The captured cavalry standard of Haider Ali is still preserved and proudly displayed, deservedly so, at the museum of the Madras Regimental Centre at Wellington.

Coote went on to relieve Vellore. Notwithstanding his successes in the campaign, things were not going well for the British. The Mysore ruler remained the master of the Carnatic at large. Early in 1782, in an action reminiscent of Baillie's defeat in the beginning of the campaign, Tipu, at the head of 600 horse, 12,000 infantry and 20 guns, surprised a force of 1500 sepoys, 100 Europeans and 9 guns, under Colonel John Brathwaite, at Annagudi near Tanjore, and forced the latter to surrender, after 26 hours of desperate fighting. Only one battalion in the rear managed to fight their way out, and reach the safety of a temple at Mannargudi. And by April Haider's troops were prowling at the gates of Madras, threatening St. Thomas Mount and San Thome. The French had chipped in too for good measure with reinforcements from home; and Cuddalore had already fallen to them and Tipu.

As the campaign lingered on, an ailing Eyre Coote sailed for Bengal, and in December that year Haider Ali died of carbuncle, while at North Arcot. Coote too died a few months later. Two great soldiers whose skills were evenly matched, they orchestrated some of the most stiffly contested battles Southern India ever witnessed; both gave their best, but neither of them could win the war. In the event, within about six months of their death, news arrived of the preliminaries of peace being signed between Britain, France and the rest of the nations involved in the war in the West, and the East India Company opened negotiations with Tipu, who had succeeded his father to become the 'Sultan'. The prisoners were released by a settlement concluded in March 1784. The Madras European Regiments involved in the war, 17 Madras Infantry Battalions, the 3rd Madras Native Cavalry, the Madras Pioneers and four battalions of the Bengal Native Infantry, received the Battle Honour, CARNATIC.

7

SERINGAPATAM

The last stand of Tipu Sultan

O f all the towns and cities which formed the seats of power in South India, Seringapatam, the ancient fortress capital of Mysore, had an aura of invincibility about it. Never in history had it been captured, though threatened on a number of occasions. In 1638 the Bijapur forces had laid siege to it, only to be beaten back with enormous slaughter of their men, and in 1679 the Marathas more or less suffered a similar drubbing. In 1755 the Nizam's troops, aided by the French under Bussy, had almost taken it when most of the Mysore Army was away at Trichinopoly; but they were bought off. Later the Marathas had attacked it twice, in 1757 and 1759, and in a third attempt in 1771, after defeating Haider Ali at Chinkurali, blockaded it for fifteen months; but still couldn't take it. It had been the ultimate British objective in the two Mysore Wars till then, but never attacked. Now in the closing decade of the 18th Century, this historic fortress capital was to become the focal point of the culmination of nearly half a century of bloody warfare in Southern India.

The Carnatic enjoyed six years of comparative peace after the 2nd Mysore War ended. Then in December 1789 Tipu Sultan invaded Travancore, one of the British allies. It was the kind of provocation the British invariably responded to, to capitalize on, and the 3rd Mysore War was soon in the making. The Governor of Madras, Major General William Medows, in command of the army himself, launched an operation from Coimbatore and Dindigul in May the following year. But it didn't come to much, with Tipu totally dominating the West Coast and the adjoining country. By the end of the year, Governor General Lord Cornwallis arrived from Calcutta where the British were now headquartered, after having roped in the Marathas and the Nizam to back the British. He moved to Bangalore, and was successful in capturing the fort there in March 1791 after a fair amount of fighting. Joined by a 10,000-strong contingent of the Nizam's cavalry there, he moved on Seringapatam, the capital of Tipu.

The British force was about eight miles short of its destination at a place called Arikere on 14 May when it was confronted by the Mysore Army, encamped on the north bank of the river Cauvery before their capital across the river. Cornwallis tried to turn the enemy's left flank with six battalions of Madras Infantry the same night, but hampered by a thunderstorm the manoeuvre was complete only by daybreak. Tipu changed his front to the left, and the two armies drew up in battle order facing each other squarely. A stiff engagement followed, at the end of which the Mysoreans were driven back; but couldn't be followed once they were under their fort guns. The Madras Army lost more than 400 killed or wounded, while the enemy losses couldn't be ascertained.

The operation had suddenly turned sour. A reconnaissance of the fort found it too well-fortified to risk an attack. Meanwhile a contingent of the Bombay troops under General Abercromby, marching from the West Coast to reinforce Cornwallis, was reported to be in deep trouble for lack of supplies, their draught animals perishing in hundreds for want of fodder. And Tipu's cavalry still ruled the roost across the open country, posing a threat to the supply lines of the main army itself. Cornwallis hung around just long enough to cover the withdrawal of the Bombay Contingent back to the West Coast, and began withdrawing his own army to Bangalore after bursting its siege guns.

The countryside neighbouring Seringapatam and Bangalore and that which fell in between were dotted by various hill forts held by Tipu's forces. Clearly, no move on Seringapatam could be sustained without neutralizing these. So instead of returning to Bangalore, the Madras Army now turned to the reduction of these forts. Some of them fell without much of a fight; but others fought on doggedly. The fort at Nandidrug held out for nearly a month, before being carried by an assault by the sepoys and Europeans. Another one at Gurramkonda was taken by the sepoys and the Nizam's troops, but recaptured by the Mysoreans who couldn't be dislodged until the end of the war. And by the time the last of these strong points, at Savandrug, 18 miles west of Bangalore, fell to a 2-battalion attack by the sepoys, it was the end of the year 1791.

Even as Cornwallis commenced his operations against the hill forts in June, Tipu had mounted a diversionary attack on Coimbatore. The garrison of about 200 Travancore troops and half as much *topass-es* under two young lieutenants, Chalmers and Nash, beat back the initial assault; and later, reinforced by some 400 sepoys and Travancoreans, gallantly held out for more than four months. But early in November, overwhelmed by a far superior force under Kummer-ud-Din Khan, the ablest of Tipu's field commanders, the garrison surrendered. Undeterred by the setback, Cornwallis moved on Seringapatam.

The Madras Army of some 18 battalions of own infantry, four of the Bengal Infantry, and four regiments of cavalry; by now joined by 12,000 Maratha horsemen and an additional 8000 cavalry from the Nizam, was finally facing the fortifications of Seringapatam by early February 1792. It was a massive show of power; some 25,000 or so of infantry with more than 30,000 cavalry and hundreds of guns. And more troops, of the Bombay Contingent, were marching to join them. For once the British were more than matching the enemy in numbers, and in the cavalry as well. In fact Tipu found himself outnumbered with a garrison of some 40,000 infantry and only 5000 cavalry, although he could match the enemy in artillery.

Seringapatam, about eighty miles southwest of Bangalore, and ten-odd miles northeast of Mysore, is an island stretching some three miles from west to east, and half that much wide, formed, like in the case of Srirangam, by the bifurcation and later convergence of the river Cauvery. The fort stood at the western end, with entrenchments and batteries protecting the eastern end. Tipu had put up his defence works across the river to the north, some three miles long and two miles in depth, facing the British advance. He had his guns positioned in two rows of redoubts, with his entire army drawn up in between.

Cornwallis made contact on 6 February and launched an attack the same night. The attackers punched a breach initially in the middle and a detachment forded across the river; but soon had to withdraw for fear of being isolated. Meanwhile the eastern and western redoubts had been carried, and the whole attacking column converged, to the plan, to the east to turn the defenders' right flank. Even as the manoeuvre was in progress, Tipu launched a counterattack in the predawn hours of the 7th, striking the rear of the middle column where Cornwallis himself was in command. More or less cut off from the main body, two battalions of sepoys and some companies of the British 74th Foot Regiment found themselves engaged in a pitched battle in the dark. The bloody contest of hand-to-hand fighting continued until the daybreak, when Tipu's troops withdrew to the western redoubts, and Cornwallis fell back with his men to join his main body, now formed up below the Karighat hill to the east.

The two opposing forces remained in a stalemate during the day, the Madras Army holding the eastern redoubts and the Mysoreans the western ones. By the next day however, Tipu withdrew his forces across the river. That evening he released two British officers who had been imprisoned at Seringapatam, with an offer of peace. But he didn't specify his conditions, and Cornwallis went on with the preparations for an assault, bringing up his batteries and constructing parallels. The Bombay Contingent, arriving after a week, crossed the river to the northwest of the fort unopposed and took up a position to the southwest by the 19th. Tipu only made a feeble attempt to dislodge them. By then negotiations were in progress, and a peace settlement was arrived at on the 24th.

According to its terms, Tipu was to cede half his dominions to the British and their allies, pay a war indemnity, release all prisoners, and give his two sons as hostages pending fulfillment of his commitments. The two children, of ten and eight years of age, remained in Madras for more than a year. Under the treaty the British obtained the possession of the provinces of Salem, Dindidul and Malabar, and the control of the province of Coorg. It was a great victory for the British, especially for Cornwallis whose military reputation got the much-needed fillip after his humiliating defeat in the American War of Independence. All the cavalry regiments, infantry battalions, and the pioneer and artillery companies, including those of the Bombay and Bengal contingents, which took part in the war, were awarded the Battle Honour, MYSORE.

In the years that followed the 3rd Mysore War, as the Madras Army found itself engaged in scattered bits of action[1] following the outbreak of war between Britain, France and Holland, Tipu kept exploring possible avenues to resume the contest with the British. He was promised French help by Napoleon himself. Things came to a head when Tipu entered into an alliance with the French, and a small party of French officers and men from Maritius landed at Mangalore and joined him at Seringapatam. Irked by the developments, the British mobilized their forces for a showdown that was to become the 4th Mysore War.

Towards the end of the year 1798 the Madras Army was ordered to concentrate at Vellore, while the British fleet imposed an embargo on the Malabar Coast to prevent the French reinforcements reaching Tipu. The Commander-in-Chief of the army was General George Harris. The British couldn't have found a better man for the job – he was the Military Secretary to Cornwallis during the last war. But he had a depleted force, with many battalions away in Ceylon or other places. This was to an

1. The first of these was more or less a one-sided campaign when the Madras troops took Pondicherry. Then consequent to Britain opening hostilities with Holland, an expedition went to Ceylon, and captured the coastal fortifications of the island by early 1796. Another expedition sailed to the Dutch East Indies, and Malaca surrendered later that year.

extent made up by the arrival of six battalions of the Bengal Native Infantry, and the promise of the Nizam's troops and that of a Bombay division. His biggest concern however, was what had been the Madras Army's principal handicap always – lack of transportation. A large number of bullocks had to be found and trained to haul the supplies and guns; and it took time, while pressure built up for an expeditious move to strike, while Tipu was still at his capital and hadn't had time to launch an offensive, which could happen any day. And it was essential that the army reached Seringapatam well ahead of the monsoon, lest the Cauvery be flooded and become impassable.

Ultimately the advance began by the middle of February 1799. Harris had about 25,000 men under his command; more than half of it the native troops of Madras, in four regiments of cavalry, 12 battalions of infantry, and the entire lot of artillery and pioneers of the Madras Army; and the rest constituted by the Bengal troops and over 5000 Europeans. The Nizam's contingent of 10,000 men under their general, Mir Alem, but operationally commanded by Colonel Arthur Wellesley, and the Bombay division of 6400 men under Lieutenant General Stuart would join him later. The advance progressed at a snail's pace, at a pitiful average of five miles a day; a massive column about three miles in frontage and seven miles in depth formed in a hollow square, enclosing a moving city of some 150,000 thousand noncombatants[2], the camp followers; and impeded by the bullock-drawn wagons and guns lumbering along clumsily. It took nearly two months for the march to be over, and on 5 April Harris put up his camp in front of Seringapatam, with his siege train in place.

Meanwhile the Bombay division, marching from Cannanore, ran into trouble as they approached the Mysore frontier. The grueling march across the mountains had cost them some 4000 bullocks, and the brigades got widely separated from each other in the jungles

---

2. It was the practice of the Madras Army during long-drawn out operations, to have even the families moving with the troops.

at the frontier. Tipu struck out and hit the leading brigade isolated near Periapatnam with a 12,000- strong force. The brigade held out gallantly, but was saved from annihilation only by the timely arrival of reinforcements. Stuart was forced to withdraw his troops to the open country, and hold the advance till some cavalry arrived. The division would finally make it to Seringapatam only by the middle of April.

No military operation in the Carnatic till then had seen the planning and preparations in a scale as that Harris undertook for the assault on Seringapatam. Commanding a natural advantage with its location on the island, the fortress was an immense structure of formidable strength. A rectangular edifice stretching a mile from east to west, and about three quarters as much from north to south, its northern and southern walls were washed by the Cauvery as it branched off to either side. With the fort occupying the western end of the island, the peninsular piece of land to the east was heavily fortified by successive lines of ditches and walls, behind a well-built glacis, securing it impregnably against any attack from the north, east or south. Harris chose to attack from the west, the only vulnerable side of the fort where, according to his intelligence, the ramparts had no traverses, and there were few bastions to give flanking fire. The position, he judged, would be difficult to defend if enfilading fire could be brought to bear.

The Madras Army was camped about two miles west of the fort. Harris commenced the operations by clearing the enemy outposts across the river to his side. As the sepoys of the infantry got in to their act with the clearing operations, brief but nasty pieces of engagement, the pioneers too swung into action, making successive parallels and linking them with zigzag trenches, offering cover to the troops right up to the forward-most trenches. Meanwhile a detachment of the cavalry made contact with the stranded Bombay troops, and escorted them to the camp. Arriving on the 14th, they crossed the river and took up a position on the north side of the island. By then Harris was falling short of rations, and was forced to send back his entire cavalry under its commander, Major General Floyd, with a brigade of infantry, to escort the supply column coming up. There loomed a fearsome possibility of it getting cut off for good, with Kummer-ud-Din Khan out there with 6000 of his cavalry, assigned precisely such a mission by Tipu; and another 8000 Mysore Horse remained available in the field under Fateh Hyder and Purnea.

By about the 25th of the month a battery each had been put up to the northwest and southwest of the fort, and they were bringing enfilading fire on the western face. The northwestern angle of the fort was chosen for the assault. It gave the easiest approach across the river, which was shallower at that stretch, and immediate access to the fort itself, being close by, once the troops had crossed over. The breaching batteries were erected towards the end of April, facing the fort at that angle at a distance of only 380 yards; and they opened up on the 30th. The outer wall of the fort to the northwest had been breached before the end of the day, and at night a reconnaissance patrol of the pioneers crossed over and ascertained that the river was fordable. The batteries, reinforced by additional guns, kept up the fire for the next couple of days, matched with equal ferocity by Tipu's fort guns, which bombarded the forward trenches relentlessly.

The heat of the battle was on, and by the 3rd, a breach, 100 feet wide, had been made. The preparations for the assault went on during the night, with the assault planned for 1.p.m. the following day when, it was judged, that in the unbearably exhausting heat of the May afternoon the enemy might not expect an attack, and probably could be caught relaxing. Two columns, right and left, of some 2000 men each, both sepoys and Europeans, were to spearhead the assault, accompanied by the artillery and pioneers, the latter carrying hatchets, scaling ladders and fascines. And the officer chosen to lead them was Major General David Baird, a man who had a personal score to settle with Tipu. Taken prisoner with Baillie at Pollilur in 1780, he had spent nearly four years in the dungeons of Seringapatam.

Tenacious and brave, Tipu was every bit as determined to defend his capital as the British were to capture it. Seven years earlier when Cornwallis had laid siege to the town, he had sought terms, because as a prudent soldier he knew his chances were slim – his armaments and fortifications were not up to the mark. Since then, with the French engineers to help, he had strengthened his fortifications and augmented their firepower enormously. Now forced to withdraw to the fort after his reverses in the field, and outnumbered (he was estimated to have had only 21,000 men within the fort and the island, with the rest of his army deployed in the field or holding the different garrisons), he made the awesome strength and firepower of the place to count. The British troops waiting in the trenches outside were hammered incessantly by fireworks of all kinds; bombs, shells, rockets[3] and musketry. Sorties dashed out of the fort during nights to skirmish with the forward troops of the enemy.

The Sultan's brave stand however seems to have had an element of fatalism[4] to it. On being counselled by the commander of his French troops, Monsieur Chapuis, that it was time to cut and run – preparations had in fact been made for Tipu's escape as the prospects of the fortress being able to defend itself successfully began to look bleak – or to seek

---

3   A study of Tipu's rocket launching sites at Seringapatam, conducted by Dr. A. Sivathanu Pillai, a top Indian rocket scientist and the Chief Controller, R & D, Defence Research and Development Organization (currently the CEO, BrahMos Aerospace), in July 2006 at the behest of President A. P. J. Abdul Kalam (under whose leadership India effectuated its first satellite launch vehicle, SLV-3), revealed that Tipu was the first to apply scientific principles to test and perfect rocket and missile technology in the history of warfare. His was the first army in the world that could boast of a rocket brigade.

4.   It is more than likely that Tipu despaired that the French help, on which he pinned so much hopes on, never arrived, and of the sad fact that he had no Indian allies. His overtures to the Nizam of Hyderabad to unite against the 'Topiwallahs', the foreigners, had gone unheeded. He had reasons to regret a lot on this score, having himself, almost a decade ago, shunned similar advice from the Maratha leader and the greatest Indian statesman of the times, Mahadji Scindia, the one man who probably had the clout in him to forge a grand alliance against the British. Mahadji Scindia had died in 1794, and with him had gone the last chance of a united Indian stand. It was the same old story of India again; of the divided house being swallowed piecemeal by the outsider.

an accommodation with the British by delivering the French troops, he rejected the options out of hand. He was also often ill advised by sycophants who let him down when it mattered. He somehow seems to have despaired and resigned to the 'will of God'. Before noon on the 4th Tipu had reports of an imminent attack by none other than the most reliable of his generals, Syyad Gaffar; but uncharacteristic of the eminent commander he was, he committed a crucial error of judgment. Far too familiar with the British preference for night operations, he ignored the reports; and not only that the threatened point wasn't reinforced, men were even permitted to leave the posts to collect their pay[5]. It was a mistake he would pay dearly for; the shortage of defenders at the breach was to give the attackers a clear advantage to begin with.

A few minutes past 1.p.m. on the 4th, after the troops had had their cheering dram, David Baird drew his sword and sprang out of his trench to lead them in a lightning charge across the Cauvery, covered by the fire of every gun that could be brought to bear. In an amazing feat, sprinting across the hard riverbed, they had ascended the breach and planted their standard on the rampart in less than seven minutes, almost to their own disbelief. But hardly had they gained the advantage, they were up against an inner rampart lined with troops, with a wide and deep ditch in between covered by gunfire. Blunted to a sudden halt, the men wheeled left and right, running along the rampart, desperate to find a way across. Someone found a makeshift platform about a foot wide spanning the ditch, and soon the attackers were crossing over in a

---

5. This part of the events remains mired in controversy, since it is apparent that for all the brilliant planning and execution of the storming of Seringapatam, the celebrated British victory wasn't devoid of a certain amount of Plassey-style treachery; strangely, with another 'Mir', Mir Sadiq, the Sultan's Dewan, enacting the role that Mir Jaffer played at Plassey, although on a much smaller scale. The British commander had fixed the time of attack in connivance with the traitor, who withdrew the troops guarding the breach at that hour under the pretence of a distribution of pay, and is even believed to have given a signal to the enemy. This alone could explain the storming party gaining the summit of the breach so swiftly and practically unopposed. However, unlike Mir Jaffer who lived to see the results of his treachery, Mir Sadiq didn't even survive the day – even as fighting raged within the fort, he was slain by men loyal to the Sultan.

single line, and charging left and right in a raging spasm. The defenders on the inner rampart, hastily assembled in a disorganized crowd, failed to stem this initial onslaught, and it was all chaos and confusion then onwards.

There was bitter fighting, and many a Mysore soldier fought steadfastly (as the considerable number of casualties among the attackers were to bear testimony to later); but they surely had lost the day even before the fighting had started. It was a scene right out of hell – the British troops in red coats and Tipu's 'Tiger' sepoys in their tiger-striped uniforms rushing at each other amidst the din and clatter of the guns and small arms. They clashed in a mortal contest, with muskets and pistols, bayonets and swords, daggers and ever bare hands. But the defenders were soon giving ground, with more and more of the attackers pouring in. One after the other they had to yield the traverses they had turned on the enemy with good effect, and soon they were fighting with their backs to the wall. There was panic and pandemonium as many of the defenders crowded the single exit of the sally-port in a bid to escape, compounding the chaos[6] and adding to their already soaring rate of casualties.

Tipu had just begun to have his lunch when the news of the attack reached him, preceded by the intelligence that Syyad Ghaffar had been killed[7]. Rushing along the rampart towards the breach, he shot down a couple of attackers; then finding his men falling back, ran back along

---

6. In an interesting development during the confusion that prevailed, Dhoondiah Wagh, a daring Indian mercenary who had been imprisoned in the fort, made good his escape to his native province of Bidnur, and putting together a bunch of horsemen, occupied Shimoga and the neighbouring forts. It took some stiff fighting, and more than three months, for the British to wrench it back from him. Even then, augmented in strength by a good part of the Mysore cavalry at large, he kept the fight going for more than a year; until at last overwhelmed by a far superior force under Arthur Wellesley in September 1800. Dhoondiah was killed, and his force dispersed for good, ending what is historically referred to as the Bidnur Rebellion.

7. In a tragic twist of fate, Syyad Gaffar had actually noticed the existence of the makeshift platform across the ditch, and turned to order its removal, when he was killed.

the rampart to the sally-port. Here was his chance if he wanted to flee, since he only had to make his way across the river to his cavalry; but he chose to fight. Mounting his horse, he tried to ride in through the sally-port, hoping to rally his men along the ramparts of the inner fort and make a stand, little knowing that the enemy troops had already made their way there. In the event, he found the gateway choked by fugitives fleeing from the attackers. The attackers were on to them even before Tipu could bring about some order, and he found himself personally engaged in hand-to-hand fighting with them. His horse was soon shot from under him. Wounded more than once, he fought on, probably his last act that of slashing with his saber at an enemy soldier, who in turn shot him dead.

It was all over in a couple of hours; the defence had burned itself out, and the attackers were fully in possession of the fort. The French troops in the Sultan's service, assembled at the entrance of his palace, surrendered without giving a fight after firing a few rounds in a symbolic gesture. The attackers now turned the captured guns onto the enemy fortifications outside the fort; but the fort having fallen, the troops there had no more fight left in them, and they just gave up or fled to the hills beyond the river. By nightfall, with the Sultan's fate unknown, the British forced the surrender of the fort by his two young sons. They were later led away in captivity to Vellore.

Tipu's dead body was found amid a heap of slain after the nightfall. He had been shot through the head and bayoneted thrice. They called him the 'Tiger of Mysore'; and he had lived up to the name every bit, fighting to the last, his sword in hand; his soldier's honour never to be disputed. Nearly 10, 000 of his men fell fighting with him. The British casualties were about 1500 killed, wounded and missing; some 800 of these Europeans, and the rest Indians; a great number of the latter, the Madras sepoys. The heavy toll of casualties among the defenders suggests certain amount of wanton killing after the fighting ended. There was also large-scale plunder, looting and rape, before order was restored the next day. Thus the victory, the greatest and the most significant so far by the Madras Army, over such a formidable enemy – Tipu's troops, trained by the French, were considered as good or better than the British sepoys – in a grimly fought battle, was to leave a stain that would do no honour to the troops, both European and Indian.

The legendary storming of the breach at Seringapatam by the Madras Army and its allies, together with the gallant if disorganized defence by the Mysore forces, created an epic military drama, probably unequalled in its ferocity and valour of the participants by any other battle fought on the subcontinent. For the descendant regiments of those that partook in the action, of both the British and Indian Armies, the Battle Honour, SERINGAPATAM, earned by their ancestors on that torrid May afternoon, remains one of the most revered accolades to pride about. The fall of the fortress capital of Mysore was also a significant turning point in India's history. The British domination of South India was more or less complete with it, leaving them free to divert their attention northward. Of the spoils, the one to accrue immediate strategic benefit to the British was Tipu's train of draught bullocks, of a special breed, which enabled Arthur Wellesley to organize his supply trains during the subsequent Deccan campaigns. The first field commander in India to recognize the significance of logistics, Wellesley was to win great victories by the thoroughness with which he planned his lines of march.

Some papers found at Seringapatam implicated the Nawab of Arcot, Umdat-ul-Umara, son of the late Muhammed Ali, in a conspiracy with Tipu. This provided the British the excuse to shed any pretence there was, and take over the direct administration of the Carnatic. But they chose to wait for the ailing Nawab to die, to make that ultimate treachery look a little less conspicuous if possible. When the Nawab died in 1801, they sent in troops to occupy his palace. The Nawab's son, Ali Hussain, kept his dignity and rejected the terms offered; a conscientious act, but one that came many years too late. They merely elevated his pliable cousin, Azim-ud-Daula, to the crown. And under an arrangement concluded with the new Nawab, the English East India Company virtually annexed the whole of the Carnatic. They were soon to emerge as the undisputed pre-eminent power in the subcontinent.

Tipu Sultan was Britain's most feared adversary in India ever. No one else gave them the kind of fight he did; and he was the only Indian ruler to have never submitted to the infamous Subsidiary system, so unashamedly promoted by Governor General Lord Wellesley, which shackled the whole of India into colonial shame. Tipu evoked mixed feelings when he lived, among his countrymen as well as the Britons he fought. Some considered him a fantastic military leader, some a fanatic, some thought of him as an able administrator, some as an Oriental despot. Antony Wild, the author of a modern day work on the times, *The East India Company, Trade and conquest from 1600,* observes:

One of the ironies of the Company's war against Tipu is that in many ways Tipu had accomplished in Mysore what the Company later aspired to achieve in India as a whole. Having inherited the state from his father, the General Hyder Ali, he had modernized the administration, improved the infrastructure through road and irrigation projects, had developed agriculture and encouraged new industries, such as silk cultivation. As a Muslim in a predominantly Hindu state, Tipu practiced a high degree of religious tolerance, and, through his tiger cult, was an avid patron of arts. He was esteemed by those he ruled over, and his armies were fiercely effective, and loyal. If he had been an ally of the Company, he would have been admired publicly by those who recognized his abilities in private, but he had vowed to remove the Company from India, and that, when it came down to it, was all that mattered. However when it comes down to his credibility as a prototype nationalist hero, against his implacable hatred of the English must be set the fact that his father had usurped the Mysore throne from an Hindu incumbent, who, ironically, it took the Company to restore, albeit on a short leash.

It is more than likely that allegations of religious fanaticism against Tipu – especially those of his having indulged in forced conversions during his Malabar campaign – could well have been British propaganda to turn the popular Hindu sentiment against him; since both Haider Ali and Tipu seem to have enjoyed the overwhelming support of the Hindu population. The fact that a large part of the Mysore Army was constituted of Hindu soldiers, and poojas and other rituals at the Ranganathaswamy Temple at Seringapatam for the army's success was a regular feature, which both Haider and Tipu were particular about before they set out on any campaign, does indicate such a trend. While there could of course be no absolving Haider of atrocities committed against Coorgs, and Tipu of those against the Hindus of Malabar, sympathetic historians point out that military or political expediency, rather than religious bias, was the motive behind both.

Controversies apart, Tipu Sultan, in India's collective psyche, remains the grandest icon of her defiance against the British imperialism in its early years; and his gallant last stand invariably admired by friends and foes alike. At Seringapatam, to the northwest angle of the old fortress, stands a lonely obelisk, on which are engraved the names of the British and Indian regiments which fought, and those of their officers who fell. And to the east end of the island lies the mausoleum, where Tipu, aged 46 when he died, was buried beside his parents.

8

POLIGAR REBELLION

The brave hearts of Panjalamkurichi

Submissiveness wasn't a trait the proud people of the Marava country were easily given to, especially when provoked by armed aggression, that too by an alien power. Formed into a loose confederacy under the leadership of their Poligars, they had been waging an unequal war for almost the entire half of a century when the British power was on the rise in the Carnatic, essentially to preserve their sovereignty over Tinnevelly. They never believed in giving up the fight.

There were over thirty Poligars in the region who, together or in separate groups, kept the fight going from early 1750s, when Nawab Mohammed Ali sent the first of the expeditions to subdue them. It consisted of a few thousand native troops, with a small detachment of British soldiers under Lieutenant Innis. Not only that the attempt proved abortive, the emboldened Poligars went on to hold Madura under Chanda Sahib's flag, when they decisively repulsed James Cope's force. This was followed by Alexander Heron's infamous expedition in 1755, after the British had beaten off the French challenge and had Trichinopoly in their firm hold. Once again, for all its initial successes, the Nawab and the British ended up looking silly, with the Nawab's brother, who commanded the native troops, treating secretly with the Poligars, and the British commander, whom he bribed off, having had to be court-martialled and sacked.

---

1. The Puli Tevan Palace at Tirunelveli, revered as a historic monument now, was the headquarters of this first Tamil Chieftain to resist the British.

The confederacy under their best known leader, Puli Tevan[1], again gained the upper hand; and joined by a contingent of the well-trained Travancore Army, handed out one humiliating defeat after another to the Nawab's forces under his discredited brother Mahfuz Khan. Although Mahfuz Khan managed to pull off a victory in the end (chanced by a pullout of the Travancoreans and a rift between the eastern and western Poligar leagues), it is only after Yusuf Khan appeared on the scene that the confederacy was contained to some extent. Even then, during the periods of his absence (first when he was recalled to secure Madura, and later when he was engaged at Madras during its siege), the Poligars, joined by Mahfuz Khan himself and the Travancoreans, held sway over the region. Ultimately, although Yusuf Khan managed to stem the tide by winning the allegiance of the Travancoreans – later they turned against each other – by ceding Kalakkad to them, his own reign proved short-lived ending in his hanging in 1764.

The strife continued unabated for the remaining part of the century, with the British occasionally succeeding to put down the rebellious Poligars, only to face yet another insurrection within a few years, assisted for some time by the Dutch at Tuticorin. So it was inevitable that the British would run into trouble with their tax collection drive in the southern provinces beyond Madura. In fact, trouble was brewing up even as they were engaged in the 4th – also the last – Mysore War in the closing years of the 1790s. The final drama of this struggle would be played out in the small hamlet of Panjalamkurichi deep south, at the dawn of the 19th Century.

Panjalamkurichi, located about 75 miles south of Madura, had for its Poligar, Kattabomman Nayak, a brave man and a sworn enemy of the British, who had been in the forefront of the fight against them for more than three decades by then. In 1783 he had gallantly fought off a determined attempt by a Madras Army division under Colonel William Fullarton, the most successful of the British commanders to have fought the Poligars, to storm his fort, before being forced to abandon it in the face of the enemy's far superior arms. While the other Poligars of the area, most of whom were also rebellious, submitted to the British authority towards the end of the century, Kattabomman led an uprising in Ramnad in 1797. In August 1798, W. C. Jackson, the British collector at Madura, persuaded the defiant Poligar to meet him at Ramnad. Either Jackson attempted, or Kattabomman suspected a trap, and the latter's escape bid turned violent; the fort commander of the place, Colonel Clarke, getting fatally wounded in the fracas. Kattabomman extricated himself with his party. The British, much as they wished to go after him, could do little, tied up as they were with the war with Tipu.

Soon after the fall of Seringapatam, a force of some 400 Europeans and two battalions of sepoys with a detachment of the Bengal artillery, commanded by Major Bannerman, moved against the fort at Panjalamkurichi. Overconfident of his superiority, Bannerman attempted to storm the fort before his artillery had taken up their posts, and was thrashed soundly; his attack repulsed with terrible losses. But he was reinforced soon, and better prepared, he opened up with his guns the next day. That night, with the fall of the fort imminent under intense bombardment, Kattabomman escaped with a few followers to Pudukotta while his two brothers and a general and confidant, Subramania Pillai, held out with the remaining men before surrendering after a while. The two brothers were taken captives; and Pillai, with whom the British had a score to settle (his having raided and plundered their post at Palamcottah nearby, not long ago), was executed. Perhaps they all had hoped to gain some time for their escaped leader, so that he lived to fight another day. But that wasn't to be; Kattabomman was caught by the Tondaman ruler of Pudukotta who was friendly to the British, and handed over to them. He was hanged as a rebel on 16 October 1799 at Kayattaru, and his fort razed to the ground.

But the flame that Kattabomman lit wasn't about to be put off that easily. Two of his brothers who were incarcerated at Palamcottah managed to escape in February 1801. One of them, born dumb (and hence known variously as Oomaiyan or Oomadurai), was a ferocious fighter reputed for his daring exploits; and the people of Panjalamkurichi rallied under him to renew the fight. In a remarkably short period of time they rebuilt the fort and formed a 1500-strong garrison to man it. By the time the British field commander in the province, Major Macaulay, was able to put together a force of about 1000 men and move against the hamlet, the garrison had swelled to a strength of nearly 5000, the people of the surrounding country having enthusiastically assembled under Oomadurai; prepared for a showdown. Outnumbered, Macaulay beat a hasty retreat, fighting off a night sortie by the rebels. Positioning himself at Palamcottah, he sent a desperate plea for reinforcements. Meanwhile the insurrection spread like wild fire, and the rebelling Poligars soon took many of the forts including that of Tuticorin.

The British reinforcements arrived on 27 March; and Macaulay, now commanding a 3000-strong force, marched to Panjalamkurichi, to appear before the hamlet on the morning of the 31st. The fort was built in an oblong form some 500 feet long and 300 feet broad, a strong, well-fortified structure surrounded by a thick thorny hedge. The British guns started a bombardment, and by 3 in the afternoon a practicable breach had been made in the northwest bastion. An assault was launched immediately.

The storming party, covered by a barrage and musketry from the rest of the force, broke through the hedge braving the odds, and made it to the top of the breach. That's as far as they got; every man who showed himself further fell dead or maimed in an instant. The defenders had played an ingenious trick. The bastions were made hollow, and the attackers, once on top, suddenly found themselves with no footing; and right when they tottered, the defenders, closely packed inside the bastions and armed with their traditional 18-foot pikes, played merry hell into them. The dead and the dying rolled back in a heap. There was no way the assault was going to succeed, and at the end of the day Macaulay's men were left licking their wounds, having lost 4 officers and 49 men killed, and 13 officers and 254 men wounded. Only at the hands of Yusuf Khan had the Madras Army suffered a drubbing of that severity in the past.

Macaulay set up camp about a mile away from the fort and awaited further reinforcements. They arrived after about two months, on 21 May – a massive force this time, with a large train of artillery, commanded by Colonel Agnew who now took charge of the operation. A well-planned assault was launched on the 24th. There was delay crossing the hedge again, but once on top the attackers were better prepared. In a hot contest that lasted over twenty minutes, they countered the pike men in the bastions by throwing in grenades. At the end of it almost the entire lot of defenders within the bastions was killed, and the attackers began bludgeoning their way into the fort. For the gallant Poligars, it was the end of the road; but they chose to die fighting like men rather than surrender. About 3000 of them who were within the fort rushed out in battle order to meet the enemy head on in a suicidal charge. And that's what it turned out to be, because they ran right into the enemy cavalry charging at them. It was mayhem all over, the Poligars adding a bit of innovation even in that last desperate bid as they unleashed their famed dogs of the Rajapalalyam breed into the fight. These ferocious canines, every bit as brave as their masters, gave the cavalrymen a run for their money as they sprang fearlessly at the riders and their mounts, biting and tearing.

The Madras Army's casualties in the battle were estimated to be nearly 200. The Poligar losses were of course much more. But the rebellion did not die off still. Oomadurai and his brother survived, and withdrawing into the nearby jungles with many of the rebels, carried on with the struggle. It took a fair bit of intense fighting for the British to quell the rebellion ultimately by October that year, when Oomadurai and his brother, captured at Sivaganga, were brought to Panjalamkurichi and hanged. The fort was once again razed to the ground; and the site ploughed over and sown with castor seeds.

The operations to put down the Poligar Rebellion cost the Madras Army nearly a 1000 men killed and wounded, including 40 or so officers. In the pages of history, this rebellion often finds itself relegated to the status of a localized conflict born of frustration among the traditionally recalcitrant Poligars, whose power and influence the East India Company tried to curtail. Nevertheless, it stands out unique in that it was the first popular insurrection of the kind in the South, in which the participation of the people, and not the diktats of any sovereign that became instrumental. The immense mass following enjoyed by Kattabomman and his brothers was definitely indicative of the overwhelming popular resentment to the crude imposition of the British authority at that time.

The British themselves admired the dogged courage of the Maravas who, poorly armed, with no formal training and with no artillery worth the name, held out against the might of the Madras Army for more than a year. No wonder in later years, heartily encouraged by the British, many of these brave fighters and their descendants found themselves in the ranks of the Madras Regiment. There is an interesting anecdote on the courage of the Poligars, quoted by Lieutenant Colonel Phythian-Adams – who authored quite a few books on the southern soldiery – in his history of the Madras Regiment, as narrated by another officer in an earlier work. The passage reads:

Col. Welsh describes how one of the Poligars fighting on the side of the British, when mortally wounded, had himself carried into the presence of the British Commander. The old man who was placed upright in a chair then said in a firm voice: "I have come to show the English how a Poligar can die." He twisted his whiskers with both hands as he spoke and in that attitude expired.

The Poligar Rebellion was also unique for being the first insurrection in the country to have displayed a degree of trans-national ethos. Marudu Pandyan, the chief exponent of the rebellion in Sivaganga, had tried to expand its scope by forging a grand alliance of the disaffected groups all across the peninsula. Besides all the Southern Poligars, the alliance generally included the Poligars of Dindigul, the Kurichias of Malabar, Dhoondiah Wagh of Bidnur, some Sardars of Nizam and even some of the Maratha chiefs including Daulat Rao Scindia. Unfortunately this popular initiative that came to be often referred to as the South

Indian Rebellion, could only bring about widespread but isolated peasant uprisings lacking cohesiveness, all of which collapsed within a year in the face of the sustained military onslaught by the British. But the resentment to alien rule continued to prevail with sporadic disturbances like the Chittoor Poligar Revolt of 1804, and major insurgencies like the Pazhassi revolt of Malabar. The Poligar Rebellion found its echo one last time, when the sentiments it evoked proved partially instrumental in inciting the sepoys to mutiny at Vellore in 1806.

Somewhat lesser known, a fierce bit of resistance against the British power took place in Canara too at the same time as the Poligar Rebellion. In what seems to have been an isolated episode, the Rajah of Bullum blockaded Mangalore, by occupying a stockaded position across the hilly tract leading to the town from Mysore, at a place called Arraikara, which was his base. The British lost 47 men in their first abortive attempt to dislodge him in April 1800. Although they succeeded in clearing the blockade subsequently with the arrival of reinforcements (taking another 150 or so casualties in the process), the hardy Rajah reoccupied his position soon thereafter, and not until 1802, when Arthur Wellesley launched a full-scale operation with some four battalions could Arraikara be finally taken. The Rajah and his brave followers were executed.

The Poligar Rebellion was the last flicker of defiance by the people of the Tamil homeland against the inexorable slide of the region into the ignominy of colonialism. More than a century and a half later the story of this gallant uprising was to inspire the making of the Tamil block buster movie, *Veera Pandya Kattabomman,* wherein Thespian Sivaji Ganesan donned the role of Kattabomman. A memorial hall for this intrepid warrior adorns the hamlet of Panjalamkurichi.

9

ASSAYE

A battle greater than that of Waterloo

In the heartland of the Deccan, some fifty miles northeast of Aurungabad, just above the junction of two small rivers, Juah and Kelna, lay the small village of Assaye. On the strip of land facing the village, a mile or so wide between the two rivers, one September afternoon in the year 1803, the Madras Army fought its first major battle beyond the borders of the Carnatic. It was also destined to be its most famous battle, and the most decisive one of what the historians came to call the 2nd Maratha War, a conflict which saw the end of the century-old Maratha power.

The leadership of the Marathas, who had organized themselves into a powerful nation under Shivaji in the 17th Century, had gradually passed on to the Peshwa, the Chief Minister. Baji Rao, the second of the great Peshwas, set up the Maratha Confederacy, by joining together the other rulers of his ilk. The members of the confederacy were Holkar of Indore, Gaikwar of Baroda, Scindia of Gwalior, Bhonsle of Nagpore and the Peshwa himself, who acted as its chief, based at Poona. After the historic Maratha debacle in the Third Battle of Panipat in 1761, fissures appeared in the weakened confederacy, presenting the British with the opportunity to make inroads into the Maratha affairs. Pitching one faction against the other, soon they were engaged in the 1st Maratha War from 1775 to 1782, a successful campaign in which they employed the Bombay and Bengal troops. At the turn of the century, having established their supremacy in the South, they were again engaged in the 2nd Maratha War, following the overthrow of their ally, the Peshwa. Early in 1803, they launched simultaneous offensives into the Deccan and Northern India.

The Deccan offensive was undertaken by Madras troops, under Arthur Wellesley, by now a major general. He marched into the Deccan early in March at the head of over 10,000 troops of all arms, supported by a 9000-strong contingent of the subsidiary force from Hyderabad under Colonel Stevenson, and restored the Peshwa at Poona in May with little difficulty, save for a forced march of 60 miles in 32 hours to beat Holkar – who was threatening to burn the city before evacuating it – in the game. In August, he took Ahmednagar, the fort surrendering after a stout defence by some Arab mercenaries on Scindia's pay. Then on 23 September, he came up against the combined armies of Scindia and Bhonsle, unexpectedly at Assaye. They had a powerful, well-trained force of 20,000 thousand cavalry, 12,000 thousand infantry under European officers and over 100 guns.

The Madras Army, marching northward, sighted the enemy drawn up in battle order across the river Kelna around 1.p.m. The Marathas had their left on the village, with the parallel stream Juah to the back. Wellesley, despite realizing that he was perilously outnumbered (separated from the Hyderabad Division at that juncture, he could field only 6000 men and 17 guns), chose to risk an attack as only the boldest of field commanders dare. He formulated his plan to attack the enemy's left, and crossed the Kelna at a short distance above the confluence of the two streams. The crossing was not contested as such, but the enemy artillery came down heavily, and most of the precious few British guns were soon put out of action. The Madras Army formed up across the fork between the two rivers, in two lines of infantry in front and one of cavalry in the rear, facing northwestward for the attack. The Marathas meanwhile deftly changed their front, facing the enemy squarely. His plan to attack the enemy's left foiled; Wellesley was left with no option but to go in for a frontal assault.

The enemy line was defended by their massive array of guns, some of them in front of the village, where there was a strong concentration of infantry. The Madras Army's first line was composed of three regiments, the British 78th Foot on the left, the 8th and 10th Madras Native Infantry in the centre, the pickets – vanguard formed of details from all the units – on the right, and four 12-pounder guns in between. The second line, 300 yards behind, consisted of the 4th and 24th Madras Native Infantry, with the British 74th Foot on the right immediately behind the pickets. The third line, of the cavalry, had three regiments of the Madras Native Cavalry, the 4th, 5th and the 7th, in that order from right to left, with the British 19th Dragoons between the 4th and the 5th.

The attacking formation advanced steadily under heavy fire. All went according to the plan until suddenly the commander of the pickets overplayed his hand. He had orders to keep out of range of the strongly held village; but either misinterpreting them or in confusion, he diverged right and went straight for the stronghold, and the 74th Foot from the second line right behind promptly followed. The consequence proved disastrous. Both were mauled by the fire from the village. And the enemy cavalry on the flank, commanded by Scindhia in person, broke through the fissure in the line caused by the divergence of the pickets. However before the situation got out of hand, own cavalry from behind came to the rescue. Galloping forward, they took on the enemy horse, and pushed them back in time, but not before they themselves had suffered enormous casualties.

The first line, meanwhile, made it right up to the line of enemy guns, and taking casualties though, drove the defenders from the guns in a do-or-die bayonet charge. The gunners stuck to their posts gallantly, many dying in the act; some even feigning death while the attackers charged through, to promptly turn around the guns and fire at their rear. The attackers pushed through and carried a second line the enemy had taken up at right angles to the first, with the Juah to the rear. Now the Maratha line broke; some of the battalions gave up entirely and fled, while others disengaged in good order, only to be broken up by the charging cavalry. The Madras Army was left in command of the field, with over 100 guns left behind by the enemy, with their dead and the dying.

The casualties were heavy on both sides. The Madras Army lost 198 Europeans and 230 sepoys killed, 442 Europeans and 696 sepoys wounded, and 4 Europeans and 14 sepoys missing; a total of 1584, more than a quarter of its 6000 combatants in the field. The Maratha losses were estimated to be 1200 men killed and 4800 wounded. The Battle of Assaye, one of the most ferocious engagements ever fought in India, stands out as a singularly unique feat of arms, because it was won in defiance of all accepted tactical principles. A vastly outnumbered force with no artillery worth mentioning, had attacked the enemy at a position of their choosing, and won the day. Initially the Marathas had everything going in their favour, including surprise, when they skillfully changed their front – a manoeuvre Wellesley never considered they would attempt – forcing the enemy to attack frontally. Wellesley's was a perilous option. He had his back to the river, and had the attack faltered, things would have ended up in absolute disaster. And his overenthusiastic pickets almost brought ruin by their preemptive action. And it was just a quirk that the Maratha infantry didn't stand their ground as their gunners did. Even then it was such a hard fought battle that if only the Marathas had chosen to counterattack, the Madras Army wouldn't have been able to sustain it, disorganized and exhausted as they were after the titanic effort.

The victory in such a battle wherein the batteries were believed to have been 'silenced by the bayonets', won the Madras troops accolades. Arthur Wellesley, later the celebrated victor of Waterloo as the Duke of Wellington, was to maintain all along that Assaye was the closest fought battle of his career. All the regiments which participated in it were awarded the Battle Honour, ASSAYE, apart from honorary colours and distinctions. The Madras Regimental Centre commemorates this victory, which has come to take the pride of place amongst the regiment's feats, on the 'Assaye Day', on 23 September every year. The device of the Assaye

Elephant, sanctioned as a special honour badge to the participant battalions, surmounts the crossed swords and shield of the regimental crest, and the cap badge, of the Madras Regiment.

After Assaye, the division under Colonel Stevenson – which had missed the battle – took up the pursuit of the retreating enemy, while the rest of the army took a respite for a few days. This division, after a month of fighting minor engagements here and there reducing the scattered enemy, came up against their hill fortress at Assirghur. Putting up his batteries, Stevenson opened fire with seven guns on 20 October; but surprisingly, this exceptionally strong fort – which was to witness an intense contest between the same adversaries sixteen years later – capitulated on the following day without as much as giving a token fight. The same afternoon however, the main army under Wellesley was to fight a sizeable field battle at Argaum, only six miles from this fort. Rather late in the act though, the Maratha forces had drawn up there to break the siege; and Wellesley, moving up to join Stevenson, went for an immediate attack.

The fight didn't go well for Wellesley to begin with, as his point battalion, emerging from a village into the enemy's range, was thrown into confusion when the enemy gunners opened up with a heavy barrage. It took some time for the men to be rallied again, and they were formed up for the attack only by 4.30.p.m. The army advanced in two lines of infantry, with the cavalry bolstering the flanks. The Arabs' and the Scindia's cavalry struck out almost immediately, fiercely attacking the flanks, only to be repulsed with equal ferocity. The lines continued to advance steadily. The enemy forces were soon proving no match for the attacking formation pushing forward relentlessly. Their line began to waver, and then they were retreating everywhere in disarray, leaving some 38 guns and their ammunition behind. 20 standards were captured. The cavalry was already in hot pursuit, causing havoc among enemy ranks. But night was already gathering, reprieving the Marathas of further loss. And the Madras Army had won yet another significant victory; and its own casualties, for the kind of battle it was, were almost negligible – 46 killed and 308 wounded.

There remained only one major Maratha stronghold in the whole theatre, standing in the way of a complete sweep by the Madras Army – the hill fortress of Gawilgarh. Perched at the end of a spur of the Satpura Ranges, its perimeter on three sides fell precipitously to the plains 2000 feet below, making it accessible only from the northerly direction. A massive wall with bastions all over blocked the approach, with a second wall behind protecting the inner fort. Positioned to sweep the narrow approach with deadly concentration were some 52 cannons and 150 wall pieces. Manning the fort was a garrison of 4000, composed of Rajputs and the Maratha infantry which had escaped from Argaum, all armed with English muskets and bayonets. Commanding them was a man of exceptional gallantry, Beni Singh, who would rather die than ever surrender. To take on this daunting objective, Wellesley had two divisions which, miserably depleted after their losses at Assaye and Argaum, barely amounted to brigades.

The divisions arrived at the foot of the hill at Gawilgarh on 5 December. After a couple of days' reconnaissance, Wellesley chalked out a plan to mount a frontal attack from the northern approach, while throwing simultaneous feints up the steep slopes to the south and the west, the two other faces where the fort had gates. Stevenson's division was to carry out the main assault, while the rest of the troops under Wellesley were to go for the feints. Stevenson's men, moving up with the siege trains, toiled for nearly a week, cutting a road and hauling up the guns. With the guns in position, they opened fire on the 13th morning. Pounding relentlessly for two days, they managed a negotiable breach by nightfall on the 14th.

Meanwhile Wellesley's men laboured desperately to haul some guns up the southern face, to no avail. The rounds fired, from two small pieces they had somehow dragged part of the way up, bounced off the stout stone wall and rolled downhill right on to the heads of the gunners. Ultimately the plan was finalized for a combined attack from all the three faces on the 15th. Simultaneous with Stevenson's main assault from the north, a party each under Wellesley and Lieutenant Colonel

Chalmers were to attempt storming the fort from the south and west faces too. The main storming party, commanded by Lieutenant Colonel Kenny, was to consist of the 19th, 21st and 22nd MI[1] and flank companies of the 94th Foot, with the 6th, 11th and 20th MI and the remainder of the 94th Foot in support. Wellesley's party would have the 8th MI and five companies of the 78th Foot, while Chalmers would have the 10th MI and the remainder of the 78th Foot with him.

The three parties moved into the assault promptly at the appointed time of 10.a.m. Kenny's main force ran into tough resistance immediately, but carried the breach with the initial thrust. Then they were in a free-for-all, furious and bloody, between the two walls. The Marathas, with Beni Singh personally in command, fought like the devils. The closed space turned to a cauldron of fire and smoke, of roaring musketry and raging battle cries. Then Beni Singh fell, as only the best of men do, fighting to the last. Even as some of his men fell back in an escape bid through the northwest gate, Chalmers' party, hauling themselves up the slope, entered that way, and the attackers had won the first round. But the inner fort was still intact, and attempts to force open the gates were finding no success. Escalade was the only option, and soon with ladders in place men were scaling their way up. They went over the wall in a dash, and into the melee again within the fort. Those who made it first drove the enemy off the wall and opened the gates; and the rest of the attackers poured in. It was all over for the Marathas; but they refused to surrender, and it turned out to be a fight to the finish. Many of the remaining defenders fell fighting, or threw themselves to their death over the walls. Gawilgarh had been taken. The Madras Army's loss was 126 men in all, among them, Kenny, the officer who led the storming of the breach.

Although major fighting came to an end with the fall of Gawilgarh, the war lingered on for another two years when a division of the Madras Army was engaged in the reduction of Holkar's possessions in Khandesh. Even after the conclusion of peace between the Marathas and the British in early 1806, Madras troops were again to be deployed in the

Deccan before the end of the decade, to discipline some of the Holkar's dependants who turned freebooters and caused trouble. And they would be back in a big way again before the end of following decade, to fight another major war, the 3rd – and the last – Maratha War.

The master stroke of the 2nd Maratha War, undoubtedly, was Wellesley's campaign. The high level of mobility he achieved by means of his supply trains contributed a lot to his success. And so did the tremendous fighting potential of the Madras Army. However, it would appear that the fighting prowess of the great Maratha armies, especially that of their famed cavalry, had somewhat diminished, by the time the war was fought. The divisive tendencies among their rulers had eaten away at the morale of the troops; and having lost sight of the grand objective of the Maratha Empire, they could no more emulate the glorious feats of their ancestors. On the other hand, unlike in earlier wars, the Maratha infantry and artillery which took the field had been extensively trained by veteran European officers employed by the various rulers, and was every bit as competent as any in the world[2]. In fact, Scindia's brigades were trained by the French general, Comte Benoit de Boigne, one of the greatest military geniuses of the 18th Century. They also had a large number of foreign mercenaries, Afghans, Arabs and Europeans, in their ranks, who fought with commendable zeal. That the Madras Army emerged victorious against such formidable foes, and often against heavy odds as at Assaye, was a thumbing commentary on the grit and cool of the southern soldier, who by then had become the cornerstone of English East India Company's supremacy over Peninsular India.

---

1. Abbreviation for Madras Infantry (Regiment) as commonly used in this book.
2. It has however been suggested that the adoption of the European model that centred on infantry and artillery might have done the Marathas more harm than good, since they were traditional cavalrymen who excelled in mobile warfare.

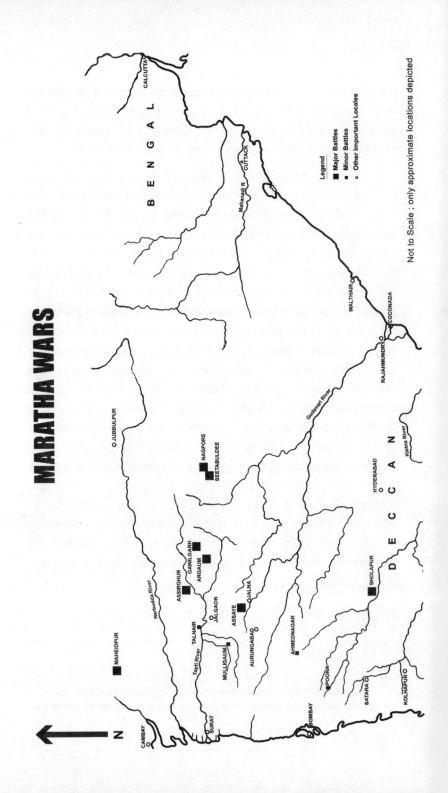

MARATHA WARS

Not to Scale ; only approximate locations depicted

Legend
- ■ Major Battles
- ■ Minor Battles
- ○ Other important Locales

10

Pazhassi Raja and Velu Thampi

Rebellions across the Sahyadri

Kerala, the strip of land beyond the Sahyadri, the Western Ghats, on the southwestern coastal belt of India, with its rivers, lakes and greenery, is renowned for its scenic splendour. Equally characteristic of the land is the deep-rooted democratic traditions of its people. So the organized resistance to the British supremacy in the Malabar, Cochin and Travancore regions, which later constituted the modern day state of Kerala, was always led by popular leaders drawing on the people's power, rather than any sovereigns with their military as such. Thus the resistance that the British met in Kerala was more in the form of rebellions than military campaigns; and by their very nature they became operationally unpredictable, and difficult to be contained. The British, with their formidable military might, were often made to look foolish by these hot-blooded revolutionaries for nearly two decades; and only by 1809, a good ten years after they saw the last of Tipu Sultan, could they finally establish their supremacy over the entire stretch of Kerala.

The earliest of these rebellions was started off by the Kovilakam Rajas, members of the family of the Zamorin of Calicut, in resentment of the sovereign submitting to the British in 1792; but was easily put down by the British within the year. But much bigger trouble awaited them in the following year, as a conflict broke out at Kottayam[1] under a popular prince turned rebel, Kerala Varma Pazhassi Raja, a descendant

---

1. This is the lesser known 'Kottayam' in North Kerala, and not to be confused with the southern district and its capital town bearing the same name.

of the Kovilakam Rajas, who took up cudgels against the crude and unjust tax policy of the East India Company. So overwhelming was the people's support to the prince that the company was forced to call off the tax collection for a year. Failing to break the impasse, the British attempted to seize the prince, who escaped to the mountains of Wayanad and launched a guerilla war. Gifted with an unusual flair for that kind of operation, and with thousands of volunteers rallying under him, he delivered such a humiliating defeat to the British in a 3-day engagement during March 1797, that they were forced to withdraw from Wayanad. Close on its heels, he ambushed a British contingent in the Peria Pass and virtually annihilated the 1100-man force. The British, finding it no more militarily or politically expedient to continue the fight, worked out a compromise formula and the two parties called a truce.

The uneasy peace lasted barely two years. After Tipu's death, the British tried to take possession of Wayanad, ceded to them by the new Mysore ruler; and Pazhassi Raja resisted the move, laying his own claim to the district. He raised a fairly big army and once again launched the guerilla campaign with renewed vigour. Arthur Wellesley, who then took command of the British operations, achieved a measure of success by improving the road network and restricting the Raja's forces to the jungles, by putting up outposts at select points. Nevertheless, they struck back occasionally and after scoring a thumping victory by capturing the fort at Panamaram, started controlling the Wayanad passes. Seizing the opportunity of a popular uprising against the British on the issue of land assessments and table of exchange, they came out into the open again, defying the authorities.

The British had so far been employing Bombay troops in the region, and the 6000-man force they had, harassed as it was by the insurgency, was also being ravaged by malaria. They were replaced by Madras troops in 1804, and they went onto blockade the Raja effectively in his jungle retreat. Finally, the *Kolkar*-s, a special police force raised by the authorities to counter insurgency, hunted him down, and shot him dead[2], on 30 November 1805. The British, on account of the popularity of the Raja, cremated him with honours befitting a 'fallen enemy'. The revolt died with Pazhassi Raja, all his lieutenants being killed, deported, or committing suicide. Thus ended one of the bloodiest rebellions in the history of Kerala; it lasted over a decade, with thousands of lives lost on either side.

That Pazhassi Raja's army was constituted of men from all classes and creeds of the society – Nairs, the traditionally martial community, as well as the Kurichias and Moplahs (Muslims) – was indicative of the amazing popularity he enjoyed among the masses. Thomas Harvey Baber, the Sub-Collector of Tellicherry, credited by the British for putting down the Pazhassi revolt, described the Raja as "an extraordinary and singular character". He testified:

In all classes, I observed a decided interest in the Pychy Raja towards whom the inhabitants entertained a regard and respect bordering on veneration which not even his death can efface.

The legend of Pazhassi Raja's martyrdom for the cause of freedom still lives on in Kerala; but sadly, even by the 200th anniversary of it in the year 2005, the people of the state were yet to build a fitting memorial for this lionhearted prince who, unlike most of the royalty elsewhere in India, chose to fight to the very end, rather than meekly submit to the foreign dominance. The British had brutally given vent to their ire by razing his palace to the ground, and building a road over it. An interested historiographer can find Pazhassi Raja's ancestral home, Patinjare Kovilakam, an ancient building in a state of disrepair, four kilometers outside the town of Mattannur in northern Kerala. In Mattannur itself, the Raja's memory lingers on, with a statue, or an art gallery or some

---

2. In the end, it was once again the same old Indian story of rank betrayal. The Mir Jaffar in this episode was a man called Pazhayaveettil Chandu, a trusted dependant of the Raja. Chandu owed his very existence to the prince, having been taken care of and brought up by the latter from the time he was a young boy on the brink of starvation, with no one else to turn to. He chose to express his gratitude by secretly revealing the hideout of the Raja to the British, for whatever miserable consideration.

sports clubs named after him, and most prominently the Pazhassi Raja NSS College and a dam dedicated to his memory. These and his tomb at Mananthawadi in the neighbourhood, with a small museum adjacent to it, are the only reminders of a great and gallant struggle, besides a small memorial stone on the bank of a rivulet, Mavila Thodu, off the river Kankara on the Kerala-Karnataka border – the spot at which he fell.

A few years after the fires of the Pazhassi revolt subsided in northern Kerala, the whole of southern Kerala erupted in a fresh rebellion, which took the British by surprise, and posed by far the biggest challenge to their authority in the region till date. It was led by a man of impeccable background in public service, Velayudhan Chempakaraman Thampi, popularly known as Velu Thampi, the *Dalawa* – Chief Minister – of Travancore, in alliance with Paliath Achan, his counterpart at Cochin. Velu Thampi had a mass following, having had led a revolt against bureaucratic misrule, which forced the King to yield to the people's demands, before he was appointed the *Dalawa*. He resented the interference in the state's administration by the British Resident, Colonel Macaulay, and joined hands with Paliath Achan, who too was facing similar difficulties with the British at Cochin. Together, they raised a force, mostly of Nairs, but joined, as in the case of the Pazhassi revolt, by volunteers from all communities. They then attempted to bring the Marathas and the Poligars of Madura into a broad-based alliance with them, while also making contact with the French at Mauritius for support.

The rebellion broke out rather extemporarily at the port city of Cochin on 18 December 1808, when a 600-man force, commanded by Paliath Achan and two of Velu Thampi's officers, stormed the British Resident's house. The resident managed to escape by a ship, which arrived at the opportune moment with reinforcements from Malabar. The rebels struck again on the 28th, when a British ship with some troops put into another port town, Alleppey, further south, wiping out a detachment of more than 30 soldiers, with sadly, a medical officer among them. Meanwhile, 50 miles to the south, at Quilon, the British garrison, comprising some three Madras Infantry battalions under Lieutenant Colonel Chalmers, was getting hemmed in by the Travancore forces advancing on the town from various directions, troops also using the Ashtamudi Lake bordering the town and other waterways to approach it in boats.

On 11 January 1809, Velu Thampi, who was by now headquartered at Kundara near Quilon, made a proclamation, indicting the British rule and exhorting the people to rally under his banner for the fight against the foreigners. The people's response was electric. They flocked in thousands to join the ranks of his forces now converging on Quilon. The garrison there, consisting of the 2nd, 4th and 26th Madras Infantry Regiments, had since been reinforced by the 36th MI and the 12th Foot. By a British estimate, Velu Thampi had nearly 30,000 men under his colours, with some 18 guns. Chalmers dug in his heels. Velu Thampi unleashed an attack on 15 January, the fiercest the Madras Army faced in the campaign. In a grim battle fought over five hours, they had the better of the Travancore forces, who were dealt a decisive defeat. Velu Thampi's losses were enormous. The debacle broke the back of the rebellion. Nevertheless, four days later the combined forces of Cochin and Travancore, numbering about 3000, launched an attack on Cochin. The defending garrison of the 33rd MI and 50 British soldiers of the 12th Foot, commanded by Major Hewitt, repulsed the attack in a gallant feat, inflicting heavy loss to the attackers. The 33rd MI was later to be awarded the Battle Honour, COCHIN, the sole distinction won by any unit in that campaign. The rebel attacks on the cantonments continued during the month, but proved futile.

In the meantime to the south, the Madras Army reinforcements, under Lieutenant Colonel St. Leger, entered Travancore through the Aramboli Pass, and managed to capture the forts of Udayagiri and Padmanabhapuram by 19 February. Later during the month, following a severe defeat at the British hands, Paliath Achan defected from the alliance. (Deported to Madras, he was never again to be permitted to visit Cochin.) The Raja of Travancore, finding St. Leger's forces assembled at the southern suburbs of his capital, Trivandrum, and Chalmers' troops on the northern side, sued for peace and ordered the *Dalawa's* arrest.

Cornered by the Raja's men at the Bhagavathy Temple at Mannadi, Velu Thampi, proud and defiant to the end, committed suicide[3] before he could be taken alive. Nevertheless, the vengeful British put his dead body on exhibition, hanging it from a gibbet at Trivandrum. His house was razed to the ground and his relatives transported to Maldives. His followers were hanged or banished from the country. The shameless act of desecration of the mortal remains of the *Dalawa* by the over-zealous British Resident (though supposedly on the orders of the Raja), was later to be condemned by none other than the Governor General, Lord Minto. He observed:

The ends of justice and the purposes of public security were attained by the death of the Dewan; and the prosecution of a vindictive policy when the object of it had ceased to exist, was repugnant to the feelings of common humanity and the principles of a civilized government.

It would seem that the British snobbery and obsession with royalty, rather than fair judgment, often dictated their attitude in dealing with whom they perceived as rebels. They had no qualms about hanging Yusuf Khan or Kattabomman, and in Velu Thampi's case, his dead body, all of whom, in their perception, were commoners; where as in the case

---

3. The Travancore State Manual narrates the end of the *Dalawa* thus: "The fallen Dalava was obliged to move from place to place to avoid the disgrace of surrendering and falling a victim to the vindictiveness of his enemies. At last he took refuge in a Potti's house at Mannati on the bank of the Kollakatavu River. The secret was soon out, and Karyakkar Mallan Pillai with a company of Nayars under a Subadar surrounded the place where the Dalava had set up a fugitive abode. The house was soon broken in. Velu Thampi, realizing the magnitude of the danger, resolved to put an end to his existence rather than allow the enemies to capture him alive. He ordered his brother to dispatch him but the latter would never commit fratricide. The Dalava therefore plunged his dagger into his own bosom. Fearing that the self-inflicted wound might prove not fatal, he cried out to his brother to complete the work. This time the brother complied with his request; and with one stroke of the sword he severed the head from the body." (The unfortunate brother, in turn, was taken captive to Quilon and hanged.)

of Pazhassi Raja, mercifully, his princely background discouraged them from insulting his mortal remains. It could also have been the case, that excepting for rare instances like that of Pazhassi Raja, they found the princely class far more amenable than the popular leaders. As it turned out, the close association of the British with the moth-eaten royalty of India in later years was to be their undoing, for it would totally alienate them from the common man.

With the rebellion suppressed, both Travancore and Cochin became subsidiary allies of the British by subsequent treaties, and the native forces of both the states were disbanded. Except for a minor insurrection in 1812 by Kurichiyas and Kurumbars in Wayanad, which was easily put down, Velu Thampi's was the last of the early rebellions against the British rule in Kerala. It was also the first mass revolt in India which made the preservation of the sovereignty of a state and the democratic rights of its people the principal cause. Velu Thampi was born a century too early. His kind of political strategy – he was the first Indian leader known to have effectively used his oratorical skills to motivate people – would one day be wholly adopted by the leaders who would eventually win India her freedom. The legacy of Velu Thampi would inspire the people of Kerala in their ideals of liberty down the lanes of history. Appropriately enough, a statue of his adorns the state's secretariat complex at Thiruvananthapuram; paradoxically though, the muddled politics of the state holds no promise for the generations to come, as the lofty ideals the great man fought for did.

11

Vellore Mutiny

The first rising of the sepoys

For nearly two centuries since the first Englishmen started trading in India, the Indo-British relations were largely one of cultural assimilation, essentially reciprocal in nature, when the British expanded their influence by a mixture of diplomacy, tact and – occasionally only – force. All that was changing by the closing years of the 18th Century. And at the dawn of the 19th Century, the English East India Company had adopted an overtly imperialistic approach, arrogantly backed by the racial prejudices of the British. Governor General Marquess Wellesley, eulogizing himself on his 'Taming the Tiger', as he preferred to describe the defeat and killing of Tipu, had set in motion policies that were bound to antagonize the Indians and erode the goodwill generations of Britons before him had built up. Embedded in these policies which created the framework for the future British Raj were, ironically, the very seeds of ruination of that institution one day.

In no sphere of activity had the British been as successful with their cultural balancing act in winning over the Indian hearts, as they had been with the creation of the sepoy armies, staunchly loyal to the East India Company. The three Presidency Armies of Madras, Bengal and Bombay, had become the cornerstones, and the symbols of, the British power in the subcontinent by early 19th Century. The men who made it happen, scores of officers, from Stringer Lawrence to Arthur Wellesley, were professionals who identified themselves with their men. A warm-hearted lot, they were alive to their troops' sensitivities and respected their customs. They led, rather than lorded over, their men. The sepoys, stout-hearted souls with strong soldierly leanings, long denied their proper dues by the callous Indian rulers, responded with absolute loyalty, priding themselves in the superior discipline and training in the 'Company's Service'; and gave their best for the sheer glory of winning battles – love of adventure of a unique kind.

Even when the East India Company's higher echelons began turning arrogant with their new imperialistic approach, the sepoys remained more or less insulated from its ill effects, because of a sensible officer corps that largely stuck to the traditional ways with the troops. But the cancer was spreading; it wouldn't be long before the officers, at least a considerable number of them, too fell prey to the ignoble tendencies of snobbery. They would start taking the sepoys' loyalty for granted. Still it would take another half a century for the malignancy to become full-blown, and things to come to a head. The day of reckoning would come for the British on the 10th of May in 1857, in the cantonment at Meerut, when the historic Sepoy Rebellion broke out. That would change India as few other occurrences ever did. Even if the sepoys could not win and overthrow the British, they made a point – India was too big a country, too serious an affair, to be left in the hands of a bunch of rapacious businessmen and crude mercenaries. It was the death-knell of the East India Company. The Crown took over the governance, and strange as it came about, India had set forth irrevocably on her path to freedom. Thus the sepoys who conquered India for the British, ironically enough, were to make the first move that would put her on the road to freedom and self governance.

More than half a century before the Meerut outbreak, the sepoys fired a warning shot at Vellore, which gave the British an inkling of what grief they could come to, should they ever be insensitive with the native troops. But they either chose to ignore it, or to underplay the episode to cover up their folly. Interestingly, the Vellore Mutiny, the first ever instance of dissidence[1] of a major nature by Indian troops against the British, resulted from the sepoys being provoked by certain orders which offended their religious and cultural sensibilities – circumstances almost identical to that which would find their brethren up north in open rebellion in 1857. A one-day affair, as bloody as any mutiny could be, it occurred on the 10th of July 1806, and takes the pride of place in history as the first major revolt by Indian soldiers against the British.

The main cause of the mutiny was the suspicion among the sepoys that the British were deliberately attempting to convert them into Christianity, fuelled to a good extent by the general resentment that was building up among the populace against the alien rule. The consternation arose from a new set of regulations introduced to bring about the uniformity of appearance of the men. These required them to shave off their beards, trim the moustaches and stop wearing earrings and painted caste-marks on their foreheads. Even more offending to the troops was a newly patterned turban, closely resembling a hat, popularly worn by the Indian converts to Christianity whom the sepoys despised.

The 2/4th Madras Infantry[2], stationed at Vellore, was the first unit to resent wearing the turbans. Ignoring their commanding officer's voice of reason, the Army Headquarters reacted with tough disciplinary measures. The battalion was shifted to another station, and 21 men, perceived to be ringleaders, were brought to Madras, court-martialled and sentenced to 500 lashes each. That only added fuel to the fire, hardening the sepoys'

---

1. Small-scale mutinies by European officers were known to happen in the 17th Century itself, the earliest having been recorded in 1674. The first known mutiny by Indian troops took place in Tellicherry in1780, which was more in the nature of a small strike and was put down easily. It was followed by a slightly bigger one in Vizagapatam during the same year, wherein the sepoys shot and killed three British officers; the first instance of Europeans being killed by Indian mutineers. The mutiny however was suppressed easily.

2. From 1796, the native infantry battalions were grouped into regiments of two battalions each, whereby each battalion came to be identified by two numerals, viz. 1/1st, meaning the 1st Battalion of the 1st Regiment, 2/1st, meaning the 2nd Battalion of the 1st Regiment, and so on.

resolve, and there were rumblings of an organized resistance to the new dress regulations. The Commander-in-Chief, General Sir John Craddock, sensing trouble, suggested to the Governor that the orders on turbans be retracted. The Governor obstinately disagreed, arguing that it would undermine the discipline of the army.

On the night 9 – 10 July, the whole battalion 2/23rd MI was permitted to sleep inside the fort in preparation for a parade early in the morning. The guards on duty for the night were from the 69th Foot and 1/1st MI. At 2.30.p.m. on the 10th the sepoys struck. Taken by surprise, almost the entire British officers and soldiers were massacred. The few who escaped fought their way to the ramparts, and perched above the main gate, managed to hold out until it was daylight. Luckily for them meanwhile, the news of the outbreak had got to Colonel Rollo Gillespie, commanding the garrison at Arcot only 18 miles away, pretty fast. He promptly rode out to the rescue, with the 7th Madras Cavalry and a squadron of the British 19th Dragoons. As soon as his galloper guns fetched up at Vellore, the gate was blown open, and the cavalry and the dragoons charged into the fort. The sepoys stood no chance. Some 350 of them perished; and the rest, though most of them escaped from the fort, were taken prisoner eventually from the countryside where they had dispersed to. More than a hundred of them were blown from the muzzle of the gun.

An enquiry conducted later, while coming to the conclusion that the new dress regulations was the principal cause of the mutiny, also suggested the involvement of the sons of Tipu Sultan and their retainers, lodged as prisoners at the fort, in instigating the sepoys. Five of the retainers were sentenced either to death or long terms of imprisonment, while the princes themselves, in the absence of any conclusive evidence against them, were sent away to Calcutta. Sepoy Mustapha Beg of the 1/1st MI, who had divulged information on the mutiny earlier (but was jailed at that time having been considered insane, as the Indian officers had successfully convinced the commanding officer), was gifted 2000 pagodas and pensioned off on the pay of a subedar – he couldn't have survived long among the sepoys anymore. The 1st and 23rd Regiments were disbanded, though the 1st was to be re-raised later. The offending turban was however withdrawn, and so were the other troublesome regulations; while the Governor and his officials responsible for the fiasco, the Commander-in-Chief, the Adjutant General – Colonel Agnew, who drafted the half-witted regulations – and his deputy, were all unceremoniously sacked.

The rescinding of the offending regulations, immediately after the suppression of the mutiny, contained the resentment that had been building up in other cantonments. However the authorities eventually found ways to introduce the dress regulations throughout the sepoy armies, cunningly advancing a theory that the Vellore Mutiny was part of a larger plot by the Muslims to overthrow the British. Nothing could have been farther from the truth, for the simple fact that almost the entire lot of mutineers were Hindus – a typical instance of the British indulging in fissiparous propaganda to gain points. Essentially the mutiny was the result of oafish obstinacy and blunder on the part of the top guns of East India Company. (At least one officer is known to have saved the situation by merely being sensible; Colonel Montressor, commanding the Subsidiary Force at Hyderabad, nipped the trouble at the bud by simply cancelling the offending orders on his own responsibility.)

Paradoxically, for all the fears of attempts at conversion of troops to Christianity, the British officers of the sepoy armies seemed to have been generally disinterested in any such initiative, if not totally against it. The general perception among the officers were that they would be much better off commanding the sepoys without the 'nuisance from the damned missionaries', since they – the sepoys – 'had their own religions they were perfectly happy with'. And they were sensible enough to be respectful about the religious sentiments of their men, which was one of the cardinal points that won them the loyalty of the troops at large. Therefore it is only logical to assume that the mutiny would have had a lot to do with extraneous factors related to the contemporary socio-political unrest, precipitated by the establishment of an alien power.

The religious bit probably came in as a convenient detonator. Be that as it might have, the tradition of the officer making his men's religion his own, continues to be one of the most powerful motivating factors that maintain the Indian Army's discipline and fighting edge to date.

12

THE THIRD MARATHA WAR

Madras Army's last great battles in the subcontinent

They rode in like the devils out of nowhere, looted and murdered at will, and vanished as fast as they came; the mere mention of their lot sent chill up the spines of the inhabitants of Central India where they roamed – they were called the Pindaries. Obscure freebooters in the beginning, they were wandering hordes of mercenary horsemen of different Asian races, acting as auxiliaries to various Maratha Chiefs. It was their wont – with the blessings of those Chiefs – to plunder and ravage the states of Central India unchecked. Sir John Malcolm, one of the field commanders who were to fight them, wrote of their modus operandi:

When they set out on an expedition they were neither encumbered by tents nor baggage; each horseman carried a few cakes of bread for his own subsistence and some feeds of gram for his horse. The party, usually consisting of two or three thousand good horse, with a proportion of mounted followers, advanced (as secretly as they could and without plundering) at the rapid rate of forty or fifty miles a day, turning neither to the right nor left till they arrived at the country meant to be attacked. They then divided and made a sweep of all the cattle and property they could find; committing at the same time the most horrid atrocities and destroying what they could not carry away. They trusted to the secrecy and suddenness of the irruption for avoiding the troops who guarded the frontiers of the countries they invaded, and before a force could be brought against them, they were on their return. Their chief strength lay in their being intangible. If pursued they made marches of extraordinary length (sometimes upward of sixty miles) by roads almost impracticable for regular troops. If overtaken they dispersed and reassembled at an appointed rendezvous; if followed to the country from which they had issued, they scattered into small parties, and nowhere presented any point of attack.

The Pindaries invited the wrath of the British when their activities began spreading into the Company's territories, from 1812. They were based in the territories of Scindia and Holkar, and the British expected these Chiefs to restrain them. Finding them unwilling to oblige, and the Company's garrisons too thin on the ground to contain the menace, the Governor General took recourse to war. Troops were mobilized in early 1817 under two field forces, the Army of the Deccan in the south with Madras troops, and the Grand Army in the north with troops from the remaining presidencies. The former, commanded by Lieutenant General Sir Thomas Hislop, had 70,000 men in its ranks comprising 21 battalions of the Madras Infantry, four cavalry regiments along with the Governor's Bodyguard, and detachments of the artillery and the pioneers, besides some European troops. The Madras Army was going to a major war again, after more than a decade.

The campaign opened with a brief engagement at Patree above the ghats of Khandesh in April when the 27th MI surprised a Pindari gang, and another one thereafter at Dossanah when the 43rd MI, backed by some cavalry and four guns, captured a fort. And by November the stage was set for a major confrontation with Appa Sahib, the Rajah of Nagpore. The British garrison at Nagpore, under threat from the Rajah's army of 16,000, had been forced to withdraw to the suburb of Seetabuldee. The place featured two small knolls about 100 feet high and 300 feet apart. Anticipating an attack by the Rajah's forces, two battalions of the Madras Infantry occupied these features on 25 November; 1/24th Battalion with one six-pounder gun holding the smaller of the hillocks, and the 1/20th with three six-pounders holding the larger one. On 26th afternoon, the Rajah's army, mostly of Arabs, attacked the positions.

Strongly defended as the knolls were, the initial attack was easily repulsed. But the Arabs were game and kept on with repeated attacks through the night, only to be thrown back every time. On the 27th morning however, they made a breakthrough and carried the smaller feature, overwhelming the fatigued defenders of 1/24th. But their victory was short lived, as the Governor's Bodyguard and three troops of the 6th Bengal Cavalry came charging down on the enemy cavalry drawn up at the foot of the hills, creating utter mayhem. The enemy cavalry dispersed, abandoning the guns that were firing at the hills. As own cavalry promptly took those guns, 1/24th, buoyed up at the turn, counterattacked and drove the Arabs back. Even as the battalion reoccupied its position and the enemy began regrouping for another attack, the cavalry made a second charge, delivering the enemy a deadly blow. The Rajah's forces were dissipated hopelessly this time, and failed to form up for another effort. Their fire slackened, and by noon they had entirely given up the fight.

The casualties of the Madras Army in this hot contest numbered 121 killed and 239 wounded, including 17 officers. Although the Rajah was estimated to have had 12,000 cavalry, 8000 infantry and 35 guns in the field, the entire force did not join the battle, and the number of casualties suffered by them was not known. The two infantry battalions which held the features, along with the Governor's Bodyguard and the 6th Bengal Cavalry, were later to be awarded the Battle Honour, SEETABULDEE.

By December the much awaited reinforcements, including some Bengal and Hyderabad troops, started arriving and by the middle of the month the British had a considerable force commanded by Major General Doveton, poised for an offensive. On the morning of 16 December Doveton ordered a demonstration of his troops. The Rajah, appearing intimidated, agreed to surrender by noon, but had an ace up his sleeve. Three parallel ravines separated his troops from the British force, as it moved forward to take the surrender at the appointed time. The advance posts along the second ravine with some 36 guns duly surrendered; but as Doveton's troops moved into the third ravine, the main enemy force, with its guns well positioned, opened up with a heavy cannonade. Caught out in the killing ground, men reeled, taking heavy casualties, but rebound smartly to charge the forward enclosures. The cavalry galloped forward to silence the most effective batteries, while the infantrymen, forming up, advanced steadily, until they were close enough to the enemy to fire a volley and charge. The enemy fled, leaving more than 70 guns and some 50 elephants behind. Nearly 150 men of the Madras Army had been killed in that brief but deadly encounter, almost all of them hit by cannon shots, which seldom wounded without killing.

The enemy withdrew into the city, and the division laid a siege. Effecting a breach by 23 December, they launched an assault. But it proved an ill-fated move. There were far too many obstacles, and the Arab garrison fought tooth and nail. The attack was repulsed with over 300 casualties. But by the time the fight was over, the Arabs had had it too. No longer enthusiastic about the prospects of a prolonged siege, they sought terms. The battle ended with the surrender of Nagpore to the Madras Army and its allies – yet another feather in its cap, one that was to earn all the participating units, which included one from the Bengal Native Infantry and one from the Berar Infantry of the Hyderabad Contingent, the Battle Honour, NAGPORE.

Meanwhile an attempt by another three divisions of the Madras Army to take Malwa, the headquarters of the Pindaries, failed due to the intervention of Holkar's army. The two armies met each other again on 21st December at Maheidpur on the banks of the river Supra, to fight, what was to be the last of the great battles that the Madras Army was to fight in India, and under its own distinct identity, which also happened to be the biggest battle of the 3rd Maratha War. The enemy – about 10,000 infantrymen in ten battalions, with 50 guns, and their cavalry behind them – was drawn up across the Supra, a stream fordable at some points. The Madras Army of a little over 6000 men, commanded by Hislop himself, consisted of five regiments of infantry, a volunteer battalion titled the Madras Rifle Corps, some pioneers, 600 or so Europeans of all arms, a detachment of the Mysore Horse, and an artillery of 18 six-pounder guns.

The operation began with four companies of infantry, supported by horse artillery, clearing the ford. It was a tough job with its inevitable toll of casualties. The troops then crossed over in three successive brigades under intensive fire, taking heavy casualties. The horse artillery was shot up badly, but the lines were formed, and a three-pronged attack launched. Fierce fighting ensued. The enemy gunners, most of whom were Pathans, stood to the last pouring in a fusillade of grape and chain shot, as the infantry bayonet-charged their line, and the Mysore Horse hacked at their flanks routing their cavalry. By the end of the day the Madras Army had won a decisive victory over Holkar's forces. With the cavalry in hot pursuit after his forces, a shaken Holkar surrendered, and signed a treaty on 6 January 1818, agreeing to relinquish his Pindari connection and support the British. The Madras Army's losses in the battle were nearly 200 killed and more than 600 wounded. This decisive battle, the anniversary of which is still celebrated by the descendant battalions of those who took part in it, won for all the regiments and detachments involved the Battle Honour, MAHEIDPUR.

The principal objectives of the campaign having been achieved, two of the Madras Army's divisions were transferred to the army in the north where the operations were still on, while Hislop began his return march southward with the remaining division after the battle of Maheidpur. But sporadic fighting was to continue for another year until all the Maratha pockets had been reduced. These mopping up operations, spread over a large area, often saw large-scale battles, wherein the Bengal troops from the northern divisions found themselves fighting alongside their Madras brethren. Three of these battles, when the Madras Army captured the forts at Talnair, Mulligaum, and Sholapur, stood out for their ferocity.

The fort of Talnair was a Holkar's possession on the bank of the river Tapti. The advance guard of Hislop's 1st Division, returning to the Deccan, was fired at by this fort on 27 February. With the Killedar remaining defiant even after being reminded of his master's commitment to surrender the fort, the division's artillery opened up. But the fire, from the ten 6-pounders and two howitzers they had, proved too inadequate to make an impact. The fort though small appeared strong, with walls about 60 feet high and only one entrance with five successive gates. After some hesitation and reconnaissance a storming party of the Royal Scots and the Madras Europeans made a thrust. They penetrated the first four gates, but found the fifth one closed. Now chance and confusion played a role as the defenders met them for a parley at the gate. A number of men from the storming party who were permitted to enter through a wicket were suddenly pounced upon and butchered. Their enraged comrades opened up with a volley and charged in. Most of the garrison, of some 250 Arabs, was put to sword. The Killedar was hanged. Unnerved by this arbitrary action, two of the neighbouring forts at Galna and Chandore immediately surrendered, but the garrison of a third one at Mulligaum, the capital of Khandesh, chose the opposite – to defend itself.

The task of tackling Mulligaum fell on a brigade under Colonel Macdowall, left behind for the mopping up operations by Hislop, as he carried on with his march to the Deccan. The brigade came up against the place on 15 May. It had a strongly built fort situated on plain ground above the confluence of two rivers, accessible only from one direction. Occupying the approach lay a township, close up to the outer fort built of mud and stone, forming a quadrangle of some 350 yards, with 12-foot high walls and flanking towers. A ditch, some 25 feet deep and over 15 feet wide, separated it from the inner fort that was 60 feet high and built of tougher masonry. Bordering it was a 12-foot wall, with plenty of embrasures to cover the ditch with effective fire. The garrison was estimated to be constituted of some 400 Arabs. Macdowall had little over 900 men in all with four heavy guns, one mortar and two howitzers.

Preparations for the assault began on the 18th evening, with working parties moving up to put up batteries. The work was almost put paid to as the enemy struck out with a powerful sortie around 8.p.m., and the entire brigade found itself engaged before it could be fought off. The breaching batteries opened up the following day, and by the 26th the outer fort had been breached to an extent, and a practicable breach made at an angle of the inner fort. There was no more ammunition left for the guns to widen the breaches, and an assault was firmed up for 28 May, as recommended by the Senior Engineer, Ensign Nattes. 500 sepoys and 100 Europeans, led by Nattes himself, assaulted the breach under a hot fire from the flanking towers. They made it successfully to the top of the breach, only to be confronted by the deep ditch which they had no knowledge about. Nattes was the first to fall, with five balls through him, even as he called out 'Impracticable', and the recall was sounded. But it was too late, and men fell like ninepins, cut down by the merciless fusillade. Those behind managed to withdraw, but their dead and wounded piled at the breach. The Arabs had drawn the first blood; but with soldierly honour, held their fire for the attackers to evacuate their casualties in the end.

The siege was now converted to a blockade, as Macdowall awaited the arrival of battering guns and stores from Ahmednagar to make the next move. They arrived on 9 June and fire was reopened on the 11th. As the shelling continued, in a terrible setback for the garrison, the main magazine of the fort blew up, the explosion ripping off some 25 yards of the inner fort right from the foundation, and the debris filling that part of the ditch. With the path wide open for an assault, the Arabs sought terms; but gallantly refused to lay down their arms until they had had a safe conduct, lest they be meted out the same treatment as was the garrison at Talnair. It was agreed upon in a reciprocal gesture to the chivalry shown by them earlier; and the entire garrison marched out, leaving Macdowall's brigade the masters of the fort. The brigade had lost 34 men killed and 175 wounded.

Even as Talnair and Mulligaum fell, Brigadier General Thomas Munro's division, earmarked for northern operations, was busy clearing up the Southern Maratha country, capturing a number of enemy strongholds like Badami and Belgaum. Then in May the division was facing Sholapur, the biggest remaining Maratha stronghold, manned by the remnant forces of the Peshwa. The Peshwa himself had surrendered during the previous month, on being hemmed in between the pursuing force of Doveton and a northern division of Sir John Malcolm coming down from Mhow, while attempting to join forces with the Rajah of Nagpore. Sholapur had an oblong fort, some 400 yards long and 300 yards broad, surrounded by a deep wet ditch. A walled, somewhat quadrangular township, spread over an area of over 1500 yards by 1200 yards defended by small bastions at regular intervals, occupied its northern face. The garrison of nearly 12,000 men of all arms had a Portuguese officer, Major de Pinto, commanding its infantry, and Ganpat Rao, the hereditary commandant of the Peshwa's artillery, commanding the rest. Munro's division, rather depleted of regular troops, was made up of local levies to a good extent.

Arriving in front of Sholapur on 8 May, Munro launched a dawn attack on the township on the 10th. The assault force comprising mainly men from the 11th and 15th MI stormed the place by escalade, and swiftly taking the forward bastions, opened the town gates for the rest of the division to enter. Even as the reserve troops were making their entry, Ganpat Rao, who by now had assembled a strong body of horse and foot with five guns on the eastern half of the town, opened up on them, forcing them to withdraw behind the wall. As the fighting raged within the town, an enemy tumbril blew up. Confusion prevailed for a while, and Munro, grabbing the opportunity, led the reserves in a charge himself. Right when the contest hung in balance, Ganpat Rao fell severely wounded, and his next two in command were killed one after the other. There was confusion in the Maratha ranks, and their main force pulled itself out of the fight.

By the afternoon some 5000 of their infantry and 700 horse had managed to move off unobserved and were marching on the road to Seenah, where they could make a stand. But by about 4.p.m. the move was known to Munro, and his cavalry and the galloper guns were in hot pursuit. Five miles out of Sholapur they intercepted the withdrawing column. The enemy horsemen made good their escape, leaving the infantry to its fate. Nearly 1000 men were killed and the rest dispersed hopelessly. The once formidable Peshwa's infantry had ceased to exist as a fighting force. The taking of Sholapur was more of a formality now. The siege of the fort commenced on 11 May and by the 14th, with the enfilading batteries pounding heavily, the remaining garrison surrendered. The Madras Army had paid a price of almost a hundred casualties for the victory.

The last engagement of the war the Madras troops was to fight was at Assirghur in the midst of the Mahadeo hill country, the last bastion of the Marathas; where Appa Sahib, the ex-Rajah of Nagpore, was believed to have taken refuge after escaping from the British. The fortress of Assirghur stood atop an isolated hill feature nearly 800 feet high, two miles away from one end of a major range of the Satpura Hills. It consisted of an upper fort over 1000 yards long from east to west, and about half that broad at its widest part, surrounded by a lower fort some thirty feet high with towers at intervals. The summit was armed by several very heavy guns – one of them a 384-pounder, while another six fired balls weighing anything from 68 to 140 pounds – and the only access to it was by steep steps leading through five successive gateways. The whole hill was scarped all round to a depth of over 100 feet from the foot of the outer wall. Below it to the western side lay a walled town occupying the main approach. Defending the fortress against the combined might of the two divisions of Doveton and Malcolm was a garrison of 1200 Arabs, Sindhis and Mekranis, under its defiant Commandant, Jaswant Rao Lar.

The operation began at dawn on 18 March 1819, when the two divisions stormed the walled town and laid a siege. The following day a breaching battery of six 18-pounders and two 12-pounders opened fire on the lower fort. That evening the defenders made an attempt to counterattack, but was repulsed. The cannonade continued, forcing the defenders to evacuate the lower fort. Then in a sudden reverse on the 21st one of the magazines of the breaching battery blew up accidentally, killing and wounding nearly a hundred men, most of them from the 2/15th Bengal Battalion. The defenders saw their chance, and reoccupied the lower fort in a rush. Nevertheless two more batteries were erected during the succeeding week, and by the 29th the lower fort had been effectively breached. But by the time an assault went in on the 30th, it had again been evacuated.

For the next one week the divisions laboured on doggedly to a man, assisted by elephants, dragging the heavy guns uphill until they could fire effectively into the upper fort. On the morning of 8 April no less than seventeen 18-pounders and two 24-pounders opened fire, with the mortars and howitzers adding their bit. The effect was devastating inside the fort with buildings and other structures crumbling. In the end it turned out to be an all-artillery show. Threatened with the total destruction of his garrison, Jaswant Rao surrendered unconditionally. It appeared an easy victory; but it wasn't. Altogether the two divisions had lost more than 300 men killed and wounded during the siege, as against the defenders' loss which turned out to be negligible in comparison.

The Peshwa's surrender and the destruction of his forces during the previous year had virtually signalled the end of organized resistance. And with the final act at Assirghur, the war now came to an end. It was also the end of the Madras Army's campaigning days in the subcontinent. With the Marathas subdued, British domination of the peninsula was complete. It would take another three decades and a lot more of fighting in the North, culminating with the Sikh Wars, before the British could establish their supremacy all over India. But the Madras Army had played out its role in the drama. The East India Company had its other two Presidency Armies, the Bombay and the Bengal ones, closer at hand for the North Indian campaigns; and the day was emerging when the Madras Army would seek its battle fields beyond the shores of India.

Nevertheless, even after the Madras Army had launched itself on major overseas campaigns, commencing with the 1st Burma War in 1824, it would fight one last operation on Indian soil in early 1830s. This brief but heated engagement fought in the picturesque country of Coorg would be the last major conflict South India would witness, before the British authority was fully established over the entire region.

13

COORG WAR

The last bit of defiance south of the Vindhyas

During the fifteen years that followed the 3rd Maratha War, except for the 1st Burma War in 1824, the Madras Army was generally left to cool its heels, with nothing better to do than quelling local disturbances. These small-scale actions – thrice in India, at Kittur near Dharwar, Sholapur and Bidnur in Mysore, and one overseas at Malacca – were hardly the stuff the army was used to. Then there occurred a fiery bit of action, when in 1834 the hardy fighters of the hilly country of Coorg chose to challenge the British power. This was to prove the last effort at resistance against the British power Southern India was to witness, until almost a century later when national movements for independence gathered ground.

Chikkavirarajendra Wodeyar was enthroned the Raja of Coorg in 1820, following the death of his father and predecessor Lingarajendra. The new king does not seem to have lived up to the legacy of able governance left by his father. While this could very well have been an impression[1]

---

1   A pen picture of the Raja drawn by William Jefferson, an officer of the East India Company who spent some time in Coorg during his reign and later published a book, *Coorg and its Rajas,* vastly differ in perception from what the later European historians would have us believe by demonizing the man deliberately. Jefferson writes: "We are particularly gratified at finding that this prince was easy of access to his ryots, listening patiently to their grievances and manifesting towards them the utmost consideration and kindness; this ensured him in return their loyalty and affection as a proof of which whenever we travelled with the Raja into interior of the country, hundreds of natives, men, women and children with curiosity crowded my companion and me – an Englishman being a rara avis in those parts – and received the Raja with every demonstration of respect and attachment. It gives me the greatest satisfaction to mention this, being aware that the most sinister reports for interested purposes were industriously propagated to the Raja's prejudice."

created by the British to meet their ends, the Raja, to a great degree, did fail to command the loyalty of all the headmen. Worse, he wasn't all that inclined to maintain the cordiality with the British as his father was. In 1825, following some executions carried out by the Raja, the British resident at Mysore called for a report from him. The Raja refused the demand on the ground that he was an independent sovereign, and that the British had no business to interfere in the affairs of his state. The British, probably not too keen on precipitating an outright confrontation, ignored the snub. But matters came to a head in 1832, when Chenna Basavappa, a nobleman turned dissident whom the Raja was about to imprison, escaped and took refuge with the British resident at Bangalore. The British refused to cede the Raja's demand to hand over the fugitive, and the incensed Raja amassed his troops for a showdown with them, issuing a proclamation calling the people of the neighbouring countries to join him in the fight against the foreign power.

Although the British authorities at Madras sensed a confrontation unavoidable, and resolved to tackle the Raja by early 1833, it was only the year after that they actually got down to business. The inaccessibility of the area due to bad roads and difficult terrain posed immense problems in troop deployment and logistics for an advance into the country – a factor the Raja was heavily banking on, and which gave him a somewhat false sense of security.

Early in April 1834, 6000 Madras troops with the British 55th Regiment, organized in four columns, moved in on an offensive. The Northern Column, comprising the 9th MI, the 31st Trichinopoly Light Infantry and the British 55th, set off from Hoskote on 1 April. Brushing aside some enemy opposition at Kodlipet, they came up against a strong stockade at the Buck Pass on the 2nd. In a fierce encounter that lasted four and a half hours, the Coorgs under a gallant commander, Madanta Appachu, fought back and repulsed an attack by the sepoys, and then went on to foil a flanking move by the British 55th. The Madras column had to beat a retreat and camp several miles behind. They had lost nearly fifty killed and over a hundred wounded. The day surely belonged to the Coorgs.

Meanwhile the Western Auxiliary Column, having had earlier advanced from Kumbla on the coast to Sulya, and taken the stockade there on 29 March, ran into trouble too. A reconnaissance party they sent out towards Mallur on 1 April was mauled and driven back, and the commander of the force, Colonel Jackson, finding it inadequate for the task, withdrew to Kasargod, arriving there on the 6th. This column too had suffered considerably – 2 officers and 30 men killed and another 36 wounded.

The advance of the Western Column, comprising the 20th and the 32nd MI, which began marching up the Heggala Ghats from Cannanore on 31 March, went unchecked until 2 April, when its advance guard was repulsed at the Stony River. However the force fought its way up the following day – losing an officer and 12 men killed and 36 wounded – and took Virarajendrapet. Here it was joined by a part of the Eastern Column, which had advanced from Periyapatna that day unopposed. A detachment was now sent to take possession of the palace at Nalknad, where the Raja had moved into at the commencement of the hostilities; while the rest of the column advanced on the capital town of Mercara, and encamped seven miles south of it. The fight was more or less over with that.

The Eastern Column, constituted of the 4th, 35th and the 48th MI, along with the headquarters of the whole force, had by then marched from Bettadpur and made rapid progress, facing hardly any opposition. (Probably the Coorgs holding these approaches had received orders not to offer resistance. The Raja is believed to have had a change of mind in the eleventh hour, and sent out orders not to put up any fight; but they either didn't reach the troops on the rest of the approaches in time, or the troops chose to ignore them; and fight they did.)

The Raja saw the writing on the wall, and sent in a flag of truce to the Madras Army camp on 4 April. The fort at Mercara was occupied on the 6th, and the Raja gave himself up on the 10th. What followed was a typical British ruse for the annexation of the country. This is how the Mysore State Gazetteer on Coorg District puts it matter of factly:

Before the Raja was deposed and pensioned off, he pleaded that he might be allowed to remain on the throne under the close supervision of the British Resident. But the British who had known the strategical importance of Coorg in controlling the neighbouring districts of Mysore, Malabar and South Kanara and who liked the pleasant and temperate climate of Coorg, were determined to bring Coorg directly under their rule. Therefore, to justify the rather unjust and hasty deposition of the Raja, Col. Fraser, who was the officer in over-all command of the British forces and the political officer of the Company, made a pretence of consulting the wishes of the people as to the future administration of the State. He called for an assembly of the headmen and principal officers of the State in front of the European guest house at Mercara. When the headmen and officers found that they would be treated as if they were the masters of the country, they were greatly pleased with the sudden change from abject servitude to a kind of consequential independence and readily agreed to be ruled by the Company. The upshot was that Col. Fraser issued a proclamation, which declared that Coorg was annexed because it was the express wish of the people of Coorg to be ruled by the British Government.

Intolerance of any kind of opposition seems to have been the undoing of Chikkavirarajendra (and his predecessors), which made him unpopular with many of his own people and brought about his downfall. The pensioned Raja was first sent off to Benares and in 1852, permitted to go to England with two of his wives and his favourite daughter, Gauramma. He was the first ever Indian prince to sail to England. He died in London on 24 September 1859.

Pre-dating the Coorg War, the Northwest Canara had witnessed a heroic but tragic struggle at Kittur. Following the death of the reigning Raja in September 1824, the British tried to annexe the state by subterfuge, on the pretext of there being no male heir to succeed. The queen, Rani Chennammal, put up a brave fight and even gave the British a drubbing in the first round. Within a couple of months however she was subdued by far superior forces, and imprisoned. The gallant queen died a prisoner after five gruelling years in the fort at Bailhongal. One of her subjects, Sangoli Rayanna, tried to continue the fight after her death through guerilla warfare; but was captured and executed in 1830. Thus with Kittur in their bag, the British had only Coorg to contend for when they moved against Chikkavirarajendra four years later.

However the victory in the Coorg War didn't really turn out to be the end of their troubles in the region. At the conclusion of the war, certain taluks which had been ceded to Coorg in 1799 were retransferred to South Canara. A rebellion broke out in these areas in 1837, following discontent over the collection of revenue by the British. Mangalore was garrisoned by the 2nd MI, and a detachment of 180 men from the battalion under Major Dawkes, escorting a collector, was attacked and suffered some 50 casualties. With the whole countryside in a state of revolt, reinforcements – 4th MI under Colonel Green – were rushed in and the uprising contained. That ultimately put a cap on the hostilities in the region.

The South was finally and firmly a wholly British domain. However the resentment to the alien rule among the common people had merely gone dormant. Sporadic outbursts kept occurring all through the days of the East India Company and later the Raj. Localized small-scale affairs though, the Karnataka region witnessed a series of revolts until as late as 1867. In Andhra, a major uprising at Cuddapah under Uyyalawada Narasimha Reddy in 1846 had to be ruthlessly suppressed. In a shameful act of sacrilege, the British, after the execution of Reddy, kept his corpse hanging in chains in a cage even after it had turned to skeleton, to deter anymore dissent. They are believed to have had the grisly show going on for almost thirty years. Nevertheless Southern India witnessed armed revolt against the British even in the 20th Century, with the Moplah outbreak of Malabar in 1921.

Nothing in history perhaps highlighted the intensity of the anticolonial feelings of the ordinary South Indian, as did the enthusiasm with which a large number of plantation labour of South Indian origin – mostly Tamils – in Malaya and Burma flocked to the colours of the Indian National Army, during the 2nd World War to fight the British. Most of them who took up the clarion call of *'Dilli Chalo'* didn't even know where *'Dilli'* was; and born and brought up in the plantations, had never set foot on the Indian soil. Yet they took it upon themselves with such fiery passion – though goaded to an extent by the appalling injustice meted out to them by the British planters – to liberate a country which they called their motherland, even if she had nothing to offer them. And these untrained fighters were to form the hardcore of the INA in its campaigns, as many of its cadre recruited from Indian Army prisoners of war with the Japanese often proved unreliable with divided loyalties.

All that was to be in the future. The Coorg War marked the last occasion when military muscle was needed in the South in any substantive manner. Whatever rebellions were there thence would amount to nothing more than trifling episodes to be swatted down. And the mighty Madras Army would once again be seeking its avenues of action overseas.

BOOK II

THE EMPIRE'S WARS

Book II

THE EMPIRE'S WARS

1

THE FIRST BURMA WAR

A grand conquest overseas

The Madras troops had begun to pick up a flair for overseas action right from early 19th Century, when they had found themselves stranded with little to do by way of action after the Mysore Wars. In the 1790s itself, when Britain and Holland were at war, an expedition of theirs sent to Ceylon had captured the coastal fortifications of the island, and another one which sailed to the Dutch East Indies had brought about the surrender of Malacca.

The Madras Pioneers had the honour of being the first South Indian troops to serve outside Asia, when in 1801 a company of the Corps sailed with General Sir David Baird's expedition to Egypt to drive the French out. Arriving in June that year, they made an epic march from Red Sea to the Nile across the desert, but could not see action since peace was signed with the French. EGYPT WITH SPHINX finds its place in the long list of battle honours the Madras Engineers hold.

The Madras Infantry was in overseas action the second time after Ceylon when they captured the French bases of Bourbon – later Reunion – and Mauritius in 1810, earning themselves yet another battle honour, BOURBON. Another expedition mounted together by Bengal and Madras troops took Java in 1811, winning them both the Battle Honour, JAVA. But not until 1824, when the British invaded Burma, would the Madras

Army be involved in a major operation overseas.

By 1820s the Madras Army had grown into a formidable fighting force[1]. More than half a century of continuous warfare had brought it to the top of its form. The expedition to Burma, the biggest overseas one so far, under General Sir Archibald Campbell, comprising 17 Madras Infantry Regiments together with the European Regiment and some elements of Cavalry, Artillery and Pioneers, sailed from Madras in April 1824. Arriving at Rangoon in May, they took the town easily, but could progress no further. There were no transports to be had as was expected, to take up an advance; and Ava, the capital city and the principal objective of the campaign, lay 400 miles to the north. The force was stranded for transports and supplies to fetch up from India, and the rainy season to pass. Nevertheless, limited forays were attempted to dislodge the Burmese from the stockades they were holding in the countryside around.

These stockades, 10 to 20 feet tall, were built of teak or other wooden beams, and often surrounded by ditches and fencings of bamboo spikes. Earthen platforms inside enabled the occupants to overlook the surroundings, and bring down effective fire through embrasures cut in the wall. Being made of wood, the stockades were not resistant to cannon shot, but neither could they be breached since the shot passed easily through the wood, causing merely a hole. The only way to storm them was by using scaling ladders; a daring proposition, and the first such major effort ended in disaster. An assault on an important post in a place called Kemmendine on 3 June was repulsed. But a second assault on the following day carried the stockade, forcing the Burmese to withdraw to Donabyu, some distance north.

---

1. By an estimate of 1826, it had eight regiments of Light Cavalry (The Madras Native Cavalry having had changed its designation to 'Madras Light Cavalry'), a Corps of Artillery, two European Infantry Regiments, two battalions of Pioneers, and fifty two regiments of Native Infantry, each having only one battalion (as against the earlier arrangement of two battalions to a regiment).

They were back however in force by the end of the month, attacking the Madras Army pickets. The pickets of the 7th, 43rd and the 12th MI came under attack on successive days; but the attacks were easily repulsed, the enemy often driven back with bayonets. The skirmishes continued for the next five months or so, with the Madras Army generally maintaining an upper hand. Then on 5 October the Light Brigade[2] suffered a terrible reverse at Kyaikalo, some 14 miles from Rangoon. They had staged an attack on the pagoda there, trying to storm the Burmese stockade without scaling ladders. The enemy held the fire until the last minute for the attacking troops to reach the foot of the stockade, and then let fly. 7 officers and 91 men, mostly belonging to the 34th Light Infantry, were killed or wounded. Strangely, the enemy abandoned the post on their own the following day.

By November, with the British advance still held up at Rangoon, the Burmese took the initiative. Assembling a massive army of some 60,000 men under their renowned general, Maha Bandoola, they advanced on Rangoon arriving in its vicinity on the 30th. Paradoxically the Madras Army which had set out to invade Burma found itself in a defensive role, outnumbered and none too familiar with the terrain of jungles and swamps. Early morning on 1 December the Burmese attacked the post at Kemmendine, wrested from them six months ago. The defence of this post for nine days from then on, by the 26th MI under Major Yates and 58 men of the 1st Madras European Regiment under Captain Page, with an artillery detachment of two 6-pounder guns and one 12-pounder cannon, was to become the stuff legends are made off.

---

2. Prompted by the spectacular performance of the Light Brigade – formed of units with lighter equipment – in the Peninsular War in Europe, the Madras Army earmarked four of its units as 'Light Infantry Battalions' in 1812. Their identities were later signified by naming them – besides their numbering – after places relevant to them by origin or history. Thus these four units came to be known as the 3rd Palamcottah, 23rd Wallajabad, 31st Trichinopoly and 34th Chicacole Light Infantry Battalions (3rd PLI, 23rd WLI, 31st TLI and 34th CLI, respectively). Not all of these battalions exist today, and those who do have changed their designations following various reorganizations down the years.

Kemmendine was a riverside post, and the Burmese had chosen to spearhead their move by an amphibious assault, while the troops closed in from the countryside around for the land attack. At 4.a.m. on the 1st, preceded by massed fire rafts, a large fleet of their war boats moved down the river towards the stockade. The one cruiser the British had anchored close by the post was forced to pull away downstream as the fire rafts descended on it; but the war boats themselves were dispersed once they came under fire from the guns of the post positioned to guard the riverfront. Meanwhile the land troops had gathered all round, attempting to storm the stockade by escalade. Fighting raged through the day as attack after attack was beaten back. Then as darkness fell the Burmese entrenched themselves at a short distance and delivered an assault at 8.p.m. simultaneously from all three sides. The defenders had a nightmarish struggle at hand, holding on desperately, barely able to see the enemy even when they were as close as thirty yards. In the end, the musketry of the Madras men, steady and skilled, won the day. The attack was repulsed.

Frustrated, the Burmese kept up incessant fire through out the night and the following day, while their war boats kept attempting to close in on the face of steady gunfire from the shore. By the afternoon, with casualties mounting, right when things were getting a bit too sticky for the defenders, help arrived in the form of a British war ship, H.M.S. *Arachne*, accompanied by a gun brig and two gunboats. The pressure from enemy war boats eased, and Yates used the reprieve to withdraw some of the men from the riverfront to strengthen the weak points of the stockade. Further help arrived during the night, when 50 more Madras Europeans came in to replace the casualties. The Burmese meanwhile had succeeded in planting a gun some fifty yards from the stockade, and were bringing down fire. A sortie by the defenders to capture the gun on the 3rd morning couldn't succeed, and during the next two days the Burmese built more entrenchments and erected fresh batteries. By the 5th evening their guns were playing havoc with the stockade, and reinforced with more troops, they launched fresh assaults on the southern and eastern faces; but once again the defenders doggedly fought them off.

With their amphibious attacks making no headway against the firepower of the British warships, the Burmese amassed their forces for yet another land attack. It came on the 7th, simultaneously from all the three land faces of the stockade, the attackers throwing in everything they had. The embattled garrison fought back fiercely. The fighting went on, grim and bloody, for more than 24 hours with both sides unrelenting; until at last the heavy toll of casualties began to tell on the morale of the attackers, and their efforts slackened. Finally towards the predawn hours on 9 December they chose to quit – the troops retired, abandoning their trenches. The battle of Kemmendine was over.

The heroic defence of the post came to be recognized as one of the finest feats ever by the men of the Madras Army. The fighting was so intense that during its entire period of nine days, not a single man had had a change of clothing; and every man who could carry a musket, no matter wounded or sick, kept to his post. The 26th MI was later awarded the Battle Honour, KEMMENDINE, 'as a perpetual record of their distinguished and persevering gallantry on that occasion'.

Even as the fighting raged at Kemmendine, the main Burmese Army was closing in on the main body of the Madras troops positioned round the Shwe Dagon Pagoda, in preparation for an attack. But their plans were preempted, as at this stage, finally the Madras Army assumed the offensive. A general attack launched on 7 December was a resounding success. The defeated Burmese made a stand at Kokine, where they were handed yet another drubbing on the 15th. Early in 1825 the Madras troops advanced up the river Irrawaddy, and in April, took Donabyu, the main base of the Burmese where they had retired to and were reorganizing. Bandoola was killed in this action, and the Burmese army went into full retreat thereafter. However with the monsoon hampering the advance, it took another year which saw heavy fighting off and on, notably at Prome and Pegu, for the

Madras forces to get to Yandaboo, 60 miles short of the capital, when the Burmese surrendered on terms. The last bit of action took place on 11 January 1826 at Sittang farther south, a month and a half before the end of hostilities.

A detachment which made the first attempt to take the place earlier in the month was badly mauled, and had had to withdraw with considerable loss. Then a second task force under Colonel Pepper, consisting of 450 men from the 3rd PLI and the 12th and 34th MI with 70 Madras Europeans, landed in the vicinity of the stockade around 8.a.m. on the 11th. Awaiting them was the gory sight of the naked and mangled bodies of their comrades, suspended by the heels from gibbets on the river bank. Without a pause the force split into three columns carrying two scaling ladders each, and moved in for a multi-pronged assault. The stockade, about 14 feet high, was constructed entirely of teak wood, with plenty of loopholes to fire from, and occupied a commanding site atop a hill, with steep slopes to all sides that made it practically inaccessible. Along its northern face lay a creek about 50 yards wide, fordable only at low current; and delayed at the crossing, the column approaching from that face could not form up with the others till 2.p.m. As the three columns began closing in on the stockade through an intervening patch of jungle, they were fired at by enemy skirmishers. But they pushed through, and emerging from the jungle, found themselves facing the stockade barely 70 yards away.

The troops hurled themselves forward on the double. The Burmese waited for them to get halfway across to the stockade before opening up. It was murder and mayhem for a while, as the attackers were cut down mercilessly. But the attack didn't waver. The ladders were dropped, picked up again, and incredibly, carried up the steep ascent. And finally those who made it to the foot of the stockade raised the ladders and planted them against the teak wall, even as the enemy tried to ward them off by spears thrust through the loopholes. Then the escalade began, men often crowding the ladders in a mad rush. One ladder broke, overcrowded, but the men, possessed by the rage of the battle, kept scaling by the rest. Then they fell on the enemy with a vengeance. All their pent-up fury unleashed, there was no quarters given; and the enemy dead when the fighting ended, amounted to some 500 out of the 1500-strong garrison. The Madras Army lost 86 men including 7 officers in the battle.

There was no more fighting. The peace treaty was signed on 24 February, and the troops began falling back along the river Irrawaddy to Rangoon for the journey back home. One battalion, the 18th MI, alone was detached and sent on a mission to explore a route across the mountains into Arakan. The battalion, commanded by Captain David Ross, with 50 pioneers and some elephants, traversed the route in twenty days, before proceeding to Amherst by river for their embarkation back to Madras. The route they explored was to come in handy more than a century later, in the allied advance into Burma during the 2nd World War. The 1st Burma War was almost exclusively won by the Madras troops, since the Bengal contingents, advancing from Assam and Arakan, could not make much of headway. The main battle honour for the war, AVA, was awarded to all the Madras Infantry Regiments which took part, the Madras European Regiment, the 1st Light Cavalry and the 1st Battalion, the Madras Pioneers.

BURMA WARS

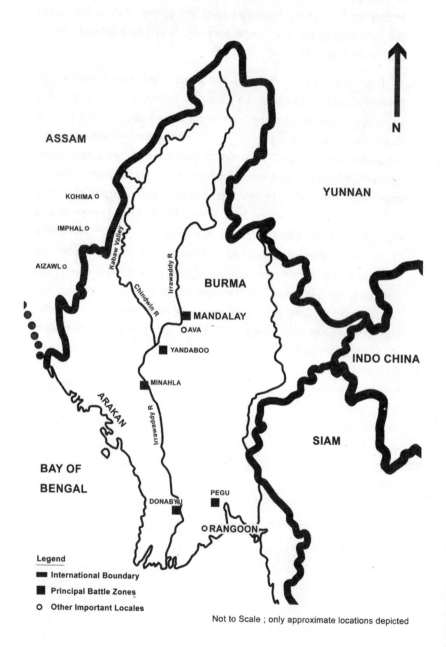

ASSAM

YUNNAN

KOHIMA O

IMPHAL O

AIZAWL O

Kabaw Valley

Chindwin R

Irrawaddy R

BURMA

■ MANDALAY

O AVA

■ YANDABOO

■ MINAHLA

ARAKAN

Irrawaddy R

INDO CHINA

SIAM

BAY OF
BENGAL

PEGU

DONABYU ■

O RANGOON

N

Legend
■ International Boundary
■ Principal Battle Zones
O Other Important Locales

Not to Scale ; only approximate locations depicted

2

SUBDUING ASIA

The mailed fist of the empire

For the Madras Army which revelled in its legacy of having been constantly in action for almost three quarters of a century, the decade and a half that followed the end of the 1st Burma War must have been terribly frustrating, having been left – excepting for the brief interlude of the Coorg War – with nothing better to do than being engaged to quell petty local disturbances. Then came along the opportunities that were to earn them laurels, as the most aggressive fighting force available to the British in Asia at that time. These were the major overseas missions in the form of China and Burma Wars, and the role they played in the Sind War in Northwestern India and the Persian War beyond the country's border.

The two-year long Sino-British conflict from 1840 to 42 following differences between the two on opium trade, which came to be referred as the 1st China War, was to become a watershed in Indian military history. This was the first time the Indian troops were engaged in an operation not directly concerned with India. Unlike the 1st Burma War which was more or less an escalation of the border disputes between India and Burma, this was an operation intended solely to further the aims of British expansion in the Far East. The empire was very much in the making. And in the saga of the Madras troops, it was to become yet another milestone, because this war too, very much like the 1st Burma War, was almost exclusively fought and won by them.

The expeditionary force was commanded by Major General Sir Hugh Gough. In July 1840 they seized the island of Chusan, after which peace initiatives were attempted with China. These made no headway, and in January 1841 reinforcements were called in. Eventually the force comprised some seven Madras Infantry regiments and two companies of the Madras Sappers and Miners. (The Madras Pioneers were converted to 'Sappers and Miners' in 1831.) One more company of the Sappers joined the force later. The operation was re-launched with the capture of the forts guarding Canton, and in May Canton itself was taken. Despite poor logistics that caused more casualties than the fighting itself, the force made it to Yangste in a year's campaigning to threaten Nanking. The Chinese then agreed for peace under which Hong Kong was ceded to Britain and five Chinese posts were opened for foreign trade.

It was splendid fighting all the way. Two pieces of action stood out to highlight the grit and gallantry of the men from Madras; the first one by the 37th MI at Canton and the second by the 2nd and 6th MI at Chin-Kiang-Foo. On 30 May 1841, the 37th MI, cut off from the rest of the force in a thunderstorm which rendered their muskets useless, held off repeated attacks by several thousand Chinese soldiers. The Duke of Wellington was so moved by the feat that he made a special mention of it in the House of Lords, and the regiment was individually honoured by being renamed the 37th Madras Grenadiers. The turn came of the 2nd and 6th MI to distinguish themselves when on 20 July 1842, in company with the British 55th Foot and the Sappers and Miners, they escaladed the walls of the fortification at Chin-Kiang-Foo under heavy fire and blew the gates open.

The mettle of the Madras soldier was on eminent display during other actions of the campaign as well; and there were many of those – Hong Kong, Bogue Forts, Chinhal, Shanghai, Ningpo and Chapoo. The mutual confidence between the British soldiers and the Madras sepoys contributed a lot to the success of the operations; so did the gallant endeavour of the newly formed Sappers and Miners who were there in every battle fought, right alongside the infantry. The Battle Honour, CHINA, and the emblem of the Chinese Imperial Dragon were awarded to the 2nd, 6th, 14th, 37th and the 41st MI and 'A', 'B' and 'F' Companies of the Madras Sappers and Miners. The 2nd MI continued to be a part of the Chusan Field Force until June 1845, and 'F' Company of the Sappers which joined the campaign in later stages remained in Hong Kong until 1846.

Back home, yet another decade of inaction awaited the main army, a period interrupted only by minor missions they had to undertake occasionally, to reinforce the troops of Bombay Presidency. Even then the Sappers and Miners began blazing their own trails. The 'C' Company of the Sappers was engaged in the 1st Afghan War from 1841 to 42, unaccompanied by any other Madras troops, even while the 1st China War was still going on. The Sind War that followed soon thereafter saw the same company reap glory in the battle of Meeanee on 17 February 1843. They formed part of Sir Charles Napier's 2500-strong force which took on the Baluchis ten times their number that day.

When the advance was checked at the river Fuleli by heavy fire, some 50 Madras Sappers under Captain R Handerson, covering the right flank of the guns, made a road for the artillery across irrigation canals, and later breached the high wall skirting the Shikargarh forest, whereby the gunners were able to poke the guns in and sweep through. And in the heat of the moment, they spontaneously joined the charge of the British 22nd Foot – later the Cheshire Regiment – across Shikargarh. In an equally spontaneous display of camaraderie, the soldiers of the 22nd exchanged their caps, the 'shakos', with the Sappers, which in modified form, still constitute the distinctive headgear of the Madras Sappers. The mutual bond continues to date.

The Sappers found themselves in the vanguard of advance as Napier continued with a forced march to Hyderabad, where he attacked and dispersed the enemy who had besieged the residency on 24 March. The war was virtually won that day, although minor operations continued for another six months until the whole of Sind was subdued. The exploits of the Sappers in this operation when most of them were yet unarmed[1], made a strong case for issue of weapons to them, and won them the Battle Honours, MEEANEE and HYDERABAD.

The Madras troops as a whole, both infantry and sappers, were to be in action again by early 1852 when the 2nd Burma War broke out. Although the Anglo-Burmese relations were getting sore once again from early 1840s, the British, preoccupied with the Afghan and Sikh Wars in the northwest, could turn their attention to Burma only after 1850. Once more the larger part of the field force mobilized – numbering 5800, commanded by General Godwin – was constituted by troops from Madras, with only a spattering of British troops and the Bengal Native Infantry.

This time they attacked and subdued the Burmese at Martaban before proceeding to Rangoon. The Burmese did put up a stiff fight at Martaban, but proved ineffectual. The invaders, moving up the river, landed on 12 April to take Rangoon. Although they skirmished with the enemy with ships in fire support, they could advance to the enemy stronghold of Shwe Dagon Pagoda to launch an attack only by the 14th. Confronting them once again were the inherent problems of fighting in Burma, a hostile terrain, the intense heat, and the inevitable stockades. The Pagoda was taken in the end at the cost of 149 casualties, and Rangoon secured. A flotilla was immediately dispatched to the next enemy position at Bassein with 700 British and Madras troops. They arrived off the Burmese position on 18 May. The enemy was well-entrenched in a mud fort with several guns. They held their fire with remarkable tact before opening up at close quarters. Nevertheless the attackers carried the day in a determined storm. But there they were to stay until reinforcements arrived three months later.

They arrived in August and the force moved on to Prome which fell without much ado. The advance continued till the troops arrived off the next objective, Pegu, on 20 October. Cutting their way inland for two

---

1. The Sappers were still being considered more or less a work force, rather than combat troops and hence not provided with personal arms; but Meeanee changed that perception, and they were to be armed as regular troops subsequently.

miles across the jungle on the 21st, they came up against the Burmese fortification. It was strongly held and the enemy opened up with heavy fire, but was driven back from their defences when the attackers took the bayonets to them. And as the attackers pressed home the advantage in a thrust for the main Pagoda, the Burmese abandoned the position.

The British commander was rather flattered by the meek show on the part of the Burmese so far, that he now grossly underestimated them. Leaving behind a garrison of merely 400 men – 200 of the 5th MI and 200 of the Madras Fusiliers – to hold the place, he retired to Rangoon with the rest of the force. The inevitable followed, as the Burmese besieged the place in strength. An attempt at relief was stoutly beaten back, and eventually Godwin himself had to move in again at the head of a 1300-man force to break through the cordon. The enemy was routed and thereafter the whole province of Pegu was annexed when the advance was abruptly halted. There had been a revolution and change of regime at Ava that had opened the prospects of peace, the new ruler, Mindon Min, being averse to war.

The war ended so, but the troops continued to be engaged for another two years in establishing law and order, which had broken down in the province with the disappearance of the Burmese Army. All the infantry regiments and sapper companies (the 1st, 5th, 9th, 12th, 19th, 26th, 30th, 35th and 49th MI, and 'A', 'B', 'C' and 'E' Companies of the Sappers) which took part in this war – which proved to be somewhat lesser contested than the earlier Burma War, owing to a disorganized enemy – were later awarded the Battle Honour, PEGU.

The combat- hardened army that returned home was in for another long spell of inaction, one which was to prove terribly disastrous to its grand reputation as a fighting force. Mercifully, the Sappers and Miners were spared such a setback, since their specialized skills continued to be in great demand. A couple of years after the 2nd Burma War, 'B' Company of the Madras Sappers joined Lieutenant General Sir James Outram's Bombay Army contingent, which evicted the Persian forces that had occupied Herat in Afghanistan during the Persian War (1856-57), to earn the Battle Honour, PERSIA. That was just one of the many they would earn down the years, as they grew into a legendary force that was to scale the heights of glory in every operation the Indian troops ever saw.

3

THE RISING AND AFTER

The disintegration of a great fighting force

In 1857, a hundred years after they had won the Battle of Plassey, the British faced the biggest challenge to their supremacy in the subcontinent in a large-scale rebellion by the soldiers of the army they themselves had raised, which came to be called the Sepoy Mutiny by the British, and variously interpreted[1] by the Indians and portrayed as the 'Rising', the 'Rebellion', the 'First War of Independence' et cetera. The conflagration, started by the sepoys of the Bengal Army at Meerut in May 1857, soon set the whole of northern and central India ablaze, with heavy British losses. However it was more or less confined to the Bengal Army, which was the largest of the three armies at that time, with more number of troops than what the Bombay and Madras Armies together had in their ranks. Most of its troops joined the rebellion, with only few of the Bombay troops and none at all of the Madras troops[2] giving them company. The British, depending more on their own troops and the ones that remained loyal to them from those recruited in the north, like the Sikhs and the Gorkhas, deployed only limited number of Madras troops, two regiments in all.

---

1. Whatever may be the interpretations of what happened in 1857, the failure of the sepoys to overthrow the British should be mainly attributed to their attempt not gaining a trans-national appeal. The concept of Indian nationhood began gaining ground only later, towards the end of the 19th Century, thanks to the nationalist movement. By coincidence, around the same period, the separate Presidency Armies were amalgamated to form the Indian Army.

2. There were no instances of mutiny among the Madras troops, bar one, when the 8th Light Cavalry refused to embark – whether sympathetic to the rebels or for some other reason – for service in Bengal in 1857, which led to its immediate disbandment.

The 17th and 27th MI joined action at Cawnpore with General Windham's force in November 1857. While the 17th was dispatched to Fatehpur to keep the line of communication open between Allahabad and Cawnpore, the 27th went on to reinforce Outram's force at Lucknow. Here it was part of a small force of 4400 which held out at Alambagh against massive rebel attacks for three months. Although the residency was finally evacuated and could be retaken only in March 1858, the saga of the British stand at Lucknow earned the admiration of both friend and foe alike, and the 27th MI and the Madras Sappers were awarded the Battle Honour, LUCKNOW, with the rest of the troops that served in that theatre. Towards the end of the rebellion and in the period immediately following it (1858-59), a number of Madras Infantry regiments and Sapper detachments formed part of various field forces which continued to be engaged in minor operations, mainly in Central India, until peace returned, earning them the Battle Honour, CENTRAL INDIA.

Almost simultaneous with the Sepoy Rebellion the 2nd China War broke out. Again the participation of Madras troops were minimal with just one regiment representing them. (This was more or less going to be the pattern in troop preference by the British for the next half a century or more.) The 38th MI formed part of the force dispatched to capture Canton in December 1857, which it did in the following month. After a period of negotiations and an unsuccessful attempt to capture the Taku Forts guarding the approaches to Tienstin and Peking in 1859, an allied force of British, Indian and French troops was assembled in HongKong in 1860. They defeated the Chinese at Palikao and occupied Peking. The war ended with the Chinese agreeing to abide by the treaty of Tienstin, by which more of their ports were opened to foreign trade. Additional troops from Madras – which included 2nd, 12th, and 21st MI – joined the campaign in its latter phase. 'A' and 'K' Companies of the Madras Sappers and Miners under Captain HMJ Stuart, which formed part of the second expedition under Lieutenant General Sir Hope Grant, served with distinction and were awarded the Battle Honours, TAKU FORTS and PEKIN.

After the Sepoy Rebellion when the power was transferred from the East India Company to the British Crown, the Madras Army, though it had remained loyal to the British, was not only downsized, but downplayed as well, being relegated to internal security duties. South India in any case, had become somewhat of a backwater militarily, with the area of operations having shifted to the north and northwest, and recruitment of troops from those areas proving convenient. A period of stagnation followed – excepting for the Sappers, who continued to be engaged – when, away from action, in low morale, and officered by low-calibre Britons shunted off for the job, the army lost its fighting edge drastically; so much so when it was called back to action after nearly 30 years when the 3rd Burma war broke out in 1885, it could not live up to its reputation of the yester years. (It came as no consolation that the rest of the troops – both British and Indian – fared equally bad or worse.) The only other instance of the Madras Infantry being operationally involved during that period, was in the 2nd Afghan War from 1878 to 1879, when a few of their regiments took part in minor engagements, which won them the Battle Honour, AFGHANISTAN 1879 – 1880.

The British policy of recruitment was always formulated to meet their own objectives of empire building. Southern India was their chief recruiting base while they fought their initial campaigns in the Carnatic and the peninsula. After the fall of Tipu Sultan and the end of the Maratha Wars, the focus gradually shifted northward. It was easier and more economical for them to recruit men from the north for operations in the north and northwest, more so because of the easy availability of recruits, especially from Nepal and Punjab after the end of the Gorkha and Sikh Wars. It certainly stood to logic to recruit these men for operations closer to their homes, rather than transporting troops from far south, given the prohibitive costs and the delay involved with the means available those days, apart from the problem of having to get the troops acclimatized to unfamiliar climatic conditions. Added to this was the difficulty the British began experiencing to find enough recruits from the south. A fairly long period of peace and prosperity, which created an environment conducive to better education, had begun to unfold new avenues of employment for the youth in the area. The comparatively better levels of education among the southern youth was, in fact, to encourage the British to recruit whatever number of them available to technical arms and services, rather than as infantry troops, who could be easily recruited elsewhere.

The fact that the Madras Sappers and Miners continued to be some of the most sought after troops from the subcontinent over the years, and have come to be rated among the finest combat engineers in the world today, leaves no doubt per se on the tremendous fighting prowess of the South Indian soldier. However the British military brass in India, too eager to glorify their own commands in the selfish pursuit of their career progress, began promoting a myth on the superiority of the Northern Indian soldiers, in what they called the martial traits, over their brethren from the South; which also perfectly suited the essential British policy of nurturing divisive tendencies wherever possible. The myth was to be totally exploded by the gallant performance of the South Indian soldiers during the two World Wars and after. But for the time being the damage was done. What was essentially a matter of logistics and socio-economics to begin with, came to be completely misinterpreted over the years, inducing the top echelons of the British military in India to regard the South Indian to be somewhat lacking in soldierly traits. The end result was the down sizing of the Madras Infantry so drastically, that by the dawn of the 20th Century, the once proud fighting force had been reduced to a scanty, insignificant part of the military establishment in India. Colonel DM Reid, a long-serving British officer of the Madras troops, aptly states their case in his book, *The Story of Fort St. George.* He wrote:

Remember that they took part in the victories of Plassey, Seringapattam, Assaye, and in quelling the 1857 Mutiny. The same men are in the Madras Sappers and Miners, which has always been, and remained, the 'Corps d'elite', and was not disbanded. Somehow the military reputation of Madras fell away. The Presidency was far from the Frontier, the traditional training ground of the Indian Army.

Retrenchment forced reductions and the Madras regiments went.

The war of 1939 saw a speedy revival of Madras recruitment, which, by the beginning of 1945 had produced the remarkable result of 22 percent of the Indian Army being from the Madras Presidency.

Even as such ignominy was being heaped on the Madras Infantry, the Madras Sappers and Miners continued with their harvest of glory, and were engaged in four different operations, all of them overseas. The first of these was in Abyssinia, in 1868. They were part of the 32,000-strong expeditionary force under Sir Robert Napier, which had set out against King Theodore of Abyssinia who was holding several British hostages. Landing on the east coast of Africa in January 1868, they fought their way inland and captured the stronghold of Magdala, whence the king committed suicide. The 400-mile journey across the mountainous terrain, often under heavy tropical showers, with 36,000 thousand pack animals, mules and elephants, took the troops almost three months to complete. The campaign, described as an 'engineer's war', saw the Madras Sappers improvise a ten-foot wide road by ramping the boulders and obstacles instead of blasting, employing ropes and pulleys to move stores and equipments in the absence of trails. They won the Theatre Honour, ABYSSINIA 1868.

Yet another Battle Honour, AFGHANISTAN 1878 – 80, was to come their way, having been involved in both phases of the 2nd Afghan War, mostly doing road works and demolitions. Six companies in all were engaged; 'B', 'E', and 'K' Companies in the first phase and 'A', 'C' and 'I' Companies in the second phase. During 1878 they were also in Malta as well as Cyprus ('G' and 'H' Companies), with an Engineer Brigade, forming a part of the force deployed to forestall any threat to the recently opened Suez Canal. They were almost everywhere pitching in with their expertise, from naval works and survey to visual signaling, or working on camping sites and water supply.

In 1882 they were in Egypt for the second time, as part of Lieutenant General Sir Garnet Wolseley's Indian Division, mobilized to suppress the military revolt led by Arabi Pasha against the ruling Khedive. Of primary concern to the British was the safety of the Suez Canal. After three weeks of landing at Ismailia in August, the division surprised the Egyptians by a night attack on Tel el Kebir, resulting in Pasha's surrender. Initially employed for repair of railways, telegraph system and fresh water canals, the Madras Sappers – 'A' and 'I' Companies – worked alongside the Royal Engineers during the battle of Tel el Kebir, earning the admiration of the veterans in the latter's ranks. They won the Battle Honours, EGYPT 1882 and TEL EL KEBIR. Again, a company of the Sappers was with General Graham's force sent to Suakin during the 1st Sudan War, and took part in the battle of Tofrek and destruction of Tamai. They were to win the Battle Honour, SUAKIN AND TOFREK.

The stage was set for the 3rd Burma War by 1885, with relations strained between the British and the new King, Thibaw. An amphibious operation was launched from lower Burma by the middle of November that year, up the Irrawaddy, by a force of 19,000 troops under Major General HND Prendergast, which included five Madras Infantry regiments[3] and three companies of the Madras Sappers. They took Mandalay before the end of the month, facing little resistance except at the fort of Minahla where the 12th MI suffered some 30 casualties. The king was soon deposed and made a prisoner, but a general insurrection broke out in the country with the dispersed Burmese Army soldiers at large, and sporadic fighting continued for almost six years before the British could be firmly in saddle.

Large reinforcements were marshalled from all the Presidencies including Madras[4] to sustain the fighting. This long drawn out campaign in Burma in an extremely difficult terrain, although successful in the end, found most Indian troops ill prepared for it, with malaria claiming more lives than the fighting itself. While the performance of the entire army the British fielded for the campaign proved rather shoddy, it would

---

3. The 23rd Wallajabad Light Infantry and the 1st, 12th, 21st and the 25th MI
4. The Palamcottah Light Infantry and the 13th, 14th, 15th, 16th, 17th, 26th, 27th and the 30th MI

appear that the top brass chose to unfairly single out the Madras troops for many of the pitfalls. All the troops who participated in the war were awarded the Battle Honour, BURMA 1885 – 1887.

During July 1885, the Madras Sappers raised a company in Burma from the natives of that country (Kachins, Karens and Shans), seconding it with officers and NCOs[5]. These 'Burma Sappers and Miners', initially stationed at Mandalay, was renamed 15 (Burma) Company in 1903, and saw action in Mesopotamia during the 1st World War. In 1938 the Company's 53-year old link with the Madras Sappers was severed, when it was re-designated 'The 4th Burma Sappers and Miners'.

For more than forty years, from 1861 to 1903, the British Indian Government had been constantly preoccupied with the 'Frontier Wars' in the northwest of the country. This included innumerable defensive and offensive operations to contain the incursions by the warlike tribesmen. There were major outbreaks from 1895 to 1898, and the Madras troops, both infantry and sappers, did their bit too. A company of the sappers was part of the force which relieved the besieged garrison of Chitral in western Kashmir. They built a 944- foot bridge over the river Swat, an accomplishment that stood out beyond their normal sapper tasks. Later in 1897 they were among the troops defending the camp at the Malakand Pass, and the ones who relieved Chakdara. In the same year they were working on the improvement of communications as well as demolition works with Sir William Lockart's force, which stormed the entrance to the Tirah Valley at Dargai in October.

During this last operation which lasted until the following April and led to the occupation of the Afridi Territory, the 21st MI (Pioneers)[6] fought a gallant rearguard action at Burg during one of the reverses, earning

---

5. Non-Commissioned Officers

6. In 1883, two of the infantry regiments, the 1st and the 4th MI were converted into pioneer units. The justification given by Sir Frederick Roberts, C-in-C Madras, for such a move was, in his own words: "----Madrassis as a rule are more intelligent and better educated than the fighting races of northern India....the Sappers and Miners are a brilliant exception to the Madras Army, being indeed a most

a special commendation. Both this regiment and the Sappers won the Battle Honours, PUNJAB FRONTIER and TIRAH, while the Sappers alone were awarded two more, MALAKAND and CHITRAL.

The Madras troops found themselves in field again during the 3rd China War in 1900, following the Boxers' Uprising. The Theatre Honour, CHINA 1900, for this brief operation was awarded to the 1st, 3rd, 28th and the 31st Regiments of the Madras Infantry, and No 3 and 6 Companies of the Madras Sappers and Miners.

No 12 Company of the Sappers were part of a force under Colonel Francis Younghusband which went to Tibet in 1903, to thwart the plans of that country to forge an alliance with Russia. They marched 400 miles from Siliguri to Lhasa over arid, windswept plains, negotiating passes at 17,000 feet in wet weather, and finally crossing the river Tsangpo (Brahmaputra as it traverses India) in flood, braving a current of more than five miles an hour. They worked on the Rangpo-Gangtok Road in Sikkim, and carried out the demolition of the fortified post of Palla and a building called 'Chinese House', prior to the storming of Gyantse Zong. The Company returned from the mission via Nathula in 1904.

The last occasion any Madras troops were in action before the 1st World War broke out in 1914, was when the 79th Carnatic Infantry was deployed in the Persian Gulf in 1911 to suppress gun running, a mission in which they displayed a remarkable degree of adaptability to varied

---

useful efficient body of men but as no increase in that branch was considered necessary, I obtained permission to convert two Infantry regiments into pioneers on the model of the Pioneer corps of the Bengal Army." (The Sappers were also raised as Pioneers, but in this case regular infantry was converted to pioneers, and formed into a separate corps, other than the Sappers and the Infantry.) The implication that its infantrymen were no more held in high esteem did not augur well for the Madras Army. Yet another battalion, the 21st MI, was converted to pioneers within a decade. Roberts, originally an officer of the Bengal Army, went on record as C-in-C India later, to make even more disparaging remarks about the Madras Infantry, which starkly reflected the growing predisposition among the senior officers. The elementary aspect that the same class of men served in both sappers and the infantry, but sappers got the best officers and infantry the worst (which made all the difference), was deliberately overlooked.

assignments.

An army commission set up by Lord Lytton in the last quarter of the 19th Century, to find ways to improve the military efficiency of India, recommended the abolition of the separate presidency armies and amalgamation of all of them into a single army of India. The recommendation was implemented in 1895, and thus the Indian Army was born. In the beginning it had four commands, Punjab, Bengal, Madras and Bombay, each under a lieutenant general. Prior to this amalgamation all the presidency armies had been downsized, in a process of streamlining undertaken after the end of the 2nd Afghan War in 1880. Many regiments were disbanded. The Madras Army which had already lost a dozen regiments in 1860s was the worst hit. It lost another eight, and was left with only 32 regiments under its colours. The display of the bias against the South Indian soldier had become blatantly naked. Between 1890 and 1903, 17 Madras regiments were converted into Gorkha or Punjabi ones. Ironically, the Madras Sappers were earning one honour title after the other during the same period. In 1876, they were titled 'Queen's Own Sappers and Miners'. They became '2nd Queen's Own Sappers and Miners' in 1903, and 'Queen Victoria's Own Sappers and Miners' in 1911.

The reorganization of the Indian Army undertaken by Lord Kitchener, C-in-C India, in 1903 proved further unfavourable to the Madras soldiers, with even more reduction in the number of their battalions. Many battalions were also reduced in strength to 600, making them suitable for garrison duty only. All the regiments of the Madras Infantry and Pioneers had also had 60 added to their numbering, so that the 1st became 61st, 5th became 65th and so on, in a final bit of bureaucratic demeaning.

4

THE FIRST WORLD WAR

A call to arms well responded

Never before had Britain had to mobilize the military resources available to her across the empire in a scale as she did at the outbreak of World War I in 1914. And the stigma that had haunted the Madras soldiers for more than half a century had to go. The Madras Infantry, as well as the Pioneers and the Sappers and Miners, were mobilized in a big way, to join the various Indian Expeditionary Forces headed for overseas operations. The first Madras troops to get into action were the 61st Pioneers and the 63rd Palamcottah Light Infantry, which sailed from Bombay in October 1914 with the expeditionary force to East Africa. The 61st was one of the first to land at Tanga on 3 November, taking the brunt of the fighting, losing 4 officers and 57 men killed, and 22 wounded. The following day when the offensive resumed after the remainder of the force landed, the regiment suffered another 38 casualties in day-long engagements. During the next three years they continued to be engaged in the East African campaign, mostly on pioneer work, while their sister regiment, the 63rd PLI, manned the garrisons.

Another regiment, the 75th Carnatic Infantry, was deployed at Aden from 1916 to 1920, almost continually engaged against the Turkish forces. They were at the dawn attack by which Jabri was captured on 7 December 1916. On 3 October 1918, they fought another stiff action at Handley Hill; a deadly piece of fighting when hopelessly surrounded they extricated themselves, keeping the enemy at bay through bayonet charges. After the operations, a Turkish commander was to admit that the Indian unit most feared by his troops was the 75th CI, 'because they were not afraid to go in with the bayonet.' The regiment suffered nearly 100 casualties in Turkish operations, more than a quarter of them killed.

Yet another Madras regiment to see a good deal of action was the 81st Pioneers, deployed at the Northwest Frontier in 1915. Their endurance and grit came to the fore when, in company with the Corps of Guides, they fought a memorable rearguard action, covering 24 miles in a day while the British soldiers collapsed of exhaustion and had to be carried. They were later engaged in the Marri operations in March-April 1918. Another pioneer regiment, the 64th, was engaged in suppressing a Kachin uprising in upper Burma, before proceeding to Mesopotamia the following year. They were continually engaged in pioneer work from March 1916 when they arrived at Basra, until the armistice. Their casualty figures were considerable in the fight for Hai Salient.

A number of infantry regiments (the 73rd, 79th, 80th and 88th CI, the 83rd WLI and the 1/156th Infantry) were also involved in the Mesopotamian campaign, manning various garrisons. Of these the 80th CI joined the 17th division in 1919 for operations in Kurdistan. In the following year they saw a lot more fighting in Iraq during the Arab rebellion, when one of their subedars earned a Military Cross. Some of the Madras regiments – the 63rd PLI, 79th CI, 81st Pioneers, 83rd WLI, and the 88th CI – were in the thick of action in Persia and Iraq too, in 1919-20. Meanwhile two regiments, the 61st and 81st Pioneers, were also engaged in the 3rd Afghan War from May to August 1919. Two other regiments, the 64th Pioneers and the 73rd CI, continued to be engaged in this theatre for another five years when fighting continued.

The Madras Infantry and the Pioneer regiments were to win almost a dozen Battle Honours for their feats during World War I (1914-18), and in operations that followed immediately. The list embraces practically the entire lot of Asian and African campaigns fought during the period;

NORTHWEST FRONTIER 1914 – 18, EAST AFRICA 1914 – 18, KILIMANJARO 1914 – 18, MESOPOTAMIA 1915 – 18, BAGHDAD 1915 – 18, KUT-EL-AMARA 1917, NORTHWEST FRONTIER 1917, PERSIA 1918, ADEN 1918, BALUCHISTAN 1918 and AFGHANISTAN 1919.

The Madras Sappers' contribution to the war effort began well in advance of the war, when Major RL McClintock improvised the 'Bangalore Torpedo' at their training centre in 1907. This device – an iron pipe of adjustable length filled with TNT, which could be inserted into barbed wire entanglements and exploded to create a passage for the assaulting troops to charge through – perfected subsequently after years of experimentation and trials, found successful use in both the world wars, and is still an accepted device to breach wire obstacles. It was used with tremendous impact by General Pershing in the US Army's first action at Saint Mihiel during World War I, and used extensively at El Alamein during World War II.

The Madras Sappers and Miners opened their account in World War I with their No 2 Field Troop joining the Cavalry Division of the Indian Expeditionary Force 'A' to France in October 1914. They landed at Marseilles on 10 November and proceeded to Orleans mounted on 30 'Gwalior' tongas (a novelty in France), each carrying three men or four maunds of equipment besides the driver. Initially they were busy manufacturing bombs and conducting bombing lessons, and were at the defence line at St.Vanant-Robeq in 1915, before joining the 1st Cavalry Division in Belgium. Their roles varied from trench work at Hazebrouck to erecting wire entanglements and making hand grenades at Ypres. They sailed from Marseilles for Mesopotamia in December 1915, arriving at Basra the following month.

By then No. 12 Field Company[1], the first unit of the Madras Sappers to join the Mesopotamian campaign, had already been in action for

---

1. The Sappers had done away with the battalion system from 1885 onwards, since it was found convenient to have the company as the standard unit for independent combat role. These units came to be called 'Field Companies' ('troops/squadrons' with cavalry or airborne formations) from 1909 onwards. This system continued till 1965, when they were grouped under different regiments.

good part of a year, having arrived at Basra in March 1915. Initially employed in constructing roads and bridges, they were at the battle of Shaiba on 12 April 1915 as part of the 12th Division, ferrying guns and howitzers between Basra and Shaiba, on rafts made out of Arab boats. Later advancing up the Euphrates with the 12th Infantry Brigade, they were at the capture of Nasiriyeh on 24 July. Their contribution to the speedy movement of troops and stores – whether constructing numerous bridges across the creeks, or blowing up the Euphrates bund at Hakika to permit steamers to move through – was outstanding. By then the company had already bagged 12 gallantry awards including four Military Crosses. They moved on to Amara in October, where they converted the existing buildings into a marine workshop, and remained there until the Turks closed in on General Townsend's 6th Division at Kut el Amara in December 1915.

Kut el Amara had to be surrendered in April 1916 following a Turkish siege, but was retaken in February the following year when the Madras Sappers played a daring role. In a major opposed river crossing, three field companies, 12, 13, and 15 (Burma), forming part of the 14th Division along with half a company of the Royal Engineers, ferried the 37th Brigade across the Tigris at Shumran on 23 February 1917 for the attack on Kut el Amara. The flooded river, 300 yards wide with a current of six knots and eddies all over, had its far bank strongly held by the Turks.

Three ferries, No. 1 upstream, No. 2 in the centre and No. 3 downstream, each of 13 bipartite bridging pontoons, were launched at 5.15 a.m. No. 1 carried the Norfolk Regiment with rowing parties of their own men and the Royal Engineers. No. 2 carried the 2/9th GR (Gorkha Rifles) with rowing parties from 12 Field Company, a section of 15 Company and 100 men of the Hampshire Regiment. No. 3 carried the 1/2nd GR with rowing parties from 13 Field Company and 100 men from the Hampshire Regiment. While No. 1 was lucky to surprise the enemy, the other two ran into heavy machinegun fire. Out of the 13 pontoons of No. 2, only 10 made it to the far bank in the first run, 3 drifting downstream with the entire crew killed. Only 6 out of the remaining 10 made it in the second run, out of which only 5 returned. Of the 140 Gorkhas the No.3 ferry carried, only 50 could reach the far bank. One pontoon recovered later had 100 bullet holes on it. Rowers were the worst hit, many of the crews getting completely wiped out. 18 Sappers in all lost their lives, and another 28 were wounded in the operation.

Another unit of the Madras Sappers, 10 Field Company, landed at the Suez in December 1914 as part of the Indian Expeditionary Force 'E' to Egypt. They were at the defence of the canal during January-February 1915, and later put up works at the advanced defence line from Gebel Nurr to Ayun Musa. During 1917 they worked on various other defensive positions, and in March 1918, took part in the offensive to capture Rafat. They were also part of the forces which captured Aleppo subsequently, bringing about the surrender of half the Turkish forces in Palestine, before embarking for home at the Suez in December 1920. 10 Field was the only Sapper Company to be in Egypt throughout the duration of the war.

About the middle of 1918, with the Mesopotamian campaign over, Northwest Persia became strategically significant, and many Sapper units were deployed in the area. 12 Field Company was engaged in the construction of a number of roads and bridges at the Turkish-Persian Border. A detachment from 9 and 14 Companies at Quetta had been operating with the 'Cordon Force' in eastern Persia from 1915, suppressing the rebellious tribes of the area. A newly raised unit, 63 Field Company, was with the 'Sykes Force', involved in similar operations in Southeast Persia. 12, 13, 15, 61, 63 and 65 Companies were all engaged in the Persian theatre, making significant contribution in improving the lines of communications and making troops' accommodation, under severely inhospitable conditions of climate and terrain.

World War I was fought at a time when the military infrastructure was still quite rudimentary, what with motorized transport still not having fully replaced the bullock and elephant carts[2]. And the sappers often found themselves engaged at parts of the globe where any assignment proved almost exploratory in nature, filled with the kind of stuff that could be right out of one of today's rip-roaring adventure movies. Towards the end of the war, 14 Field Company of the Madras Sappers joined a Railway Battalion, and took part in the campaign in the German East Africa with a bridging train of the Bombay Sappers. An account of the operation there, narrated in the 'History of the Corps of Engineers', makes interesting reading:

The war there was fought under exotic conditions. Lions attacked men at work, rhinoceroses charged columns marching by night, giraffes broke telephone lines, elephants delayed motor convoys and once a crocodile swallowed the football during a friendly match. On another occasion a rhino charged through a squash court built from aeroplane packing cases. The anopheles mosquito, the tse-tse fly, the spirillum tick and the jigga flea were the local terrors.

---

2. Animal transport was an integral part of the Sapper warfare. The story of the 'Grey Mule', revered as the most travelled mule in the world, enjoys a legendary status in the lore of the Madras Sappers. The Grey Mule joined the Madras Sappers in 1891 and served for 31 years, during which it took part in expeditions to Chitral, Tirah, Malakand and Tibet among others. Having had served in Egypt and Palestine during World War I, the old mule was about to be sold off along with thousands of other mules to Egyptians in 1921, when the Expeditionary Force was due to return to India. But Colonel Basset, who was commanding 10 Field Company interceded and obtained a special permission from the Force Commander, Sir Philip Chetwode, to take it back home. On arrival at Bangalore it was pensioned off and given the complete freedom of the lines. Fed and cared for by whichever unit was stationed there, this honoured war veteran lived a quiet life for more than a decade, wandering at will but never leaving the neighbourhood of the lines. At the 150th Anniversary Reunion in 1930, the Grey Mule headed the march past of the pensioners, accompanied by the same Sapper Driver who, as a young man had led him up the Malakand Pass, 33 years earlier. The Grey Mule wore his campaign ribbons on his brow band. When the column passed the spectator stand, everyone stood up to pay tribute to the gentle animal. That was his last parade. The Grey Mule passed away in 1933, at the ripe age of forty-seven. Four ink stands made of the hooves of the grey mule are preserved, one each at the MEG Officers' Mess and the 'Monkey House' (the Headquarter building of the Centre, so named jovially for the numerous monkeys that occupied the premises at the time of its commissioning), and one each in 4 Engineer Regiment and the Officers' Mess, Royal School of Military Engineers, Chatham (UK). The Grey Mule lies buried in the unit lines of the Regimental Centre at Bangalore.

The Madras Sappers and Miners won the Battle Honours, FRANCE & FLANDERS, NORTHWEST FRONTIER, SUEZ CANAL, EGYPT, BAGHDAD & MESOPOTAMIA, TIGRIS, KUT-EL-AMARA, INDIA, GAZA, MEGIDDO, SHARON & PALASTINE, PERSIA, EAST AFRICA and AFGHANISTAN, during the War. They were also accorded the rare distinction of being Honour Titled 'Queen Victoria's Own[3] Madras Sappers and Miners' (removing the prefix of '2nd' and adding 'Madras' to their earlier title).

The last occasion on which the Madras troops were employed on an important operational role prior to World War II, was when the 64th Pioneers and the 83rd WLI were engaged in a brief action to put down the Moplah outbreaks in Malabar in 1921. (On a lesser scale, a pioneer battalion had also had to be briefly employed later in Burma during a rebellion there in 1931-32.) The outbreak, popularly known as the Malabar Rebellion, was actually a large scale revolt against the British authority, which broke out when the government tried to stem the tide of the historic Khilafat Movement from overwhelming Malabar. The Moplah (Muslim) rebels put up a ferocious fight with good amount of success, even establishing their authority in some areas. They were eventually put down rather ruthlessly by the army, employing Madras as well as Gorkha and British troops.

A tragic episode which came to be called the 'Wagon Tragedy' came to epitomize the callous attitude of the authorities. In the incident, described by some historians as the 'Black hole of Podanur', 61 of the 90 Moplahs who were being transported as prisoners, in a closed railway goods wagon from Tirur to Coimbatore on 20 November 1921, died of

3. The esprit de corps of the Madras Sappers was such that serving in the Corps was a family tradition, with as many as eight successive generations entering the rolls. They called themselves 'Quinsaps' – when they became Queen Victoria's Sappers – and it is believed that their sons were encouraged to marry only 'Quinsap' girls. A Sapper once asked to name his caste by an officer, promptly replied, "Sapper caste, sir". Their long association with the British soldiers and officers was often laced with a touch of humour too. A senior British officer, addressing the Sappers in high-flown Urdu, noticed their blank faces and asked their subedar to interpret the speech in a language they could follow. The subedar rendered the speech in fluent English.

suffocation by the time the train made it to Podanur. The revolt somehow lost its patriotic sheen later with the Moplahs indulging in atrocities towards Hindus, providing ample ammunition for the British to paint the whole thing as a communal flare up. It ended with the rebel leaders being captured and shot, and hundreds of others being imprisoned or deported. An estimated 10,000 lives were lost in the uprising; no mean an attempt against the British power. The army casualties were also considerable in numbers, the Madras troops alone losing some 165 men killed and wounded. All troops engaged were later to be given a medal and other gallantry awards.

As much as eight additional battalions of the Madras troops – two of the pioneers and six of the infantry – were raised during 1917 and 1918, but all of them were disbanded after the war in 1919. In the following year, despite the recognition earned during the war, the size of the Madras infantry was whittled down once again – nearly by half – and when the Indian Army was reorganized in 1922, Madras was allotted only one regiment each of the pioneers and the infantry. The pioneer regiment, comprising three battalions, was named the Madras Pioneers, and the infantry regiment, comprising five battalions, was named the 3rd Madras Regiment, the first time the regiment was designated so. It was numbered 3rd, because the 1st and 2nd Battalions had by then been converted to Punjab units.

The bias against the Madras soldier, nurtured by those in the higher echelons of the army for more than half a century, found its expression one last time when the axe came down again on grounds of economy, and by 1928 the whole of the 3rd Madras Regiment was disbanded[4]. Closely followed by this, the pioneer battalions were also mustered out in 1933 on the formation of a single Corps of Pioneers in the Indian

---

4. No monument tells the story as sadly as does a tablet in the historic St. Mary's Church within Fort St. George at Chennai, 'Erected by the Officers, past and present', of the Madras Regiment, towards 1930s, 'on the final disbandment of the 1st Battalion, the 3rd Madras Regiment, the last remaining Battalion of the Madras Infantry'. One of the last pieces to find a place inside the church, it is a reminder of the darkest phase in the history of the Madras Regiment, which was reactivated later during the Second World War, and finds her rightful place among other infantry regiments of the Indian Army today.

Army. Thus the only remaining descendants of the old Madras Infantry in the Indian Army at the outbreak of World War II in 1939 were four territorial battalions – the 11th, 12th, 13th and the 14th – suitable only for internal security duties, and one university training corps formed in 1921-22; not counting yet another territorial battalion, the 15th, that was to be formed later in 1939.

5

SECOND WORLD WAR

The Burmese Campaign

As the curtain raiser of World War II was enacted in Europe in1939, Britain once again turned for fighting men to her traditional recruiting bases, of which the Indian Subcontinent was the largest and the most favoured. Men from all over India promptly flocked to the British colours, to put on field, before the war was over, the largest voluntary army the world had ever known. The Southern Indian troops, infantry as well as the rest of the arms and services, were to form nearly one third of that army. Like a phoenix, the re-raised Madras Infantry was to blaze its way up and scale the heights of glory during the war. In 1941, the 3rd Madras Regiment was reconstituted, and the 11th, 12th, 13th and 15th territorial battalions, converted to regular ones, became its first four battalions, with another three, the 5/3rd, 6/3rd and 7/3rd, being newly raised. A Recruits Training Centre – forerunner of the Madras Regimental Centre – was also formed at Madukkarai near Coimbatore during the following year.

The 4th Battalion was in action by 1943 in Burma, the first theatre where Madras infantrymen were operationally committed during World War II. Following the British withdrawal from Burma in 1942, an Allied defence line was built up along the forest clad hills and valleys of the Indo-Burma Border. Joining the 20th Division in October 1943 at Imphal, the battalion moved forward to Moreh in the Kabaw valley, the notorious 'Valley of Death'. They took up position at this border post, through which the only motorable road to the Imphal plain passed, patrolling the enemy positions along the Chindwin River. The post fell right in the way of the Japanese offensive unleashed in March 1944. As the 20th Division fell back to Imphal from Tamu before the enemy's overwhelming strength, the battalion fought off heavy enemy attacks repeatedly.

Two encounters stood out for their ferocity; one at the Shark Piquet where a platoon inflicted nearly 100 casualties on the attacking Japanese, and another at Sita Ridge where Captain RS Noronha held out with his company for 16 days. The latter action won the officer a Military Cross, four of his men Military Medals and many others certificates of gallantry. The battalion was eventually withdrawn to Palel in Ukhrul sector to defend an airfield, and was stranded at the Imphal plain with the rest of the 20th Division as it was cut off by a Japanese outflanking drive. In September 1944 the battalion joined the 268th Infantry Brigade in its offensive towards Sittang on the Chindwin. They made it to Sittang by a four-day march in severe monsoon, often plodding through knee-deep mud, pushing the advantage of the enemy's demoralized state from heavy losses and exhaustion. Despite the river being flooded the battalion crossed over, making itself the first Indian battalion across the Chindwin in the great offensive that was to end in Rangoon.

As the advance continued, the battalion covered 200 miles during December 1944 and January 1945, clearing pockets of enemy all the way to arrive at Shwebo in early February 1945. Moving further to Thetseingyi, a village on the west bank of Irrawaddy, they launched an attack on an enemy stronghold on an island formed at a fork of the river. The attack, a feint to ease the pressure on the bridgehead of the 19th Division to the north, proved successful but the battalion had to withdraw later against heavy opposition. Captain Noronha – by now promoted a Major – won a bar to his Military Cross in this battle, and Jemadar Thomas won yet another Military Cross for the battalion.

Shortly the Japanese delivered a night attack on the battalion as it approached their defences at Pegado, six miles west of the river Sagaing, which was repulsed. Three days later the battalion staged a full scale attack with artillery and tank support, forcing the enemy to abandon the position, their last line of defence north of the river. Moving to Sagaing, the battalion went on to capture the Ava Bridge. As the southward advance resumed against enemy resistance and they arrived at Myingyan in April, the 1st Battalion, which had joined the campaign in February 1945, made contact. The latter was temporarily brought under the 268th Brigade and dispatched on an outflanking mission round Mount Popa, an extinct volcano between the Irrawaddy and the town of Meiktila fortified by the Japanese. They succeeded in surprising the enemy from behind their lines on the 13th, but were pinned down under artillery fire for five days.

Meanwhile the 5th Brigade, which was already facing the position, launched an attack with the 268th for company, and the Japanese, threatened from the rear as they were, abandoned the position without a fight. The 268th Brigade took up the pursuit, chasing the enemy in flight and mopping up all the way up to Kama, the last possible crossing place for the Japanese who were retreating down the west bank of the Irrawaddy. The 4th Battalion suffered some casualties in the fighting around the crossing, and was involved in the patrol clashes that followed as several thousand Japanese dispersed into the jungles beyond. These were the last actions of the battalion in World War II, and it returned to India on 31 July 1945.

The 1st Battalion continued to be in the operational area with the 5th Division, preparing for Operation Zipper, the amphibious assault on the Malayan peninsula, which did not take place because of the Japanese surrendering in August 1945. They were among the first troops to land on the Singapore Island when it capitulated, and was present at the ceremony of the formal Japanese surrender on 12 September. Subsequently for the next six months or so the battalion was engaged in suppression of the rebellion in Indonesia, involving severe clashes at times, especially at the town of Sourabaya where they assault landed from British Marine craft. They suffered 72 casualties of which 20 were dead, mostly from sniping and mines during intense built-up area fighting. Major CPA Menon (later Lieutenant Colonel) won a Military Cross. Another gallantry award was won by Lance Naik Perumal. This fiery NCO, on being slashed across the face with a sword, pursued and killed three of his assailants before bothering about any medical attention. The battalion returned to a heroes' welcome at Madras in May 1946, where they were felicitated by the Governor of Madras, Sir Archibald Nye and Lieutenant General Lockhart, GOC-in-C Southern Command.

The 3rd Madras Regiment won the Battle Honours, MOUNT POPA, TAMU ROAD, UKHRUL, AVA and KAMA, and the Theatre Honour, BURMA 1942-45, during World War II.

As early as August 1939 15 Field Company of the Madras Sappers had been dispatched to Malaya. 46 Army Troops Company and 6 Bridging Section joined them during the next two years, and together they formed the 11th Division Engineers by the time the Japanese invasion came in December 1941. As the division withdrew, they were engaged in demolishing bridges and destroying facilities in the face of the enemy. Early next year when the Japanese unleashed their Burma offensive, 58 and 60 Field Companies and 50 Field Park Company were part of the 17th Indian Division which took the brunt of the onslaught, having taken the field to reinforce the 1st Burma Division.

In the fighting withdrawal of over 1000 miles that ensued, the Sappers had the same difficult task of denying facilities to the enemy, often getting encircled in the process and having to fight their way out. They operated many ferries, and civilians having run away, had to maintain the essential services like the power and railways. 50 Field Park lost heavily when their harbour was attacked in May. It was also an ordeal which stretched the troops to the limits of their endurance.

Such overwhelming odds however couldn't break the Sapper spirit. 60 Field Company maintained its marching discipline so well during the retreat that General William Slim was to comment that it was the best he had seen.

The division fell back across the Assam border to Imphal, and the Japanese themselves, with their supply lines overextended, halted at the Chindwin River. During the next two years of standoff when the British attempted the Arakan offensives and Chindit – behind the enemy lines – Operations, many new raisings of the Sappers poured in with the new formations. They had the arduous task of opening proper lines of communications in a hostile terrain by improving – and often building new – roads, bridges and airfields. Consequently many units were specialized in their tasks. There were the road roller sections, bridging platoons, quarrying companies and airfield construction units, all raised to cope with the mammoth engineering challenge. And overcoming the rigours of climate compounded by malaria and the lack of labour and equipment, the Madras Sappers left their mark, making their singular contribution to the Allied victory in the east.

Early 1945 as the Allied offensive gained momentum and Slim's XIV Army crossed the Irrawaddy, 422 and 309 Field Companies were with the 20th Division, one of the leading formations. 58 and 60 Field Companies, advancing with other divisions, found themselves restoring the facilities they themselves had destroyed during the retreat. 36 Field Squadron of the Sappers rode with the 255th Tank Brigade which spearheaded the advance of the 17th Division to Meiktila. Meiktila fell after a four-day battle in March. 58 Field Company, advancing with the 36th British Division, put up a spirited defence at the bridgehead across the river Shevli against Japanese counter attacks, an action for which Lieutenant MR Rajwade was awarded the Military Cross. 60 Field which had suffered the humiliation of the retreat with the 17th Division, now surged forward with the same division, leading the IV Corps advance to Rangoon. They were barely beaten by the 26th Division which took the city by an air and sea assault. As the XII Army pursued the Japanese withdrawing to Thailand in August, the war ended with the dropping of the atomic bomb over Hiroshima and Nagasaki.

The Madras Sappers won the Battle Honours, BISHENPUR, MEIKTILA and TAMU ROAD, and the Theatre Honours, MALAYA 1941-42, and BURMA 1942-45, for the campaign.

6

SECOND WORLD WAR

The North African and Italian Campaigns

Few military outfits anywhere in the world were deployed on such versatile missions and saw action on so many fronts, as did the Madras Sappers and Miners during World War II. And true to their glorious reputation, they made their contribution count memorably wherever they were engaged. The Madras Sappers were represented in the North African campaign from the beginning itself by 11 Field Park and 12 Field Companies with the 4th Indian Division, and 44 Field Park, 16 Workshop and Park, and 101 Railway Construction Companies with the 5th Indian Division, both the divisions forming part of General Wavell's VIII Army. The 4th Division took part in the brilliant counter-thrust which destroyed eight Italian divisions in Egypt in December 1940.

Both the divisions then joined the allied attack on the Italians in Eritrea and Abyssinia. They defeated the Italians at Agordat and pursued them to Karen. The breakthrough at Karen by the Indian divisions came after severe fighting, and led to the fall of Addis Ababa and the surrender of Italians a month later. Company Havildar Major Sampangi of 12 Field Company was awarded the Indian Order of Merit for the gallantry displayed in the extensive mine clearing operations the company undertook. The 4th Division was recalled to the western desert in March 1941 after Karen, and the 5th Division followed after the Italian surrender.

The Germans, who had entered the fray by now, were on the offensive, and in June 1941 the 4th Division was engaged in Operation Battleaxe, the abortive attack on Rommel's position on the Sollum and Halfaya Passes. Sir Claude Auchinleck, who replaced Wavell, launched Operation Crusader in November, and drove Rommel back to his starting point at El Agheila, but was pushed back to the Gazala-Bir-Hacheim line in the German counterattack. The 4th Division, replaced by the 5th, withdrew to Egypt to refit, but was hastily brought into line again, as Rommel outflanked Bir-Hacheim in May 1942 and captured Tobruk. He pursued the Allies back to El Alamein where he was halted.

Montgomery replaced Auchinleck, and the 5th Division having left for the Far East, the 4th Division fought on, joining the 12-day battle of El Alamein which commenced on 23 October, to end in Allied victory. An extract from the war diary of 12 Field Company, quoted in the 'History of the Corps of Engineers', amply describes the vital role the Sappers played at El Alamein:

23 October, 1942, 1600 hours 12 Field Company moves to battle positions north of 4 Divisional Headquarters 2130 hours. A compressor of 11 Field Park Company is going full blast on the front wire. Its object is to preserve the normal atmosphere up to the last possible moment and to drown the noise of the carriers. Counter-battery fire begins. The compressor is as loud as ever. 2155 hours Company of 1/2 Gurkha Rifles passes through the wire in brilliant moonlight. The Sappers follow. The compressor reaches a crescendo of noise on the hardest rock it can find. 2200 hours 600 Guns open fire from Ruweisat to the sea. The compressor packs up, its task accomplished.

Rommel withdrew out of Libya into Tunisia, and in the pursuit, the 4th Division's expertise in mountain warfare proved immensely valuable. In April 1943, the I British Army, fighting its way from Algeria, joined up with the VIII, and together they launched the final attack on Tunis. Early in May the Axis forces in North Africa surrendered.

The units of the Madras Sappers with the 4th and 5th Divisions contributed their might throughout the campaign, mainly clearing mines, destroying obstacles and restoring the roads and water supply. How tough would have been the Sappers' job in the pursuit to Tunisia is abundantly clear from what Rommel himself had to say about the tactics he employed: "Throughout our retreat we called on all our resources of imagination to provide the enemy with ever more novel booby traps and thus to induce the maximum possible caution to his advance guard. Our Engineer Commander General Buclowius, one of the best engineers in the German Army, did a splendid job."

After Africa the 4th Division joined the Italian campaign (having been moved in between for a while to the Middle East to protect oil supplies), landing at Taranto in December 1943. They were moved to the Sangro sector and placed under the 5th US Army operating on the west coast. Both the companies, 11 Field Park and 12 Field, joined action at the capture of the mountain monastery of Cassino, the focal point of the German Gustav Line 100 miles south of Rome, and were then engaged in mine clearance, and cutting a jeep track on the hill face under fire. Cassino was to witness the ultimate in a Sapper's – or any soldier's – valour when Subedar K Subramaniam of 11 Field Park Company made the supreme sacrifice, by throwing himself down on a mine which was about to explode, in a desperate bid to save the lives of his comrades. The gallant VCO[1] was awarded George Cross (posthumous), making him the first Indian recipient of this award. Havildar Bhushan Rao of the same company won a Military Medal. Later the two companies advanced along the Adriatic Coast close on the heels of the retreating Germans, bridging streams, making roads and clearing mines. They constructed the 'Jacob's ladder', the steepest jeep track ever, climbing 1150 feet at a gradient of 1 in 10.

---

1. Viceroy's Commissioned Officer, re-designated Junior Commissioned Officer – JCO – after Indian Independence; these are officers of the rank of Naib Subedar to Subedar Major, commissioned from the ranks and subordinate to the Second Lieutenant, the lowest ranking Commissioned Officer.

10, 14 and 61 Field Companies, which were part of the 10th Division, joined the campaign in March 1944, and worked on improving the communications for the VIII Army's assault on the Gothic Line, under testing conditions of terrain and weather. The Sappers of the 10th Division were constantly busy with the construction of bridges and operation of ferries and rafts. 10 Field Company developed a submersible suspension bridge called the 'Houdini Bridge', which could be lowered into water by loosening cables, and could be made completely invisible by camouflaging the approaches. As the Allied offensive ground to a halt at the Gothic Line, the troops spent a chilly winter in trenches facing the German positions. In April 1945 the Gothic Line collapsed and the VIII Army broke into the Po Valley; and early in May the Germans in Italy surrendered.

The Sappers of the 10th Division – including 52 Army Troops Company which was on construction work throughout its tenure in Italy – continued to be engaged in reconstruction until November, when they embarked for India. Meanwhile 11 and 12 Field Companies moved to Greece, and were occupied with the suppression of the civil war in that country before returning home in February 1946.

The Madras Sappers won the Battle Honours, MERSA MATRUH, NGAKYE DAUK PASS, and CASSINO, and the Theatre Honours, ABYSSINIA 1940-41, NORTH AFRICA 1940-43, IRAQ 1941, SYRIA 1941, and ITALY 1943-45, during these campaigns.

Book III
INDIA AT WAR

1

FREE INDIA'S PROUD SOLDIERS

Partition riots and the war in Kashmir

Indian independence, August 1947: Like the rest of the nation, for the Indian Army too, the days that followed the great event were to prove traumatic. While on one side the army went through the agony of being split into two, as the Indian and Pakistani ones, on the other it was charged with the unenviable assignment of maintaining peace amidst the holocaust of the partition riots. The soldiers from the south, whose forefathers had more than 200 years earlier – as mercenaries and unwittingly though – rallied under the British colours, to fight and win the earliest battles that would put India on the inexorable path to unification as one country for the first time ever in history, were, appropriately enough, to play the crucial role of being the guardians of peace at the national capital of a free India, which was being torn asunder by the murderous riots. And these men, professionals[1] to the boot they were, rose up to the challenge to do a magnificent job, the nation would be hard put to forget.

---

1 Professionalism and discipline have always been the biggest assets of the Madras soldier. It wouldn't be out of context to quote what Colonel Reid, that great South Indian enthusiast, had to say about what made a Madras soldier click: 'They were not massive impressive warriors. They never appeared as great subjects for the author or the artist. They never advertised themselves. They were just plain Madrassis, Naidus, Mudaliars, Naickers, Pillays, Muslims and Christians. Quiet, hard working, intelligent, efficient, disciplined, eating the same food, with no animosity towards each other, they were the men of South India, grand stuff.'

As the riots erupted, the 2nd and 4th Battalions of the 3rd Madras Regiment were chosen[2] to maintain peace at Delhi. They did it unbiased without fear or favour, keeping with the highest traditions of military discipline. The crucial role played by the Madras soldiers in the riot-torn national capital in those difficult days found its echo internationally, when the New York Herald Tribune paid a handsome tribute by writing that, "Whether popular or not, the Madras Regiment, fully backed by the Government of India, seems today to maintain peace in the area of Old Delhi, which, three weeks ago, was littered with corpses." Within India, Prime Minister Nehru himself was prompted to state that, "But for the Madras Regiment, India would have lost Delhi." The regiment received great public acclamation in the end, when the 4th Battalion led the march-past of the troops in the first ever ceremonial parade held at the free India's capital on 22 March 1948.

Even as the Madras Regiment fought to keep the capital in one piece, the Madras Sappers were out in Punjab, providing succour to the multitude of refugees moving both ways across the border. Interestingly, 36 Para Field Squadron, forming part of the 2 Airborne Divisional Engineers, helped in Pakistan's Independence Day festivities at Karachi. On the same day, August 14, 14 Field Company rushed to the rescue of some 5000 people stranded, when their Jammu-bound train from Lahore derailed en route, and helped accommodate the survivors in a camp. As Sialkot went up in flames with the fury of the riots, 14 and 15 Field Companies – commanded by Major WH Walker and Major RN Kumar respectively – were the two main units to provide security to the thousands of people seeking refuge at the Sialkot Cantonment. When the local police proved unworthy, Major Kumar simply took charge of the law and order.

The Punjab Boundary Force, entrusted with the task of maintaining law and order in Punjab, was finding itself too inadequate for the job.

---

2. There seems to have been a preference for troops like Madrassis and Gorkhas, who hailed from places far from the riot torn areas, for cardinal tasks, in view of the sensitivity of the situation.

Denied military protection, the Sikhs of Narowal and Shakargarh burned down their villages and marched to India; 40,000-odd people plodding along with their cattle and belongings in a huge column. Heading in the opposite direction was an equally big column of Muslims bound for Pakistan. A clash which was inevitable was averted sheerly due to the vigilance of 14 Field Company escorting the Sikhs. In the subsequent days as columns of uprooted people trudged along the monsoon ravaged roads, causing massive congestions, the Company kept working tirelessly to alleviate the misery of the people. There were other units of the Madras Sappers too, 9, 10 and 13 Field Companies and 36 Para Field Company, contributing their might to guard the refugee columns.

The saga of the railway sappers was equally heroic during the carnage. 101 Railway Construction Company, along with a Railway Operating Company, braved the odds of terror and sabotage to run a number of shuttle trains between India and Pakistan. The scale of the task involved in rail movement was unprecedented. Nearly ten million people – 30 lakhs Hindus and Sikhs from West to East Punjab, and over 50 lakh Muslims the other way – had to be shifted in three months' time, to meet the deadline for the completion of history's most unnatural relocation of population. The contribution of the sapper companies to the effort was stupendous.

Barely two months after independence, even as the embers of partition riots were still smouldering, India found itself engaged in a war – the first one of the half a dozen it will fight before the century was over. The inglorious 'Tribal Invasion' of Kashmir, the first of the many cynical ploys Pakistan would attempt in the Subcontinent and Asia in the next half a century, began in the early hours of 22 October, forcing the shifty Maharaja of the state to sign the Instrument of Accession with India; and the first contingent of Indian troops had air-landed in Srinagar by dawn on the 27th of the month. It was only a miniscule instalment – 329 men of the 1st Battalion, the Sikh Regiment – of over a lakh Indian soldiers who would fight in the snowy highlands of Kashmir, first to stem the tide of the invasion, and later after their tanks had fetched up, to rout the raiders and drive them back up the valley they had come from in disarray.

The Pakistan regulars joining the tribals' ranks disguised would do little to check the avalanche of Indian counter-offensive, until eventually an inept Indian political leadership reined it in with a ceasefire, permitting Pakistan to keep the parts of the state still in its possession and referring the matter to the United Nations. Thus of our own doing, Kashmir would end up a disputed territory (and a source of constant grief for the people of Kashmir and the whole of India to date), despite the Indian Army winning the first ever war after the independence hands down, giving a bloody nose to its troublesome neighbour.

The first unit of the Madras Regiment to join action in J&K was its 1st Battalion. Arriving at Pathankot early in November, it was deployed at Kathna on the Jammu border under 268 Brigade. In umpteen localized encounters with bands of raiders during the next few months, various patrols of the battalion killed at least 100 raiders. In one instance when they wiped out a group of 30 raiders, killing 27 and taking 3 prisoner, Prime Minister Nehru felt obliged to thank the unit personally. In another instance a single platoon fought off a night attack by 500 raiders. The attackers fled leaving behind 53 dead, while the platoon did not lose a single man.

The battalion was moved to Baramula under 161 Brigade in April 1948, to join the forces which recaptured Kanrauli that had been overrun by the enemy. In a sad episode on 26 April, the day before Kanrauli was recaptured, an entire reconnaissance patrol of the battalion under Lieutenant KT Philip, accompanied by the Commanding Officer of the Battalion, Lieutenant Colonel CPA Menon (who won his Military Cross during World War II), was wiped out in an ambush; bar one sepoy who survived to report. The unit joined the summer offensive in May, and after the capture of Tithwal when the advance was halted for the supplies to catch up, took up defensive positions with the rest of the formation.

They were to distinguish themselves by their gallant contribution to the defence of Tithwal in the days that followed. On 11 June, two platoons holding a feature, Ring Contour, repulsed three successive attacks by a 300-strong enemy force. Naik Raju of one of the platoons was awarded the Maha Vir Chakra for an outstandingly gallant effort during this action, when he kept manning a machinegun despite being wounded twice – the second time in his eye – until forcibly evacuated. The gritty encounter saw many more acts of conspicuous gallantry by the officers and men of the battalion, and a number of them were decorated; three of them, Captain K Venugopal, Havildar IK Gopala Kurup and Lance Naik T Ayyappan with Vir Chakras. Two more Vir Chakras were awarded to Company Havildar Major M Pushpanathan and Naik Abdul Rahiman Kunju, for exceptional acts of gallantry in engagements prior to the battle of Ring Contour; and another two were awarded to Subedar Mohammed Ibrahim and Jemadar Shaik Khader Sahib for similar acts during subsequent operations.

On 13 July the battalion suffered a reverse when Ring Contour was overrun by the enemy. The battalion withdrew across the river behind, blowing up the bridge. They held on to the home bank under enemy shelling until the ceasefire on 1 January 1949. The total casualties suffered by the battalion in the operations were 21 killed and 96 wounded. The gallantry awards won by the personnel of the unit during the operations were 1 Maha Vir Chakra, 7 Vir Chakras and 16 Mention in Dispatches. The history of the battalion is replete with the tales of its men who made a habit of heroism in the highlands of Kashmir in this war fought more than half a century ago; the images vivid and inspiring; of Company Havildar Major Pushpanathan leading a bayonet charge on a horde of sabre-wielding tribals; of Subedar Ibrahim, bleeding from his wounds, holding steadfast against the raiders; of Captain Venugopal holding out at Ring Contour with a handful of men against an enemy which outnumbered his force almost ten to one; and many more of the kind. Deservedly, the 1st Madras prides itself as the 'Fighting First'.

The next Madras battalion to see action in J&K, the 2nd, joined 77 Para Brigade at the Uri sector in May 1948, and relieved the piquets of the 4th Kumaon and the 2/3rd GR. During June, one of the companies captured an enemy post and held it against a major counterattack, but an attack on Haji Pir Pass along the road to Punch failed. In July, on being replaced by 2nd Dogra, they concentrated at Uri. Patrolling and clashes continued until the ceasefire, the battalion losing 21 killed and 51 wounded in J&K, earning 19 Mention in Dispatches.

Yet another battalion, the 4th, was to have a brief but eventful stint in the J&K operations. Arriving at Langar Camp at Jammu early in September 1948, they captured Pir Kalewa, a dominating feature near Rajauri, during night 25-26 October. On 10 November they took another feature called Camel's Hump vital to the enemy. Sepoy Sanal Kumaran Pillai, the signalman of the leading company, was awarded the Vir Chakra for exemplary courage in maintaining communications during the battle. The battalion continued to man the border posts against enemy infiltration for a year after the ceasefire before being relieved. The total casualties of the battalion in J&K amounted to 9 killed and 21 wounded. Besides one Vir Chakra they also won 12 Mention in Dispatches.

The Madras battalions which took part in the J&K operations won the Battle Honours, TITHWAL and PUNCH, and the Theatre Honour, JAMMU & KASHMIR 1947-48.

The Madras Sappers joined the action in Jammu as soon as the operation started in October-November 1947. 32 and 14 Field Companies were the first Sapper units to get to the theatre. The tribal invasion having been stopped in its tracks, when 161 Brigade launched its counter-offensive in early November, 32 Assault Field Company, commanded by Major RN Kumar, advanced with two platoons in support of the brigade. As the enemy retreated in disarray down the Baramula-Domel Road, the Company swung into action, clearing the road and making diversions where needed. By 13 November the brigade had taken Uri and was poised for a thrust to Domel, when much to the dismay of its commander, Brigadier LP Sen, it was diverted to the Punch axis; a costly error that was to result in a permanent enemy sanctuary within Indian territory, which could disrupt Uri's line of communications with both Baramula and Punch.

32 Company, which should have been clearing the road to Domel for the advancing forces, found itself working on the defensive works at Uri. The enemy counter-attacked on 22 November, but was repulsed. Braving harassing fire and casualties, the Company then went on to replace the improvised plank crossing across the river Jhelum, with a 160-foot wooden trestle bridge to take care of the increasing traffic.

Meanwhile a number of isolated State Forces garrisons, far-flung and feeble but heroically held, were being besieged by the raiders. Those of them which fell were being looted and burnt. Rajauri which fell on 12 November had 30,000 of its inhabitants slaughtered and its women subjected to barbaric brutality. The rescue of the remaining garrisons, Punch, Naushera, Jhangar, Kotli and Mirpur became desperately urgent; and Jhangar, a track junction of crucial significance, became the immediate objective. 50 Para Brigade set out on the mission on 12 November, with a platoon of 32 Field Company in support. But the bridge at Beri Pattan had collapsed and they were stranded at Akhnur, 19 miles out of Jammu, even after 24 hours.

In the absence of bridging stores, the platoon of 32 Company began to build a boulder fort 360 feet in length. It was tough going, but by 17 November they had built more than half the causeway, when they received the much needed boost with the arrival of 14 Field Company rushed from Pathankot. 14 Field got down to business straight away making the approaches manually, and the ford was complete before nightfall. The vehicles of the leading battalion were being winched across by 1730 hours accompanied by a platoon of 14 Field Company. The advance was on again after a harrowing delay of almost five days.

14 Field Company soon had its hands full clearing the road to Jhangar, to make sure that the armoured cars and guns kept up with the leading infantry, the enemy having had done everything they could to hamper the brigade's advance, be it felling the trees or burning down

the bridges and culverts. As the brigade went on to clear Naushera, Jhangar – which both fell in the next two days – and Kotli before the end of the month, the platoon of 14 Field advancing with it cleared 47 roadblocks in ten days. The whole Company then took up the repair and maintenance of the road they had traversed, and also began operating a ferry at Beri Pattan. No operation could be sustained without proper line of communication.

While 50 Para Brigade made its way to Kotli, 161 Brigade from Uri launched itself to the north to relieve Punch. The ill-maintained, one-way Uri-Punch Road, with its numerous hair-pin bends, winding up to the 8000-foot Haji Pir Pass in its first 14 miles and then descending to Punch in the next 21 miles, was a tough proposition, even without the havoc the raiders had created by burning down the bridges. And all the Sapper support that the brigade could muster was a detachment of the over-worked 32 Field Company. Nevertheless the detachment slogged on, improvising ways to keep the advance going, often resorting to such tedious expedients like filling in the gap of a burned-down bridge with boulders. Reinforced by some more men from the Company later, this handful of Sappers accomplished their awesome task to see the brigade enter Punch on 21 November.

Towards end November, Punch, which was thinly held and reeling under a huge influx of refugees, was under constant enemy threat. To meet the urgent need of sizeable engineering support, all that the Punch Brigade – as the forces there were designated – had was a one-man Sapper force in the person of Jemadar R Kanickasami. Undeterred, the JCO went on to lengthen and improve the crude airstrip; which the refugee labour had constructed by flattening out the State Forces barracks. And later during December, as the enemy stepped up their attempts to interfere with the landings by pushing in their piquets, in a brilliant display of the Sapper spirit, he mined and booby-trapped the approaches as well parts of the no man's land on his own. His exceptional courage and initiative was to be recognized by being awarded the Vir Chakra, and a promotion as Second Lieutenant.

As the newly formed Jammu & Kashmir Division – the JAK Div as it was commonly referred – under Major General Atma Singh launched its freshly planned 3-pronged offensive during December (westward beyond Uri to the north, on the Naushera-Kotli-Punch axis in the middle, and on the Akhnur-Munawar-Bhimber axis to the south), more brigades – and Sapper units – began moving in. The month was to become a memorable one for 14 Field Company for the exceptional gallantry they displayed individually and collectively. On 18 December a detachment of the unit got caught up in an ambush with a convoy on the road to Jammu. Ram Chander, the civilian dhobi of the unit, made history of sorts on the occasion when he picked up a rifle and fought it out, accounting for some half a dozen of the enemy, in a daring attempt to save the life of an officer who was wounded. The officer survived, and Ram Chander was decorated with Maha Vir Chakra.

Two days later a convoy carrying ammunition and rations for the beleaguered troops at Jhangar, led by the OC of the Company, Major HL Khastgir, was waylaid. The officer was cut down by machine gun fire in a valiant bid to charge the ambush. The next morning the Punjab Battalion holding Jhangar was overwhelmed despite a gallant stand. A detachment of 14 Field Company with them fought as infantry, to the last man and last round. There were no survivors among them. This was one of the first cases of large-scale sapper casualties in the operations. After two days the enemy launched a similar attack on Naushera where 14 Field Company was located, the first shells landing right in the Company area. But Naushera held, after a tough ordeal though, with only one Sapper seriously wounded.

Early in January the enemy renewed the attacks on the town, concentrating as much forces as he could. Naushera, the gateway to Rajauri and to the Kashmir Valley, had become his prime objective. In the weeks that followed, as Brigadier Mohammed Usman's 50 Para Brigade gallantly held out fighting some of the fiercest battles of the campaign, 14 Field Company was in the thick of action with them. By the end of the month the Company found itself engaged in anti-tank mine clearing operations, to help the 7th Light Cavalry in its mission to block enemy reinforcements finding its way to Naushera.

As the fighting continued into 1948 more and more Sapper units began to be inducted, to find themselves constantly engaged in improving the road communications and airstrips. Captain AK Khanna's 36 Para Field Company, arriving in May found itself with a rather strange mission of breaching and relaying own minefields, the earlier ones having been laid in a hurry with no proper records. A task force headed by Major NB Grant's 664 Plant Company braved the winter rains and snow, with nothing more than the angola shirts to protect the men from the elements, while some 127 machines of theirs – bulldozers, graders, scrapers and excavators – churned out 62 miles of the Pathankot-Jammu Road on a new alignment, out of reach of the enemy guns.

There was tragedy too to mar the success story of the Madras Sappers. In April 1948, a ferry at Akhnur, which was being operated by 39 Assault Field Park Company along with a platoon of 13 Field, was caught in the swirling current of the Chenab while carrying a Sherman Tank across, and went down killing the entire crew. Three Sappers, one officer and two JCOs too were swallowed by the river. One more officer who was involved was washed ashore miraculously and survived.

Once the snow started clearing in April and the operation picked up momentum in the Valley, various units of the Madras Sappers found themselves supporting the advance of one or other brigade. A detachment of 32 Field Company, mounted on carriers, formed part of the vanguard of advance to Domel, centred on a squadron of the 7th Light Cavalry and a battalion of the Sikhs. The newly arrived 433 Field Company supported 163 Brigade's advance to Tithwal. 13 Field Company supported 77 Para Brigade in its advance beyond Uri.

At this stage of the fighting while the Indian Army was steadily getting on top of the situation in Jammu, the opposite was happening to the north beyond Srinagar. Having taken possession of Gilgit by subterfuge at the time of independence, Pakistan had an overbearing advantage in the sector because of the distance involved – more than 300 miles – and inaccessibility of the area for Indian reinforcements to fetch up. The tehsil headquarters of Skardu between Gilgit and Ladakh became the initial focal point. Z Brigade formed in February 1948, under Brigadier Lakhinder Singh, was holding it against odds. They were desperately trying to form a defensive link between the far-flung Indian outposts in the sector, which extended over a mammoth front from Handwara to Kargil, Leh and Skardu. The formation, which later became 163 Brigade, was supported in its ordeal by two platoons of 32 Field Company, both working on the road links at different areas.

The enemy had succeeded in occupying Gurais, a vital track junction, during the winter months. Skardu was lost in April, after a last-ditch attempt at reinforcement by two battalions of the Kashmir Infantry ended in disaster. Other losses soon followed. Kargil was lost on 10 May and Dras on 6 June. By the end of June own troops had been pushed back to the Zojila Pass, and Srinagar itself was being threatened. The Sri Division which was to take care of the northern sector, since taken over by Major General K.S. Thimayya, ultimately swung into action.

In April a Bihar battalion had managed to oust the raiders from Tragbal, and they had withdrawn to the Razdhainangan Pass. Now the 1st Grenadiers, replacing the Biharis in a fresh counter-thrust, went for the Pass. A platoon of 13 Field Company accompanying them got the campaign rolling by making a jeep track from Sonarwain to Tragbal, one which many considered the steepest the Indian Army Engineers had built so far. The first jeep drove up to Tragbal by 21 May and the Grenadiers, well stocked for the offensive, took the Pass on the 27th without much ado.

A road to the 12,000-foot Razdhainangan Pass was no platoon job, and a month passed by the time the rest of 13 Field Company under Captain Gurney that was in Uri could fetch up. Two platoons straight away took up the road work, while a third joined the Grenadiers in a mission to take Gurais. Bad weather intervened to stall the move planned for 25 June; but joined by the 2/4th GR which staged a feint to Kanzalwan, Gurais was taken by the early hours of the 29th. Kanzalwan also fell to us in the fray, and an enemy attempt early in July to recapture it was beaten back. 13 Field completed the road from Tragbal to Razdhainangan Pass, then constructed a suspension bridge on Krishanganga, and linked it up with Kanzalwan by making a road on the left bank. They went on to make an airstrip at Gurais, and connect Kanzalwan to Bandipura by a jeep track, accomplishing all this in a record time of two months. The saga of 13 Field Company toiling through snow often as deep as 12 feet, with the men spending their nights out in the freezing cold with only a blanket each to keep themselves warm, had had few parallels all through the operation. The 'History of the Corps of Engineers' gives an eloquent commentary on the performance of this unit:

In later years when you talked to the men who worked with this unit they would recall the summer of 1948 with a glint in their eyes and a fleeting smile on their lips. They were a modest bunch of Sappers and they thought nothing of having carved a 12,000-foot high jeep track all the way into Gurais, through snows that never melt completely, through valleys that are as deep as anywhere in the Himalayas and over plateaux that are amongst the highest in the world – and all through hostile territory. All were South Indians who had never seen snow or never known such cold. Yet they did not mention the frost nor did they give any hint of the privations that they suffered. They only spoke in glowing terms of Capt Gurney Sahib who had led them in their exploits.

The Sappers were confronted by a major challenge in mid September with the inevitability of having to induct tanks for the offensive. A task force under Major MA Thangaraju comprising his own unit, 13 Field Company, less one platoon, 433 Field Company (also bereft of a platoon) under Captain Krishnaswamy, and a platoon of 682 Field Park Company (Bengal Sappers) under Major Inder Singh Manku, got down to the job, converting a five-mile jeep track between Baltal and the Zojila Pass into a tank-able road, climbing 12,000 feet, a height no tank had ever climbed before. Completed under the enemy's nose in a record one-month period, to beat the snowfall which would have closed the pass, the feat was described as 'a record in any operation' by General Thimayya.

No single Sapper task during the operations had come to assume such significance as this, since the success of Thimayya's bold tactics, to bring a speedy end to the war by taking tanks to such heights, solely depended on the completion of the road in time. Racing against the deadline, the Sappers gave such a magnificent account of themselves, that their accomplishment is still remembered as one of the best ever by the Indian Army Engineers. The 'Thambis' – meaning 'younger brothers' in Tamil, as the young South Indian soldiers are popularly referred to within the army – earned themselves a sobriquet, the 'Razor-blade brigade', as they drove themselves mercilessly round the clock, each man carrying a trademark razor blade tucked into the brim of his hat to cut the cardtex or safety fuses. As good as 25 tons of explosives were used per mile in blasting operations, where the normal requirement should have been of 3 or 4 tons. Jemadar Thangavelu of 13 Field Company was awarded the Vir Chakra for carrying out blasting work under fire. And the road, appropriately enough, was named after the soft spoken but highly competent commander of the task force, Major Thangaraju.

The Stuart Tanks of the 7th Light Cavalry, transported from the plains with their turrets removed to reduce the weight and reassembled for the operation (a spectacular overnight effort which the Corps of Electrical and Mechanical Engineers – EME – could be justly proud of), hit the road at 1030 hours on 1 November. A platoon of 433 Field Company rode alongside them to clear any anti-tank mines they might encounter. It was practically a walkover for the tank men; the enemy just took to the heels the moment the tanks opened up. It was a victory drive then onwards, of course, the Sappers having had to keep at it building the road and bridging the rivers for the tanks to push ahead. 13 and 433 Field Companies moved ahead with the advance to capture Dras and Kargil. With the winter fast approaching 13 Field Company was withdrawn by end November; and 433 Field Company, which could be withdrawn only by December, ended the campaign braving the blizzards at subzero temperature, many of their last casualties caused by frostbite and snow blindness.

Apart from their combat role during the operations, the Madras Sappers, along with their Bombay and the Bengal brethren, contributed their might to the development of the road network and airfields in J&K, a task in which a number of units were involved, and is one which continues to date.

The Madras Sappers were awarded the Battle Honour, ZOJILA and the Theatre Honour, JAMMU & KASHMIR 1947-48, for the J&K operations 1947-48.

No document could have highlighted the significance of the role the Madras soldier played in J&K in that critical period more aptly than a letter received by the Madras Government after the operations, written by none other than Chief Minister Sheikh Abdullah of J&K, paying tributes to the Madras infantrymen and the Sappers alike. It stated:

Nothing could better describe the oneness and unity of India than the fact that the South Indians should fight the North Indians' war of liberation. I have been anxious to convey my feelings to the people of the South. In the war in Kashmir, our brothers from the South have taken a leading part. They have fought tenaciously and valiantly; and although unused to the severities of a cold climate, they have held their posts on top of high snow-covered cliffs and mountains with a courage which has won them the admiration of the whole Kashmir people. Likewise, the perseverance and fortitude shown by Sappers and Miners – the majority of whom belong to the South – in keeping our long and difficult line of communication in good order, are both an epic and an exploit. The role of the 'unknown soldier' in the war in Kashmir has truly been of the Madrassi foot-soldier. The people of Kashmir will never forget the help they have received from their brothers of the South.

During September 1948, while the J&K operations were still going on, the Indian Army found itself engaged in what came to be known as the 'Police Action' – code named 'Operation Polo' by the army – by which the state of Hyderabad in the Deccan was integrated to the Indian Union, against the wishes of its Nizam who desperately wanted to hang on to his sovereignty. It was a whirlwind operation that barely lasted five days when the Nizam's miserable forces were swept aside with no great effort.

Although the Madras Regiment was engaged only for internal security duties after the operation, their mounted brethren did their bit in the actual action; so did the Madras Sappers. Forming part of the 1 Armoured Division which spearheaded the operation was the 16th Light Cavalry[3], a proud descendant of the old Madras Native Cavalry; while 9, 10 and 65 Field Companies and 11 Field Park Company of the Madras Sappers supported the advancing columns with bridging and mine clearing. 10 and 65 Companies fought on occasions in infantry role as well, the former losing two men in one of the fights. At one rare instance when the *Razakars*, the Nizam's militia, managed to hold up the infantry of the Mysore State forces at Hospet, couple of 'Ad hoc Companies', hastily formed of trainees and recruits from the Madras Engineer Group and Centre at Bangalore, helped overcome the opposition.

Following independence, 'The Madras Regiment' finally came to be christened so, dropping the numeral '3rd' that was being prefixed to its name for some curious reason even when there was only one regiment of its kind in existence. Moving the Regimental Centre from Madukkarai to Wellington, it began with four battalions, the 1st, 2nd, 4th and the 8th (many of the war time raisings having been disbanded by then); but soon another four were added from the State Forces[4], and a dozen more in the years to come.

---

3. The cavalry element of the old Madras Army suffered a temporary extinction (generally parallel to the setbacks the Madras Regiment went through), after the 1903 reorganizations when the troop composition of their regiments were changed. Consequently the 26th, 27th and the 28th Madras Light Cavalry, re-designated the 8th, 16th, and the 7th Light Cavalry respectively by 1922, had no South Indians in their ranks. In 1946, the troop composition of one regiment, the 16th Light Cavalry, was restored to make it a fully South Indian unit, the only cavalry regiment of its kind in the Indian Army, and ranked the senior most in the order of precedence.

In parallel runs the story of 'The Madras Engineers'. The Corps of Madras Pioneers, the forerunners of the Sappers and Miners, although raised in Madras, had sunk their roots in the area around Ulsoor lake outside Bangalore in the land allotted to the Madras Presidency by the Maharaja of Mysore as far back as 1865. The Madras Engineer Group, MEG[5], formed in 1933, is centred in the same location today. The group has since expanded to form 22 regular regiments and 10 smaller independent units under its colours, a 'regiment' of the engineers being the equivalent of a 'battalion' of the infantry, under a colonel's command.

The 1950s, the decade that followed the turbulence of independence and the happenings thereafter, was militarily a peaceful period for India – barring the Northeast insurgency that had begun to crop up – as the newborn republic set about the task of nation building. The lone bit of operational engagement for the Madras troops commenced in 1958, when the 16th Battalion was called up to man the border outposts in Assam against hostile incursions from East Pakistan. Effectively containing the incursions during a four-year tenure, their officers and men distinguished themselves on the assignment.

The 1960s was to be an altogether different story, with India facing quite a few military challenges. The opening bit was of course just a walkover, let alone any challenge, when an arrogant Portuguese regime stupidly holding on to their small pocket in Goa – probably out of such silly old notions that being Europeans they could still outsmart the 'Asiatics' – was unceremoniously kicked out in the matter of a single day in December 1961. Interestingly, for an operation that took place in

---

4. The final chapter of the book, 'Arms, Uniforms and the Legacy', tells the story of these units.

5. The Group assumed the name 'MEG' – Madras Engineer Group – only from 1950. It was first called 'Queen Victoria's Own – QVO – Madras Sappers and Miners Group' (1941); then changed the name thrice, QVO Madras Regimental Centre, RIE (Royal Indian Engineers) (1946), QVO Madras Group, RIE(1946), and QVO Madras Engineer Group (1948), before the current name was finalised.

Southern India, there were hardly any South Indian troops engaged at Goa. However the headquarters of 417 Engineer Brigade, the engineer formation for the operation, was raised at Belgaum by the Madras Engineer Group and Centre. Goa, for the whole Indian Army, just turned out to be a small field exercise, when compared to what was to follow during the decade.

KASHMIR WAR 1947 - 48

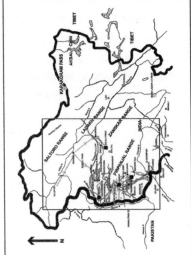

Legend

- ■ International Border
- ⇧ Pakistani Agression
- ⇧ Indian Counter-offensive
- ■ Major Battles
- ▪ Minor Battles
- ■ Passes
- ⊠ Passes
- ○ Other important locales

Not to Scale : only approximate locations depicted

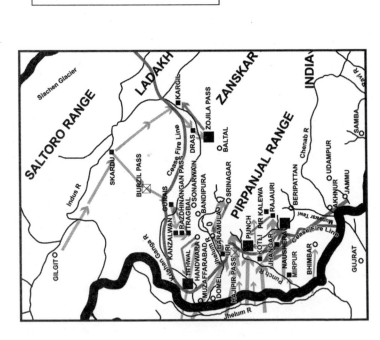

N

2

THE BORDER WAR WITH CHINA

A grand army humiliated

It was an uncalled for war forced on an unprepared army by a national leadership which couldn't have been more naive. Having provoked a powerful neighbour into open agression by its unrealistic foreign policy, the Government of India perpetrated the unpardonable sin of committing the troops for an operation for which they were least prepared and wholly ill equipped, blatantly ignoring the counsel[1] of its field commanders. The result was a catastrophe of unprecedented magnitude. The Indian Army, always exalted for its glorious victories in the field, was to be meted out a drubbing it would find hard to live down. Pummelled to withdraw from its positions on the border, it would end up ceding chunks of own territory to the enemy, as the Chinese unleashed a massive offensive in October 1962.

In the unholy debacle, the Madras troops bore its share of humiliation along with the rest of the great army. Two battalions of the Madras

---

1 The Chinese had always disputed the validity of the McMahon Line as the international boundary. A pragmatic approach would have been to resolve the matter through diplomatic channels, since the Indian Army didn't really have the wherewithal at that time to get into a contest with the Chinese while containing an inherently hostile Pakistan as well. However the Government of India, incensed by the aggressive posturing China adopted following the strained relations on the Tibetan issue, ordered the army to occupy posts to the north of the McMahon Line, on a one-sided interpretation that the water-shed beyond the line was inclusive in it. These posts, besides violating the line as depicted on the map, were tactically untenable – enough provocation, as well as tempting objectives, for the Chinese to attack. The commanders in the field did point out this folly, but the army's higher command proved too meek to prevail upon the political leadership.

Regiment, 1 and 2, were deployed in the North East Frontier Agency (NEFA), the theatre which was to witness a virtual rout of the Indian side. 1 Madras, commanded by Lieutenant Colonel K K Chandran, was one of the units which took the brunt of the onslaught. It had been rushed up from the plains of Assam where it was concentrated, to take up defences at Bomdi La at a height of 13,000 feet from the sea level, to stem the tide of invasion after the Chinese had overrun the Namka Chu Valley of the Kameng Frontier Division. Arriving at the location on 27 October, they joined 48 Infantry Brigade which formed part of 4 Infantry Division defending the heights. The battalion dug in with the rest of the brigade, and even as it was engaged in forward patrolling, the enemy was busy perfecting his approach road to Bomdi La.

The attack came on the morning of 18 November. D Company, commanded by Major Harbans Singh, which had moved to nearby Dirong Dzong to protect the Divisional Headquarters located there, was the first to come under attack. Confronted by a two-battalion force of the enemy, they held out tenaciously, men fighting from slit trenches with no artillery or mortars for support, while the Divisional Headquarters withdrew itself safely to Rupa in the rear. Outnumbered and outgunned, the company put up a desperate fight, making the enemy pay with heavy casualties; but past noon, with its position no more sustainable, it fell back in order to the battalion location at Bomdi La, where the entire brigade was reeling under intense shelling since the morning. At 1645 hours an enemy force of almost two divisions launched an attack on the two forward battalions of the brigade defences, 1 Sikh Light Infantry on the left and 1 Madras on the right. While the Sikh LI was withdrawn later that day, the Madrassis held on putting up a grim fight, until isolated and short of ammunition, they were forced to pull out by early hours of the following day.

They made it to Tenga Valley by 21 November, but found themselves cut off by the Chinese holding positions to their rear. As the battalion tried to extricate itself towards Charduar, it was ambushed. Major WNC Hensman, the Second-in-Command, leading the column, was killed along with seven of his men in the Intelligence Section, and 13 others were wounded. The CO with 3 other officers, 5 JCOs, 187 Other Ranks and 2 non-combatants were taken prisoner. Among the officer prisoners was Captain EN Iyengar, the Regimental Medical Officer of the battalion, who continued to attend to the casualties at great peril to his life. He was to be awarded the Vir Chakra on his release.

The rest of the battalion made it to Charduar in small groups in the days that followed, some of the groups having had to make a detour of more than 60 miles. The entire operation was a chaotic affair characterized by the disastrous breakdown of command and control at the formation levels, leaving individual units to fend for themselves. It saw men with no acclimatization fighting at high altitudes without snow clothing or footwear, bereft of even up to date maps, not to mention the vintage bolt action 0.303 rifles they carried against the modern automatics the enemy had; and it cost the units dearly. A severely wounded pride apart (for a unit that had fought so gallantly in J&K in 1947-48), 1 Madras had suffered some 300 casualties; 8 killed, 13 wounded, 37 missing believed dead, and 216 captured.

2 Madras, commanded by Lieutenant Colonel PT Allen, also under 4 Infantry Division, was deployed at Tuting. Although the enemy attacks on the outposts were beaten back by the battalion (losing a JCO in one of the attacks), in a typical goof up at the formation level, the Divisional HQ ordered the abandoning of Tuting on 19 November before any major attack materialized. The battalion pulled out in the early hours of the 20th, and after a torturous three-week-long march arrived at Along on 9 December. The war had ended for them even without the satisfaction of at least having fully engaged the enemy once.

15 and 65 Field Companies of the Madras Sappers, who had been engaged for engineering support at Bomdi La and Walong in NEFA, got caught up in the fiasco and had to share the miserable fate with the rest of the troops. However in the west along the Ladakh front, where the army generally succeeded in putting up a comparatively

better show, the Madras Sappers made an eminent bit of contribution with engineering support to the troops under fire. When the Chinese attacked the Sirijap Posts along the northern shores of Panggong Lake to the north of Chushul on 21 October, the Sappers of 9 Field Company fought alongside the Gorkhas who put up a last-ditch battle, and were taken prisoner when the posts were overrun. Meanwhile two entire detachments of 372 Field Company, one at Galwan and the other at Kongka, were wiped out.

In the hurried withdrawal across the lake that followed, 36 Field Company ferried the troops across at night on two storm boats. One of them sank hit by enemy fire. Naik Raghavan, a hundred yards ahead in the other boat, turned around without a moment's hesitation to rescue the survivors from the sunken boat. He managed to save three of the infantrymen, before a fast Chinese tug came at him with headlamps on. The NCO's death-defying courage was to earn him a Vir Chakra. The next day two Sappers of 9 Field were killed by enemy fire while laying mines in the area.

9 Field Company, commanded by Major SR Bagga, took up the hectic preparations for the defence of Chushul by 114 Infantry Brigade, while 372 Field Company helped prepare the airfield there. The ceasefire came into effect as the brigade had withdrawn to the defence sector west of the airfield, following the enemy bombardment of Chushul.

There were some more Madras troops – a couple of battalions of the Madras Regiment – which were also mobilized, but saw no action. 16 Madras was airlifted from Madras and concentrated near Gangtok, and 17 Madras was moved to Misamari foothills, but before either of them contacted the enemy the war ended with the Chinese declaring unilateral ceasefire on 21 November. And India let out a sigh of relief; it had been a close call – the gate to the plains of Assam, albeit briefly, had fallen open to a foreign invader. A sad and shameful commentary on a proud nation and its army, that for that moment in history, we found ourselves at the enemy's mercy.

SINO - INDIAN WAR 1962

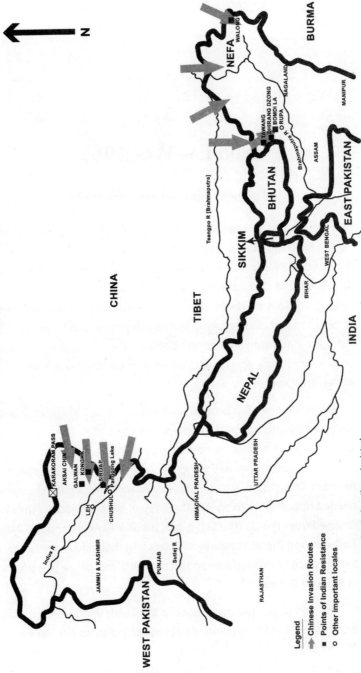

Legend
- Chinese Invasion Routes
- ■ Points of Indian Resistance
- ○ Other important locales

Not to Scale ; only approximate locations depicted

3

Indo-Pak War 1965

A glorious fight, but a stalemate alas

To begin with Pakistan had codenamed it 'Operation Gibraltar', after the Arab invasion of Spain which began with the capture of the Rock of Gibraltar. It was an ambitious plan conceived by the military dictatorship of that country under Field Marshal Ayub Khan, for the conquest of Kashmir. The Indian Army's dismal show against the Chinese in 1962 had emboldened Ayub to make the move; and he was also in a hurry. The expansion and modernization of the Indian Army was going on at a rapid pace, and he would find himself at a disadvantage if he waited anymore.

Essentially the plan propounded to have a 30,000-strong guerilla force to infiltrate through the porous borders of Kashmir, and incite an uprising in the state. But before that he had to go in for a ploy, to cause imbalance in India's troop deployment along its border with Pakistan. This would also provide his armed forces with the much-needed opportunity to try out the array of latest weaponry they had received from the US (the Sabre Jets, the Star Fighters and the Patton Tanks among them), concurrently assessing their adversary's capacity to fight back. The venue selected for this initial trial phase was the Rann of Kutch in Gujarat.

Pakistan began the game in early 1965 with small scale incursions into this vast and thinly manned segment of Indian border, forcing India to relocate its troops to bolster the defences there. However, despite some hot engagements, the affair did not come about to much, with the

British Prime Minister brokering a ceasefire to restrain the two members of the Commonwealth from fighting each other; and it ended up getting referred to the International Court of Justice for arbitration.

The second phase of the Pakistani plan got off the ground in August, with massive infiltrations into Kashmir. But Ayub Khan was in for a shock. In the first place the local population refused to play ball, and the planned insurrection just didn't materialize. Second, the Indian Army chose offence as a means of defence, and went after the infiltrators, striking at their routes and capturing a number of enemy posts along the ceasefire line of 1948, most significantly the stronghold of Haji Pir Pass. The Uri-Punch Road was now open for the first time after 1948. India had won the first round.

The Pakistan High Command reacted with its contingency plan, that of an open invasion. Operation Gibraltar was off; in its place they now launched Operation Grand Slam – its objective: cut off all of J&K north of Jammu by striking at the Chamb-Akhnur front, and take Jammu itself. They unleashed the blitzkrieg with a massive tank and infantry attack in the wee hours of 1 September. By the 5th, Jaurian had fallen and Akhnur was being threatened.

The Pakistanis were in for the second surprise now. A diminutive looking but highly determined Indian Prime Minister stuck to the word of warning he had issued to Ayub Khan that India would retaliate at the time and place of its choosing, should J&K be attacked. The Indian Army opened two new fronts simultaneously, a southern one on the Lahore Sector and a northern one on the Sialkot Sector. The offensive on the southern front was under way by early morning on 6 September; three infantry divisions of 11 Corps pushing forward on three different axes, the GT Road axis from Amritsar, the Khalra-Barki axis and the Khemkharan-Kasur axis. Capturing enemy territory in their drive, they were to converge on Ichhogil Canal – the 47-mile long obstacle which protected Pakistan—to threaten Lahore. The northern thrust by 1 Corps which got off the ground thirty-six hours later, with 1 Armoured Division

– India's only armoured division at that time – spearheading the advance of its three infantry divisions, would threaten Sialkot.

The Indian offensive didn't exactly turn out to be a roaring success as it was expected to be; but we did snatch a victory of sorts, grabbing sizeable chunks of enemy territory by the time the war ended with the ceasefire coming into effect on 23 September. The Pakistanis who had started it all, ended up looking downright silly. They were hit for a six in their much-planned infiltration game under Operation Gibraltar. In Operation Grand Slam that followed too, they failed to exploit the initial advantage gained with their successful foray into the Chamb area. And if they didn't end up losing Lahore and Sialkot, it had more to do with the fumbling[1] of the situation by Indians rather than their own merit. And in armoured warfare – the war saw some of the fiercest tank battles after World War II – the Indians certainly got the better of their adversaries. The Indian tank men, riding their vintage Centurions, Shermans and AMX-13s, knocked off an awful lot of brand new US built Patton Tanks the Pakistanis were equipped with. Their armoured division was virtually written off. The story of their Sabre Jets in the air wasn't any better either. Thus at the end of the day, India had managed to undermine the massive arms buildup Pakistan was pursuing. (The territorial gains or losses didn't amount to much for either side anyway, since the pre-war status was eventually restored.) And it gave the Indian Army the much needed shot in the arm after the demoralizing ordeal of 1962.

Across every battle front, the war of 1965 saw the Madras Regiment in action in a big way, with as many as ten battalions taking the field. 1 Madras, commanded by Lieutenant Colonel CPA Menon (the nephew of

---

1. What by all counts should have been a resounding victory for the Indian side turned out to be more or less a stalemate, with both sides making rival claims, sheerly for want of aggressive senior-level leadership within the army. Lieutenant General Harbaksh Singh, one of India's finest soldiers ever, who during the war was the GOC-in-C of the Western Command, the formation that handled most of the fighting, candidly observed in his book about the operations, War Dispatches, that but for a lack of boldness by the commanders at various levels to seize an opportunity when it presented itself and exploit the situation to our advantage, we could have achieved a decisive victory.

the officer of the same name killed in J&K in 1948), was engaged from early August itself in the search-and-destroy operations against the infiltrators in the Rajauri Sector of J&K, where it did a commendable job of rounding up scores of infiltrators, before being shifted to Naushera by the end of the month to throw defensive piquets along the Ceasefire Line. Later by 10 September, the battalion joined the 1 Corps offensive in the Sialkot Sector as it got under way, forming part of 52 Mountain Brigade under 26 Infantry Division. Concentrating at Fatehpur by the 12th, the unit was assigned for an attack on Tilakpur, a village across the Ceasefire Line, 12 kilometres short of Indo-Pak Border.

The brigade attack, which materialized only on 18 September, went in an hour before midnight, 1 Madras forming its left point and 2 Mahar the right, with 5/11 GR in reserve. It was a gritty battle with the enemy artillery coming down murderously on the attackers. The brigade successfully took the objective, albeit at the cost of a considerable number of casualties. A squadron of tanks from 18 Cavalry drove in by daybreak to reinforce the infantrymen, who had dug in by then to take on the counter-attacks. During the next four days, before the ceasefire came onto effect in the early hours of 23 September, the enemy – mostly Baluchi troops – staged three powerful counter-attacks, backed by armour, artillery and air-power; but the battalion, with the rest of the brigade, doggedly held on, beating the enemy back every time, inflicting heavy casualties on them, including one of their tanks knocked out by anti-tank guns.

Soon after the ceasefire, the battalion was diverted for operations in the Akhnur-Chamb-Jaurian Sectors, first for penetration into enemy territory for establishing forward defence positions, and later to take up the defence of the Jhung Feature overlooking Sunderbani. On 30 September it was called up to go in for another attack, that of an important feature, Malla, in the Kalidhar Range, which had been lost to the enemy two days earlier. The attack was launched at 0330 hours the next day. Pounded by artillery and mortars and braving machinegun fire, the men had a job of clearing the false front the enemy had put up; and by the time they made it to the actual objective it was broad daylight. A nasty bit of fighting ensued with fierce hand-to-hand combat; but the assault carried the day, and by noon the objective had been taken. The enemy brought down heavy artillery with a vengeance; but the battalion stuck to the position, and later went on to secure a forming up place for another unit to attack a neighbouring feature. 1 Madras was to man the Kalidhar Defences for more than three months, until relieved in early January 1966. The battalion suffered 88 casualties in all during the course of the war; 2 JCOs and 28 men killed, and 3 officers, 2 JCOs and 53 men wounded.

2 Madras, commanded by Lieutenant Colonel CV Donoghue, based at Ambala before the war, joined the 11 Corps offensive towards Lahore right at the beginning. Forming part of 29 Infantry Brigade, which had been assigned to guard the northern flank of the offensive, the battalion found itself engaged in one of the most significant battles when it was earmarked, along with 1/5 GR, to attack the Dera Baba Nanak Enclave. Formed of a salient extending about a kilometre and a half into the Indian territory across the river Ravi, it was encircled by an embankment along which the international boundary ran. The place was clustered by 'Sarkhanda' grass growing ten to twelve feet all over. A massive steel-and-concrete bridge, about 800 metres long spanning the river, linked the enclave to Pakistan. The enemy had deployed about three companies of regular infantry – 3 Punjab – and a company of the Sutlej Rangers along with a battery of 25-pounder field guns, a platoon of mortars and a squadron of medium tanks to defend the place. The main body of the infantry with the field guns and mortars held the enclave, while the tanks with the rest of the infantry remained in reserve across the river.

The attack commenced sharp at 0400 hours on 6 September, the H-hour for the entire Corps, with 2 Madras going in from the right of the bridge and 1/5 GR from the left. Assaulting on a two-company front, the Madras men ran into a tough defence line refusing to yield ground. The fight that erupted was ferocious, but by daybreak the attackers had wrested a victory, occupying the objective. 32 Pakistanis lay dead and another 10 had been taken prisoner. The Gorkhas were victorious as well. The Indian Brigade had won the first round. The enemy had been driven to the far side of the river.

Almost immediately they counter-attacked with massive artillery and armour support. There were anxious moments when one of the Madras companies were almost overwhelmed and had to be reinforced by men from the reserve company; but finally the enemy was beaten back for good. Meanwhile the Gorkhas found themselves in a spot of trouble as the day wore on, with the counter-attacks on their side gaining momentum[2], and two of their companies getting overrun. Alarmed, the brigade threw in its third unit, 3 RAJ RIF (Rajputana Rifles), by nightfall. The RAJ RIF men, in an interesting ruse, drove in in a huge convoy of vehicles with headlamps on, simulating the arrival of a much larger force. They then mounted an assault at 0200 hours on the 7th, and dislodged the enemy troops who had come to occupy the embankment by the river. The Pakistanis, having fallen for the ruse, panicked, and fearing an

---

2. Every so often, battles leave behind untold episodes of courage under fire. One such tale is that of Sepoy Ayalaiah of 2 Madras at the Battle of Dera Baba Nanak. A master gunner, Ayalaiah was manning his 106 mm Recoilless (RCL) Gun after the capture of the objective, when three Pakistani tanks made a push across the bridge to boost up their counterattack on the Gorkha position. They were tempting but tricky moving targets for Ayalaiah, with the steel girders of the bridge denying him a clear field of fire. His first two shots hit the girders and the lead tank made it through; but with his third shot he knocked out the second tank which came to block the bridge. An armoured recovery vehicle (ARV) soon drove up to pull it aside, and Ayalaiah made his second hit knocking out the ARV. Panic gripped the Pakistani tank men, and the lead tank, which had crossed over, turned around and tried to dash back to safety. Ayalaiah promptly engaged it but missed. That was the last round he fired. An RCL gun easily gives out its position with the mighty flash it whips up in place of recoil; and it didn't take any wizardry on the part of the Pakistani tank gunner to swivel around his turret and blast the troublesome gun out of existence. There was no escape for the tank crew either. With the knocked-out tanks blocking the bridge, they abandoned their own machine, and on foot, tried to run for it, only to be mowed down by the machineguns of Ayalaiah's comrades. Ayalaiah's war was over; an unsung hero, he died doing what he was good at – scoring hits with his anti-tank gun. The three stranded tanks blocking the bridge, two of them smouldering, stood testimony to his valour.

Indian thrust across the river, blew up a span of the bridge once it was daylight. They had blunted any more Indian offensive in the area, but the Dera Baba Nanak Enclave was firmly in Indian hands.

With the northern flank of the Indian advance so secured, 2 Madras and 1/5 GR were pulled out the next day – leaving only 3 RAJ RIF to hold the enclave – for deployment in other sectors where battles were raging. With the typically confused scenario most military operations create, the two units were moved about from one location to another for almost a fortnight, often under shelling and air attacks, until they found themselves together once again on 21 September, poised to attack Khemkaran, where we had suffered reverses in the face of a major offensive by the enemy. It proved to be a disastrous mission, wherein the battalion started taking casualties from intense enemy shelling[3] even as it was establishing a firm base. Despite heavy odds the attack went in at 1400 hours on 22 September, only to make very slow progress against the fierce resistance the enemy put up. The next morning Pakistanis intensified their air strikes and artillery fire to a saturation point; and with its forward position no more tenable, the battalion was pulled back some 800 metres. The ceasefire was declared that afternoon; and the unit remained facing Khemkaran till relieved on 29 September. 2 Madras lost 27 lives in all, including those of 3 officers in its two major engagements of the war, at Dera Baba Nanak and Khemkaran.

3 Madras, commanded by Lieutenant Colonel BK Bhattacharya, and 4 Madras, commanded by Lieutenant Colonel HL Mehta, were inducted into the operations together, along with 9 Kumaon (the three units forming 69 Mountain Brigade of 6 Infantry Division under 1 Corps), on 7 September for the capture of Maharajke in the Sialkot Sector. A fairly big-sized village some two and a half miles across the international border and 13 miles from Sialkot, it became tactically significant because of being the site of a major crossroads on the drive to Sialkot. The capture

---

3   Aggressive use of artillery was Pakistan's strongest point throughout the war. Obviously – considering the accuracy of their fire – they had fine-tuned their forward observation mechanism to direct the fire to maximum effect.

of the place was part of 6 Division's mission to secure a bridgehead for the breakout of 1 Armoured Division later.

The brigade attack, well-supported by artillery and synchronized with flanking attacks by other formations, went in at 2300 hours with 3 Madras and 9 Kumaon going for the right half of the objective in the first phase, so as to block the roads to Pagowal-Badiana and Sialkot. Deadly fighting ensued with the enemy machine gunners playing havoc; but the assault proved unstoppable[4], and the objective was overrun by 0130 hours. The losses of the Madras battalion amounted to 20 in all, 3 killed and 17 wounded.

The phase-2 of the attack, for the left half of the objective – to block the roads to Charwa and Zafarwal – by 4 Madras, launched at 0200 hours on 8 September, turned out to be a far bitter contest, against a rather dogged defence by the men of Pakistan's famed Frontier Force Regiment. With the initial two-company-up assault flagging, the CO was forced to commit the reserve companies as well. In the end it was a trench-by-trench bloody hand-to-hand fighting; but the Madrassis had taken the objective by 0530 hours. The amount of casualties was considerable on both sides. 16 dead bodies of the Frontier Force men and the Mujahideen were counted on the objective after the battle; the number of Madrassis killed weren't much lesser – 11 in all, which included their Commanding Officer. The wounded numbered 34.

It was the 4th Battalion's – 'Wallajahbadis' as they proudly call themselves, being the descendant unit of the old Wallajabad Light Infantry – hour of glory. Trench after trench was cleared by men closing in and lobbing grenades, often led by young officers. The Adjutant of the unit, Lieutenant Ramesh Kumar, was wounded in such a sortie. Two JCOs, Subedars, CA Madhavan Nambiar and PM Gregory, leading a

---

4. The battalion kept up a furious pace of assault, and there were acts of cool courage to overcome the odds. At one instance, a NCO, Naik Samuel Thampan, identifying a particularly troublesome machinegun post of the enemy, crawled up to it and lobbed a grenade in, silencing the weapon. He was later awarded a Sena Medal.

handful of men charged two enemy posts from the rear. They both were to be awarded the Vir Chakras later. The CO of the battalion, Lieutenant Colonel Harbans Lal Mehta, who personally led an outflanking attack by a reserve company, was mortally wounded. He was awarded the Maha Vir Chakra posthumously.

After the Battle of Maharajke, 3 Madras was engaged in clearing some of the villages in the vicinity until 13 September, when it was assigned, along with a company of 4 Madras and two squadrons of 62 Cavalry, to form the vanguard of the brigade advance to Pagowal. The enemy was contacted within two hours of the commencement of the advance at 0400 hours, and a position cleared and occupied north of Pagowal without much of a hassle. But the enemy kept the stakes high with constant shelling, and counterattacked with tanks and infantry in the afternoon. It was repulsed with the powerful support of own artillery. After holding on to the position for three days the battalion captured Pagowal itself on the 17th and cleared three more outlying villages during the next four days until the 23rd when the ceasefire was declared. The operations after Maharajke had cost the battalion 23 casualties, 4 killed and 19 wounded.

6 and 7 Madras were deployed to contain the Pakistani infiltration in Jammu and Kashmir, mainly on the Rajauri-Punch Sector. Although ceasefire had been declared by the time 6 Madras arrived, it took part in a subsequent attack on Balnoi in Punch. 7 Madras had been hunting the infiltrators from early August itself and held vital pickets in Punch during the operations. The battalion continued to be deployed in the area for another three years. The casualties of 6 Madras were 1 killed and 1 wounded, and that of 7 Madras were, 6 killed, 16 wounded and 1 missing. 8 Madras, though mobilized, could not see action since the ceasefire had come into effect by the time it concentrated in Punjab. Lance Havildar Kannappan of 7 Madras was awarded a Sena Medal for exceptional bravery.

9 Madras, commanded by Lieutenant Colonel BK Satyan, forming

part of 65 Infantry Brigade under 7 Infantry Division, was part of the 11 Corps thrust aimed at Lahore. As part of the advance guard, the battalion captured the village of Barka Kalan, a vantage point, prior to the armour-supported assault of 10 September on Barki, around which the Pak defences of Ichhogil Canal Bund were built. The Ichhogil Canal[5] being a strategically significant barrier for its nearness to Lahore (12 miles), the Pakistanis put up a stout defence. Having had to abandon their positions in disarray under the tank assault, they blew up the bridge; but before the Indian troops had consolidated their hold, managed to reoccupy a part of the Bund in strength. With the deadline fixed for the ceasefire on 23 September, the battalion (short of one company) – which has so far been holding the firm base for the attack by the other two battalions of the brigade, 4 Sikh and 16 Punjab – stormed the Bund during the night 22nd-23rd and dislodged the enemy in a do-or-die fight.

The Battle of Ichhogil Bund was by far the fiercest engagement the Madras Regiment fought in the war of '65. It was a tricky mission wherein the unit had to assault in waves, one company at a time from the flank, and clear the enemy entrenched along the Bund with colossal fire support from their comrades on the far bank barely 150 feet across. Nevertheless, in an amazing feat of arms, the battalion, endowed with an abundance of fresh youngsters and equally vigorous young leadership, made short work of it with a lightning charge that bordered on recklessness, supported eminently by our own guns and tanks which kept up a steady fire across the canal through out the engagement, effectively neutralizing the enemy fire from the far bank. The enemy was virtually routed, with a number of them jumping into the canal to escape the fury of the assault, while many of the rest were bodily

5. Ichhogil Canal, which the Pakistanis call the 'Bambanwalla Ravi Bedian Link' – BRBL for short – was constructed by them in 1950s as a defence obstacle against a possible Indian attack on Lahore. It runs close to Indian border between the rivers Ravi in the north and Sutlej in the south, blocking an advance on Lahore along that corridor from the east. 45 metres wide and 5 metres deep, and its western bank built higher with bunkers overlooking the eastern bank, it made a formidable obstacle for the advancing Indian formation.

198 Empire's First Soldiers

lifted and thrown in, if not shot down or bayoneted. It was all over in 2 hours and 30 minutes from the word go at 0030 hours on the 23rd. By 0300 hours the objective had been overrun. The enemy casualties were heavy, 48 dead and an estimated 80 washed away in the canal. 11 were taken prisoner, including one officer. An enormous amount of arms and ammunition including 2 RCL guns were also captured. Own casualties were considerably heavy too – 49 killed including one JCO and 65 wounded including one officer.

It was a night of unfettered heroism, layered with glorious acts and poignant scenes. There were the two jawans of the lead platoon, Narayanan and Bhaskaran, who volunteered to silence a machinegun and crawled forward in the darkness. The gun was silenced in 20 minutes, but in the heat of the battle no one noticed their absence. They were found after the battle, sprawled dead in front of the pillbox wherein the weapon had been located. A similar pair, Sepoys Mallappan and Ramachandran, was found dead, frozen in sitting posture manning their machinegun, one handling the weapon, the other belt feeding. Then there was Major Dharam Pal, leading his men in the assault undaunted by a splinter lodged in his leg. There was the sight of the CO, Colonel Sathyan, cheering his men on, walking up and down the Bund fully exposed to the enemy, gifted with a charming existence; as the night reverberated with the Madrassi Battle Cry, "*Veer Madrassi Adi Kollu, Adi Kollu*", a no-nonsense phrase, to the point, and deadly – "Brave Madrassi Strike and Kill, Strike and Kill." (The 9th Madrassis call themselves the "Terrors" – indeed that's what the Pakistanis would have found them to be that night.) And giving it all a sombre touch was the medical inspection room truck plying up and down non-stop, picking up the casualties, with the popular Medical NCO, 'Rasam' Thankappan, at the wheel. For 9 Madras, a unit which traces its origin to the Travancore State Forces, it was quite an *Onam*, the traditional harvest festival of Kerala that the men of the whole Madras Regiment celebrate with zest in the month of September every year.

Since the Pakistanis did not open a front in the east, 16 Madras, deployed on the East Pakistan border, saw no action. 17 Madras went into action during the night 19-20 September, forming a firm base at Dali in Pakistani territory for the advance of 85 Infantry brigade towards Khinsor. However they had to withdraw late in the evening on 21 September following an enemy attack heavily supported by air and artillery. Subsequently after the ceasefire, they captured Kinra and Point 413 in Skarbu area, both within Pakistan, during September-October. The total casualties the battalion suffered were 3 killed, 15 wounded and 59 taken prisoner.

The Madras Regiment won the Battle Honours, KALIDHAR 1965 and MAHARAJKE 1965, and the Theatre Honours, JAMMU AND KASHMIR 1965 and PUNJAB 1965, for the participation of its battalions in the operations.

The Madras Engineers had two of its field companies taking part in the 11 Corps offensive towards Lahore; 10 and 63. Major PP Srivastava's 63 Field Company, which formed part of 29 Infantry Brigade, was the first unit to be engaged. The Company found itself in the thick of action at Dera Baba Nanak as soon as the enclave had been captured by our troops – which included 2 Madras – and the initial counter-attacks beaten back. By the early hours of 7 September, the Company was called upon to demolish a span of the Ravi Bridge and mine the approach on its home side to prevent further forays by the enemy. The mines and explosives were late in arriving, and it was broad daylight by the time the work could be taken up. Nevertheless, a team led by Second Lieutenant N Chandrasekharan Nair got down to the nightmare of a job, laying mines right under the direct small arms and tank fire and artillery shelling.

The enemy himself meanwhile contributed to the effort by demolishing a span of the bridge; except that it turned out to be a shoddy piece of sapper craft – the bridge still remained usable. And adding insult to injury, the young Indian Sapper officer, Nair, in an act of daredevilry, crossed over the 'demolished' bridge all alone, captured an enemy jeep and drove it back. The officer was later decorated with

Vir Chakra.

Major MM Mathew's 10 Field Company – the second unit deployed for the 11 Corps offensive – with 67 Infantry Brigade in Fazilka and Firozepur area couldn't see much of action except for mine laying and braving constant shelling, since no enemy threat materialized in that sector.

The 1 Corps offensive towards Sialkot saw 8 companies of the Madras Sappers in action; 13, 14 and 65 Field Companies and 684 Field Park Company with the 1 Armoured Divisional Engineers at the Samba Sector, and 9, 36 and 39 Field Companies and 372 Field Park Company with the 26 Infantry Divisional Engineers at the Suchetgarh Sector.

When 1 Armoured Division launched its two-pronged offensive on 8 September, Major RC Mehta's 14 Assault Field Company advanced with the tanks of 1 Armoured Brigade headed for Phillora, and Major Gur Dayal's 65 Assault Field Company joined 43 Lorried Infantry Brigade on its way to Pagowal. On 11 September Phillora witnessed the biggest tank battle fought anywhere in the world till then after World War II, which was to turn the place into a graveyard of Pakistani Patton Tanks. Before the battle, in the brigade's advance to Phillora and later as it struck out towards Chawinda, the Sappers kept at it tirelessly developing the tracks for the division to advance, constantly harassed by the enemy air force and artillery. At least 4 Sappers were killed in strafing and shelling. Pagowal fell on 13 September, and Alhar Railway Station and the areas south to it were taken on the 15th. The operations ended before Chawinda could be taken. 13 Field Company joined the track building effort towards the end.

In the Suchetgarh Sector, the advance elements of 26 Infantry Division had reached within striking distance of Sialkot when ceasefire was declared. 39 Company was engaged to move the bridging equipment forward, which made it a favoured target of the enemy air force for strafing.

The Sappers' war wasn't without its lighter moments either. In 26 Divisional Sector 36 Field Company was carrying out the demolition of a low wall for clearer field of fire. After the charge had been fired, the demolition group was confronted by the strange sight of some 20 Pakistani soldiers and a JCO emerging from the smoke and debris with their arms thrown up in surrender. They had mistaken the demolition for gunfire. The young officer in charge of the Sappers promptly disarmed them and marched them off to captivity.

A large number of other Madras Engineer units were also rushed to the western sector from elsewhere, anticipating a long haul, but the conflict ended before they could go operational. The MEG won the Theatre Honours, JAMMU AND KASHMIR 1965, and PUNJAB 1965.

The 1965 operations also saw the South Indian cavalry regiment, the 16th Light Cavalry (commonly referred as 16 Cavalry), in action in a significant role. Equipped with Centurion Tanks, the regiment formed the vanguard of advance of I Armoured Division towards Sialkot, up to Gadgor in Pakistan. In a major tank battle fought at Gadgor on 8 September, and a subsequent engagement at Alhar Railway Station, they destroyed 16 Patton Tanks of the enemy, against a loss of 6 tanks of their own. 2 officers, 1 JCO and 14 Other Ranks of the unit were killed in these actions; and a number of officers, JCOs and Other Ranks were wounded[6].

---

6. In the lexicon of India's gallant soldiers maimed in battle, seldom comes along a tale as epic as that of Captain JK 'Chottu' Sen Gupta of 16 Cavalry, who lost both his eyes when his tank was hit. Undeterred by the devastating injury, this brilliant and popular officer – a top ranker from his days as a young boy at RIMC, through NDA and IMA – who was barely 24 at the time of the war, began rebuilding his life with the same zeal that he fought his battles with. Adapting his remaining faculties to do almost everything – be it using a typewriter or crossing the Chowringee Road at Calcutta unaided – with a level of dexterity that amazed both friends and strangers, he went on to become a successful businessman. Some ten years after the war, he found his pretty wife – or she found him – and the couple lives happily at Kolkota with their children.

The Regiment won the Theatre Honour, PUNJAB 1965. The gallantry awards won by its officers and men comprised 1 Vir Chakra, 1 Sena Medal, 8 Mention-in-Dispatches and 3 Commendation Cards from the Chief of Army Staff.

INDO - PAK WAR 1965

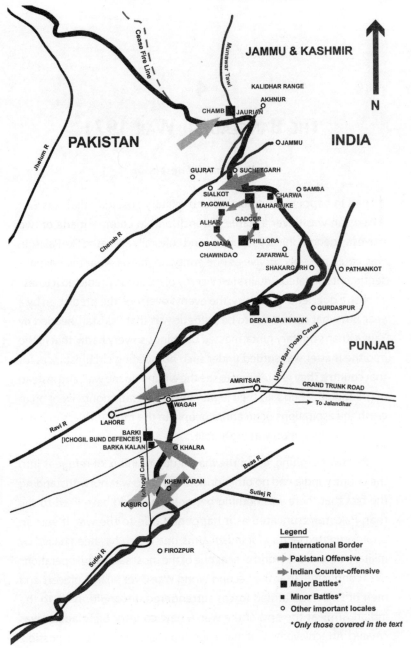

Cease Fire Line

Munawar Tawi

Jhelum R.

JAMMU & KASHMIR

KALIDHAR RANGE

AKHNUR

CHAMB JAURIAN

PAKISTAN

○ JAMMU

INDIA

N

GUJRAT ○ SUCHETGARH

SIALKOT ○ SAMBA

PAGOWAL CHARWA

MAHARAJKE

ALHAR GADGOR

BADIANA ○ PHILLORA

CHAWINDA ○ ZAFARWAL ○

SHAKARGARH ○ ○ PATHANKOT

Chenab R.

○ GURDASPUR

DERA BABA NANAK

PUNJAB

Upper Bari Doab Canal

AMRITSAR ○ GRAND TRUNK ROAD

→ To Jalandhar

WAGAH ○

Ravi R.

LAHORE ○

BARKI
[ICHOGIL BUND DEFENCES]
BARKA KALAN ○ KHALRA

Ichogil Canal

Beas R.

KHEM KARAN ○

Sutlej R.

KASUR ○

Sutlej R.

○ FIROZPUR

Legend

▬ International Border
➡ Pakistani Offensive
➡ Indian Counter-offensive
■ Major Battles*
▪ Minor Battles*
○ Other important locales

*Only those covered in the text

Not to Scale ; only approximate locations depicted

4

THE BANGLADESH WAR 1971

Indian Army's finest hour

It had to happen – the political and military absurdity that was East Pakistan was never a viable proposition. No country made of two halves so geographically separated and culturally alienated like Pakistan was, could possibly survive as one entity, no matter what the religious sentiments dictated. Britain's last Viceroy of India had predicted it to last, at best, a quarter of a century; the events overtook the prediction by a year. But what turned out to be pathetic was that Pakistan, headed by Yahya Khan's military junta, messed up things so very badly, that in the end the matter was settled under such humiliating circumstances for that country. They just refused to see the writing on the wall; and instead of granting the Bengalis their legitimate democratic rights, went on to crush the aspirations of an entire people in the most ruthless manner possible. A revolution was inevitable.

By any reckoning, given the magnitude of influx of refugees into the country, India had no other option but go to war, notwithstanding the fact that there was nothing better India would have liked to see than Pakistan truncated as it happened due to the war. It was an unprecedented victory for Indian arms, one which has been hailed by military experts the world over as one of the most successful operations ever conducted after the Second World War. Over 90,000 officers and men of Pakistan's armed forces surrendered unconditionally to the Indian Army at the end of the war. A new country, Bangladesh, was created. An achievement of that magnitude couldn't have been possible but for India's bold and sensible political leadership, complemented by a brilliant military strategy. The Pakistani junta's arrogance and stupidity came as a bonus, with a shamefully defeatist attitude of the country's armed forces in its eastern wing.

India, which started off being a sympathetic party to the Bengali cause, soon found itself covertly involved in training Mukti Bahini, the army of their freedom fighters, and was to finally go in for an all out invasion of East Pakistan. The success of the operations owed a lot to the fact that the Chief of Army Staff refused to be browbeaten to take hasty or unwise steps, and conducted the war in the time and manner as dictated by sound professional reasoning (at the time of the year when the weather and ground conditions were favourable, and after the army had had adequate time for planning and preparations). And the Pakistani establishment naively missed out on the one chance it had to avert the catastrophe – it failed to preempt the war, and force India to take the field before she was ready and under unfavourable conditions for an offensive.

Thus to start with, India had all the advantages. But then advantages alone do not add up to such a total and decisive victory. Pakistan still could have salvaged its reputation, by smartly exploiting the one inherent advantage it had – the riverine terrain of Bengal. There are few better defender-friendly terrains anywhere in the subcontinent. And India did not have the 2:1 superiority in numbers, conventionally required for an offensive to succeed. A determined and well-organized defence could have slowed down the Indian offensive and made the victory far more costly, probably offering Pakistan the bargaining power for a face saving formula. But the Pakistani army in the east had long ceased to be a professional force. The indulgence of the officer corps had abysmally eroded the morale of the men. And in the end when it came to the fighting, excepting for odd instances, most of their army just put up a token resistance for the first few days, and then fled even when they had a fighting chance. Demoralized and feeling betrayed by their own government, their only concern was to get to Dacca somehow from where they hoped to be extricated, from what they perceived to be the trap that East Pakistan had become, with the Indian Navy blockading its ports and the Indian Army formations closing in on them from every direction. (Even then, they lost over 2000 killed and some 4000 wounded in the operations, not counting an equal number of casualties they suffered during the build-up to the war since March that year.)

In contrast, the morale of the Indian troops, ready and raring to go, was on an all time high. Ultimately it was their dash and determination that reaped the glory. 1500 of them perished doing that, and another 4000 were wounded. That toll could have been far lesser and the victory far speedier, had it not been for the unfortunate – and the inherent – timidity of some of our commanders at unit as well as formation levels, who remained bogged down with their archaic textbook notions of warfare, while they should have used their imagination to unleash the younger men on a blazing blitzkrieg that the operation should have been. In fact, that was how it had been planned – brilliantly so – by the Eastern Command. And our air force had ensured – by knocking out whatever air power Pakistan had in the east within the first few hours of fighting – that the army could advance with absolutely no hindrance from the air. Yet we were often found vacillating, obsessed with an exaggerated perception of enemy strength. Our advance on many instances was held up by 'enemy strongpoints', which ridiculously enough, when 'attacked and captured' contained no enemy at all. And when it came to genuinely strong positions held by the enemy, more often than not, we went for blunt frontal assaults with disastrous results, instead of smart outflanking manoeuvres that would have threatened their rear. The lessons from the war of '65 did not seem to have sunk in on many of the field commanders.

The credit for the grant victory thus must primarily go to the indefatigable fighting spirit of the officers and men in general, and the sound strategy employed by the Eastern Command. Codenamed 'Operation Cactus Lily', the grand plan envisaged an invasion of East Pakistan simultaneously from four directions in a swift, enveloping move.

The newly raised 2 Corps made up of two infantry divisions was to move in from the Southwest; the Siliguri-based 33 Corps with two divisions and some additional brigades was to move in from the Northwest; and the Tripura-based 4 Corps with three divisions was to advance from the Southeast, while an ad hoc formation under command the Shillong-based HQ 101 Communication Zone Area, with a brigade group that was to be supplemented by a brigade or two and a parachute battalion, was to move in from the Northeast and eventually head for Dacca.

Although a full-fledged war commenced only on 3 December, sparked off by the preemptive air strikes by Pakistan in the Western Sector that afternoon, in the East the Indian troops had occupied enemy territory up to 10 kilometres across the border during November itself, in preparation for the offensive. The main operation that followed was conducted generally according to the plan. A 3-pronged advance by 2 Corps from the Southwest swarmed the entire part of East Pakistan which fell south and southwest of the river Padma (Meghna, downriver), by investing Khulna down south, and pushing eastward up to Faridpur by the banks of Meghna and northward up to Kushtia and beyond to the Hardinge Bridge on the river. Similarly a pincer movement by 33 Corps from the Northwest invested Dinajpur and Rangpur in the north, and eventually converged to capture Bogra to the south, overwhelming the enemy in the whole area that side bound to the east and south by the two rivers, Jamuna and Padma. 4 Corps, moving in from the Southeast, invested Sylhet to the north, and captured Ashugang and Chandpur, before effecting a crossing over the Meghna, to threaten Dacca. The Corps also dispatched a subsidiary force to invest the port town of Chittagong far south. Meanwhile the ad hoc force under 101 Communication Zone Area invested Mymensingh and Jamalpur in a pincer move from the Northeast, and converging further south, para dropped a battalion ahead in Tangail area and raced forward to hit the outskirts of Dacca, which, more than anything else, drove home the point to Pakistan's Eastern Army Command that surrender was their only option.

The historic surrender, *by Lieutenant General Amir Abdul Khan Niazi, Martial Law Administrator Zone B and the Commander Eastern Command (PAKISTAN), to Lieutenant General Jagjit Singh Aurora, General Officer Commanding in Chief, Indian and BANGLA DESH forces in the Eastern Theatre,* took place at 1631[1] hours IST on 16 December 1971, at the Dacca Race Course. East Pakistan was no more, and Bangladesh was born. The Indian soldiers had made it happen; but as it is their lot always, no monument in the new nation-state commemorates their role in it.

The Indian Army's moment of glory was deservedly shared by the Madras Regiment and the MEG, who both played their roles to the hilt in the operations. Three battalions of the Madras Regiment, 4, 8, and 26, took the field, all of them with formations which moved in from the West Bengal border.

4 Madras, commanded by Lieutenant Colonel SL Malhotra, which formed part of 340 Mountain Brigade under 20 Mountain Division of 33 Corps (Northwestern Sector), went into action as early as 12 November, and was one of the first units to be engaged. They began with the capture of a Pak border outpost, Khanpur Hat, some 12 miles south of Dinajpur, in a preemptive move to secure a bridgehead for the eventual advance of the brigade. The attack, mounted before dawn on the 13th after moving up during the night, turned out to be a nasty bit of action, with the enemy – a couple of platoons and some *Razakars* well-fortified with quite a few machineguns – holding out rather stubbornly. The battalion had gone in two companies short, but supplemented by a company of BSF and two companies of Mukti Bahini, the last more or less dissolving once under fire. Artillery and tank support were at hand, but with the war yet to be declared, couldn't be brought to bear. In the end a blistering assault by the battalion took the objective by daybreak.

---

1. Interestingly, Lieutenant General JFR Jacob, then Major General and the Chief of Staff Eastern Command, who organized the surrender ceremony, notes in his book on the war, *Surrender at Dacca, Birth of a Nation*, that although the time entered in the surrender document is 1631 hours, the actual signing of the document took place only at 1655 hours. The time, obviously, had been entered in advance in keeping with some scheduled time plan.

In less than two hours the enemy launched a counterattack supported by tanks, only to be beaten back by a spirited defence, aided this time by artillery and mortar fire. The bridgehead had been established. At least 12 dead bodies of the enemy were counted after the battle.

The brief engagement saw exceptional acts of gallantry by the officers and men of the battalion. Naib Subedar PO Cherian, the JCO Adjutant of the battalion, was knocked down by a machinegun burst 40 yards from the objective. He pulled himself up, and bleeding but undeterred, led his men in the charge until the objective was taken. He was awarded the Vir Chakra. During the counterattack, the Commander of the Recoilless Gun Detachment, Naik LR Joseph, was shot up by tank fire. Severely wounded but with great presence of mind he popped off two rounds in quick succession and managed to relocate the gun, before permitting himself to be evacuated.

The actual war was still three weeks away, and the battalion meanwhile went on to expand its hold on to some 26 square kilometres of the enemy territory; a factor which was to prove of immense tactical benefit when the operations commenced on 3 December. This often called for small-scale but sharp engagements. In a gallant piece of action, a single platoon commanded by Second Lieutenant Bandyopadyay overran the Ghughudanga Bridge over Gouripur Canal. The officer was decorated with a Sena Medal; so was his leading Section Commander, Lance Naik Chinnathambi, the latter posthumously. The NCO had silenced a Light Machine Gun which was holding up the advance by crawling right up to it, falling prey to the enemy fire in the act.

Once the operation commenced, the far-flung forward companies began to come under enemy attacks. On 6 December, D Company under Major Phul Singh withstood and fought off an exceptionally powerful attack supported by tanks. Subedar Perumal of the company was killed trying to take on the tanks with a rocket launcher. Major Phul Singh himself was wounded and taken prisoner with three of his men when the enemy overran a portion of the company position; but the company held out. (In an interesting turn of events, the major and his three men were to be liberated from the enemy by men of 4 Madras themselves on 16 December, after the battle of Bogra wherein the battalion partook.)

While 4 Madras kept the enemy so engaged, the rest of the brigade began moving south, isolating Dinajpur for good. With the enemy resistance fading in a couple of days the battalion was also on the move to catch up with the brigade, which had traversed 100-odd kilometres southeastward by then. Meanwhile a stalemate had developed at Hilli to the south, where 202 Mountain Brigade had launched an abortive attack on 22 November. On 10 December the Divisional Headquarters assigned a special mission to 4 Madras, to capture an enemy strongpoint to the rear of Hilli so as to threaten its defences. It turned out to be a brilliant piece of tactics, and is best chronicled by the man who conceived it and had it executed, Major General Lachhman Singh Lehl, GOC 20 Infantry Division. The General wrote in his book on the war, *Indian Sword strikes in East Pakistan*:

I ordered 4 MADRAS to move from Dinajpur area to Nawabganj and placed them under 66 Mountain Brigade........At this stage, Malhotra, an energetic and bold Commanding Officer, reported to me. His battalion had arrived in Nawabganj area in the afternoon. I ordered him to capture Maheshpur on 10 December and destroy enemy guns and Brigade Headquarters in the area. This operation would have automatically threatened Hilli from the area. I had information that the enemy had one artillery battery, one Infantry Company and Tajjamul's Brigade Headquarters in the area. I placed 63 Cavalry less two squadrons under Malhotra, and Subha Rao arranged artillery support for him from guns deployed in Nawabganj area. Malhotra moved cross country during night and surprised the enemy in Maheshpur. The tanks shot up a number of vehicles and destroyed two enemy guns and captured another two. There was panic in the enemy Headquarters where they started burning documents as they were afraid our tanks would overrun their Headquarters. However, our tanks did not know about the exact location and were content to capture enemy guns and shooting up vehicles. The raid created chaos in the enemy's rear and

Brigade Headquarters and denied artillery support to the defenders of Bhaduria in the subsequent battle. ('Tajjamul' referred here is Brigadier Tajjamul Hussain, the Commander of Pakistan's 205 Brigade which was defending the area.)

Bhaduria was an enemy strongpoint the battalion had outflanked in its move to Hilli. The enemy pulled out of both the places during the night that followed. The advance of two brigades, 66 and 202, held up so far at these points would resume on 11 December. The 'Wallajabadis' of 4 Madras, in partnership with the tank men of 63 Cavalry, had delivered a master stroke that would propel the Indian advance to surge forward to its crowning climax. Instances of unwavering courage were commonplace as the battle raged. A bullet injury couldn't stop Sepoy Chellaiah Moses from manning his machinegun when the enemy counter-attacked; only a near-direct artillery hit that did him in could. In the same counter-attack, Naik Periappa Balaraman, manning a listening post 600 yards in front of the forward defences with six of his men, imposed maximum delay on the enemy with his LMG, to be shot down in the end when he chose to withdraw.

In the mobile warfare of the theatre, the battalion found itself engaged in the Battle of Bogra (14-16 December) with the rest of 20 Division. A stiff contest which saw intense built-up-area fighting, it culminated with the routing of the entire Pak forces in the northwestern sector of Bangladesh, prior to the surrender of their whole Eastern Army on the afternoon of the 16th at Dacca. 4 Madras had paid the price for its share in the victory with a sizeable casualty toll. The final figures at the end of the war were: 1 JCO and 8 Other Ranks killed; 3 officers, 2 JCOs and 25 Other Ranks wounded; and 1 JCO and 2 Other Ranks missing believed dead. The estimated enemy casualties the battalion caused were 36 killed and 8 wounded.

As 4 Madras fought it out in Northwest Bangladesh, the other two battalions, 8 and 26 Madras, were engaged in the 2 Corps Sector to the Southwest. 8 Madras, commanded by Lieutenant Colonel NH Narayanan, formed part of 32 Infantry Brigade under 9 Infantry Division. The Division, which had launched a successful offensive in Bayra area as early as 20 November, was facing the Pakistani defences of Jessore when the war was declared. Wilting under the probing attacks of the Division the enemy abandoned Jessore by 7 December to fall back to their line of defences along Daulatpur, Khulna and across the river Madhumati. 8 Madras along with a squadron of 63 Cavalry formed one of the two groups of 32 Infantry Brigade, which took up the advance to Khulna along separate axes on 9 December. Skirmishing their way across the many delaying positions of the enemy (often skillfully prepared by demolishing bridges, and making good use of the anti-tank and anti-personnel mines as well as the marshy terrain), the groups linked up with each other by the 10th at Nawapara, a few miles short of the objective, for the final approach. On the 12th the advancing brigade came up against the stoutly held enemy defences at Siramani, a built-up area on the outskirts of Khulna.

Siramani was to witness some of the fiercest fighting of the campaign. The first attack launched by two companies of 8 Madras under Major NK Rastogi, the Second-in-Command of the battalion, with a company of 13 Dogra in reserve, from a northwesterly direction late at night, had to be called off halfway, with the water level rising precariously in a marsh the assault was to go through. Nevertheless, a second assault was put under way by the wee hours of the 13th with the other two companies taking the lead. While B Company attacked from due north, C Company with tanks in support charged from the northeast. The enemy resisted fiercely on both fronts, turning it in to a bitter hand-to-hand combat. The fight lasted more than three hours, and it was past 0700 hours by the time the attackers had made a foothold. Two JCOs of the battalion, Naib Subedars VV Rajan and PC Varghese, met a heroic end in the battle leading the assault from the front. The latter was to be awarded a Vir Chakra.

As the day wore on the unit firmed in on the captured enemy positions, and fought off a powerful counter-attack. The Siramani main defences were now appreciated to be far more impregnable than anticipated, and a divisional attack was planned for the next day. During that night, 26 Madras, fighting its way from the east under 350 Infantry Brigade, moved in and occupied the positions held by 8 Madras, relieving it to join the divisional attack. 32 Infantry Brigade on its part planned a two-phase attack, wherein 13 Dogra was to go in first followed by 8 Madras in the second phase. The attack, after the planning and preparations, was launched only on the morning of 16 December. As it turned out, once the Dogra attack went in successfully the Pakistani garrison surrendered, in anticipation of the capitulation of their whole army that afternoon. The casualty toll of 8 Madras in the operations amounted to 2 JCOs and 5 Other Ranks killed, and 34 Other Ranks wounded.

26 Madras, a comparatively young battalion raised only in 1967, commanded by Lieutenant Colonel VK Singh, was to have its baptism of fire in East Pakistan. This unit too was with 9 Infantry Division and was inducted during November itself, assigned to protect the southern flank of the main divisional thrust along the Chaugacha-Jessore axis. On 23 November the battalion occupied the village of Chuttipur, after forcing the enemy to vacate it by aggressive patrolling. Basing itself in the village they kept the pressure on the enemy by a series of probes and feints, to keep the division's flank fully protected until actual operations began and the advance progressed towards Khulna. Then following the stalemate in front of Khulna where the advance of 32 Infantry Brigade had got stalled, the battalion was assigned to press home an attack on the Siramani defences from the east on 13 December.

The attack launched in the afternoon that day snowballed into a stiff contest, with the enemy fighting tooth and nail for every inch, immensely benefitted by their built-up area defences. In a do-or die fight the battalion succeeded in gaining a toehold in the end, but for all the tenacity shown, further assault was repulsed. Eventually during the night they occupied the firm base already established by the sister battalion, 8 Madras, relieving them to join the divisional attack later.

The extraordinary grit shown by 26 Madras won them a lot of admiration. Two Vir Chakras were awarded to the personnel of the battalion, both posthumously; one to Subedar R Krishnan Nair for his resolute leadership, when he carried on with the assault even after being wounded; and the other to Sepoy KJ Kristapher who daringly dashed into a single gap in a wall, to lob in a grenade and silence a machinegun, getting himself cut down in the act. Two other men won a gallantry award each, Naik Jacob Mathew a Sena Medal and Sepoy Joseph Stevence a Mention-in-Despatches, for acts of courage which bespoke the noblest in soldiering. Though wounded themselves, they went on to rescue the wounded of the Dogras lying exposed under fire. A shell burst was to deprive Mathew of an arm later.

The battalion lost 2 Officers, 2 JCOs and 12 Other Ranks killed, and 4 Officers, 2 JCOs and 56 Other Ranks wounded during the operations, most of those in the assault on Siramani. Brigadier HS Sandhu, the Commander of 350 Infantry Brigade, obviously moved by the performance of the unit, was to write to its Commanding Officer later:

Words cannot acknowledge the tenacity, resilience, resourcefulness and bravery displayed by all ranks of your unit on the battle field of Siramani. The performance of the unit on its very first outing is laudable and praiseworthy. That such a unit should come out with such flying colours is no mean achievement, and reflects the dedication of all ranks to live up to the traditions of the Thambis. My sincere prayers for the continued success of your Battalion in future battles.

Besides the three units of the Madras Regiment which were operationally committed in East Pakistan, a fourth battalion, 2 Madras, also made its own contribution to the creation of Bangladesh by imparting training to the Mukti Bahini. One of the unit's companies remained on vigil at the Sino-Indian Border – deployed for the defence of the Lungze Ridge – during the course of the operations, with the Chinese intervention perceived to be a possibility.

For the operations in the Eastern Theatre during 1971, the Madras Regiment won the Battle Honour, SIRAMANI and the Theatre Honour, EAST PAKISTAN 1971.

The contribution of the Madras Engineer Group, along with those of its sister groups, the Bombay and the Bengal ones, to the success of the Bangladesh Campaign was monumental. Aptly described as an 'Engineers' War', the rapid offensive that it was in a riverine country with poor roads and antiquated bridges, could have made no headway but for the traditional skills of the Sappers in improvisation. There were five regiments of the MEG, 3, 4, 11, 13 and 15, besides a company of 203 Engineer Regiment, in action.

Lieutenant Colonel Joginder Singh's 3 Engineer Regiment supported 23 Mountain Division on the Belonia-Chandpur axis from the Southeast, and later supported the advance of 83 Mountain Brigade Group to Chittagong. In a remarkable show of bridging skills, they helped the medium guns and light tanks of the formation get through a terrain crisscrossed by rivulets, where even light vehicles couldn't normally make headway. An officer of the regiment, Lieutenant BM Uthappa, was decorated with Sena Medal for exemplary courage on an occasion, when he went out of his way to rescue a trapped crew member of a tank that had run over a mine and caught fire. The officer breached a lane while fully exposed to small arms fire, to get to the tank.

4 Engineer Regiment, commanded by Lieutenant Colonel DN Dass, supported 61 Mountain Brigade of 57 Mountain Division from Tripura in the same sector, facilitating the brilliant manoeuvre which saw the Brigade surprise the enemy at Comilla by appearing behind the Mynamati Cantonment. Further on in the Brigade's final push towards Dacca, the Sappers used local steamers to ferry tanks, guns and vehicles across the river Meghna, and at times improvised bridges out of country boats.

15 Engineer Regiment, commanded by Lieutenant Colonel OP Behl, a second regiment supporting 57 Mountain Division – from Agartala – went

through the battle of Akhaura, Gangasagar, Brahmanbaria and Ashugang, and was part of the forces engaged in the heli-borne operations at Narshingdi across the river Meghna. Advancing with the division all the way, it was the first Sapper unit to get to Dacca. A classic piece of this unit's work was the construction of a 400-foot bailey suspension bridge – the longest possible in the category – at Brahmanbaria.

Lieutenant Colonel SK Jain's 11 Engineer Regiment supported 6 Mountain Division advancing from Pachagarh to Saidpur in the Northwest Sector, breaching mines, repairing roads or launching bridges continually to keep the formation moving.

13 Engineer Regiment, under Lieutenant Colonel M Balakrishnan, supported 20 Mountain Division in the battle of Hilli in the same sector, and went on to convert 16 miles of rail track into a class 40 road in a matter of 18 hours. Medium guns were hauled forward over this track for the advance to Bogra.

A field company of 203 Engineer Regiment, under Lieutenant Colonel RS Kalra, supported 9 Infantry Division's thrust on Jessore and onward to Khulna in the Southwest. After the fall of Jessore on 7 December, the company undertook the repair of the badly mauled airfield there, and re-commissioned it in record time.

The Sapper effort in Bangladesh was to be applauded even by the enemy. After the surrender of the Bogra garrison on 18 December, a Pakistani Engineer officer was to express his admiration to one of his Indian counterparts of 'the way your boys brought the division virtually on your shoulders over the most indifferent and unexpected approach.' 'We', the Pakistani officer had added, 'could never imagine that such a large force could ever advance over a route which we had ruled out as impossible'. That said it all of the Sappers' saga in Bangladesh.

The MEG won the Theatre Honour, EAST PAKISTAN 1971, for the Bangladesh Campaign.

BANGLADESH WAR 1971

Legend
International Border
Indian Thrust Lines
Major Battles
Minor Battles
Other important locales

Not to Scale ; only approximate locations depicted

5

War in the West 1971

Pakistan's day of reckoning

In all fairness it should be admitted that India had given enough provocation to Pakistan to open the Western Front, and the war. Given the Indian incursions in the East, it would appear surprising why Pakistan waited so long at all, until 3 December, by which time India was all set and ready for the show. Unlike in the East, the forces of India and Pakistan facing each other in the Western Sector were more or less evenly matched. The Indian plan was basically one of defence, with the option for offensive tactics as a defensive measure. Here too there were three corps deployed under the Western Command, with two additional divisions in Rajasthan directly controlled by the Southern Command. 1 Armoured Division along with 14 Infantry Division was held in the Army Headquarters Reserve.

To the north, 15 Corps in Jammu was poised to strike out from the Chhamb Area towards the Pakistani town of Gujrat with its 10 Infantry Division, while its 26 Infantry Division advanced towards Sialkot. Immediately south, in Punjab, 1 Corps was to take up the advance up the Shakargarh bulge between the rivers Bein and Karir with its 39 Infantry Division, while its 54 Infantry Division advanced between the rivers Karir and Basantar, aiming to take Mirzapur, leaving a third infantry division, 36, in reserve. Further south, 11 Corps guarded the area from Dera Baba Nanak to Fazilka, its 15 Infantry Division holding the positions north of the Grand Trunk Road and 7 Infantry Division holding those to the south. In the southern-most sector in Rajasthan, under the Southern Command with its advance Headquarters at Jodhpur, 11 and 12 Infantry Divisions were deployed in the Jaisalmer and Balmer Areas.

If the army's role in the West was to be considered merely one of defence, by and large it was performed eminently, in that; every offensive undertaken by Pakistan was thwarted by our formations. We did however suffer some reverses, significantly at Chhamb, where we lost our territory west of the river Munawar-Tawi to the enemy (rather permanently, since unlike in 1965, areas captured by either side in J&K were not to be exchanged after the war), and in Punjab where they took the Hussainiwala Enclave across the Sutlej. Also, at the end of the day, the rank and file of the army was left with the nagging feeling that we certainly could have done better in our offensive operations. Except for Punch where we did remarkably well throwing back the Pak thrust and grabbing some enemy territory (though the situation couldn't be exploited to take the Haji Pir Pass), and for Ladakh where we captured the enemy posts overlooking our line of communication; our offensive manoeuvres lacked enthusiasm. A more determined push in Punjab and Rajasthan could have brought us rich dividends.

The uncomfortable fact also remained that the Pakistani offensive could not really be rated as all that high spirited. Once again, like in '48 and '65, they failed to match the indomitable fighting spirit of the ordinary Indian soldier. As it turned out, Pakistan ended up losers in the West as well, where they were neither outnumbered nor outgunned, as they could plead to have been in the East. They lost some 3000 square miles of their territory – 1200 in Sind, 850 in Kutch, 830 in Shakargarh and 30 on the Punjab Border. India had lost merely 50 square miles in Chhamb and Hussainiwala.

Eight battalions of the Madras Regiment were in action on the Western Front, four on the Punjab Border, three in Rajasthan, and one in J&K. The 3rd, 6th, 16th and the 17th Battalions of the Madras Regiment fought on the Punjab Border. 3 Madras (belonging to 65 Infantry Brigade under 7 Division of 11 Corps), commanded by Lieutenant Colonel

Jitendra Kumar, was deployed to hold the border posts in the Khalra area from October. The battalion found itself in an offensive role with the enemy thrust towards the Upper Bari Doab Canal (UBDC), as soon as the war broke out in December. It was assigned to retake the village of Kalsian Khurd by the UBDC some 400 yards from the international boundary, which had been lost to the enemy initially along with a border outpost sited there.

The single platoon that could be spared – with restrictions in force on the minimum strength to be maintained for defence – under a sharp-witted JCO, Subedar Perumal Pillai, set off on the mission in the wee hours of 6 December. Pinned down by shelling and automatic fire, Pillai split the platoon into two groups and encircled the village in a two-pronged move. With timely marksmanship they knocked off the observation post of the enemy artillery and rushed the objective. The enemy fell back in panic, abandoning the village. Elated, the battalion rushed in a mobile combat team with a recoilless gun under a hardy officer, Captain K Chandrasekhar, boosted by a troop of 3 Cavalry operating alongside. By the afternoon, Chandrasekhar, now in command of the force, had established a strong defensive position in the built-up area. Before nightfall he was reinforced by a section of 3 inch mortars and two sections of BSF.

The enemy counter-attacked during the night, only to be thrown back; to a great extent owing to the courage of one man, Havildar Shantayya, the Platoon Second-in-Command, who took it upon himself to enfilade the enemy assault, by opening up from the left flank single-handedly with a LMG. Through out the next day, 7 December, intense bombardment by the enemy artillery and tank fire as well as air strikes rocked the place, before they launched another counter-attack, a powerful one by two companies, during the night. Once again they were repulsed.

The shelling and air strikes continued during the following day, and during that night, 8/9 December, the enemy mounted a third counterattack. Both sides fought desperately. Enemy assault was often stopped short by bringing down our own artillery fire barely ten yards in front of the defenders, who made every small arms volley count with deadly effect by holding their fire to the last and firing with the enemy in their sights at close quarters. The position held. After this attack, though they kept the village under shelling, the enemy did not attempt to take it, and the war ended with 3 Madras still holding Kalsian Khurd. The battalion had lost 7 killed and 9 wounded, some of them mine casualties. Captain Chandrasekhar and Havildar Shantayya were both awarded the Sena Medal for their gallantry in the battle.

6 Madras, commanded by Lieutenant Colonel Ratan Singh, was concentrated in the Samba Sector at the commencement of the operations, under 91 Infantry Brigade of 39 Division with 1 Corps. After it had successfully withstood the initial onslaught of the enemy and captured a chain of villages across the border in counter strikes, the battalion was re-allocated to join 47 Infantry Brigade of 54 Division for operations on the Punjab Border. The brigade, along with 17 Poona Horse, had been assigned to secure a bridgehead across the river Basantar. 16 Madras, also with the same brigade, led the attack by storming the enemy position successfully, late in the evening on 15 December in the first phase of the operation. 6 Madras, earmarked to stage the fourth and final phase of the attack, was moved up early next morning to reinforce 16, by now being thronged by counter-attacks.

For the next more than thirty-six hours until the ceasefire fully came into effect, the battalion fought off one counter-attack after the other. A Company which was occupying the extreme right corner of Lalial, the locality to the right half of the captured objective, faced the worst, peppered constantly by aimed and effective automatic fire from close range. The Recoilless Guns Detachment Commander, Naik Jojula Sanyasi, was to turn a hero during the stand-off when in a single-handed exploit he took out an enemy machinegun. He was awarded the Vir Chakra. The battalion suffered 27 casualties in all, 6 men killed and 21 wounded, including an officer.

16 Madras, commanded by Lieutenant Colonel VP Ghai, did some of the toughest fighting the Indian Army saw in 1971. The battalion was part of 47 Infantry Brigade under 54 Infantry Division of 1 Corps, which launched the offensive in the Shakargarh bulge of Pakistan's Sialkot district. Leading the advance from the beginning, they captured various outposts. In a memorable action in the early hours of 7 December, a combat group of one company of the battalion and a squadron of 4 Horse surprised the enemy at Bari, overrunning the post. In subsequent actions on the 10th and 11th, they went on to capture two more posts, Baher and Nakki Gujran. But the most significant battle they fought – and one of the bravest and the bloodiest by any one unit in the whole war – was at the Lalial-Sarajchak complex across the Basantar, during the two nights and two days that followed the evening of 15 December.

The battalion, along with 3 Grenadiers, was assigned the task of securing a bridgehead across the river to induct tanks the following day. A two-phase attack was planned in which 16 Madras was to go in first and capture the twin features of Lalial and Sarajchak, followed by 3 Grenadiers taking Jarpal to the south of them. The enemy was well fortified in his defences in the two features, some 1000 yards from the western bank of the river. The river itself was heavily mined on either side and effectively covered by automatics' fire, rendering it a formidable obstacle. Unknown to the attackers, yet another line of enemy defences running along a parallel obstacle to the north, the Supwal Ditch, extended almost up to Lalial, imposing a factor that would add an ominous dimension to events as the battle developed. Two companies led the attack launched at 1930 hours; Major PV Sahadevan's C Company on the right going for Lalial, and Major CBS Krishnia's D Company on the left going for Sarajchak.

It was hammer and tongs all the way, right from the word go. The men raced across the obstacle in a hailstorm of bullets and shell bursts. The commanders of both the leading platoons of C Company had been wounded by the time the column had made it across the river. The company was being mauled by machineguns sited at the pillboxes of the Supwal Ditch, a nightmarish development no one had anticipated. Even with own artillery hammering the enemy up front and close, the going got so tough that some 400 yards short of the objective the assault almost floundered.

The hard-pressed Company Commander, Sahadevan, chose to turn the enemy's flank. He dispatched his No 8 Platoon under Havildar Thomas Philipose – the Platoon Commander, Naib Subedar Bhaskaran Nair, having been wounded and out of action – to swing off to the right and strike the enemy from up north. Philipose, a no-nonsense man with a never-say-die spirit, moved swiftly to lead a fierce flanking charge. Twice wounded and bleeding, he kept going until the platoon had stormed the troublesome bunkers and subdued the enemy; later to hold on to the captured area regardless of his wounds.

Sahadevan himself, crawling up close to a recoilless gun with a handful of his men, set its jeep ablaze by lobbing a grenade. There was panic in enemy's ranks, and Second Lieutenant PA Somaiah, following right behind with his No 9 Platoon, sensed the chance and unleashed a charge. The enemy fire withered, and the whole company pounced on the objective with bayonets. As the mortal hand-to-hand combat raged across the objective, Naik A Sahadevan, a namesake of the Company Commander, rushed an enemy machinegun in a daredevil bid and hurled a grenade to silence it. The gun indeed was silenced; so was the brave NCO, cut down by a burst that he took fully in the chest. The fighting continued for good about an hour before the enemy could be cleared off the entire objective, and the C Company's success flare went up at 2130 hours. 14 enemy soldiers were killed on the objective; and of our own, 9 had been killed and 30 wounded.

D Company, assaulting on the left, ran into almost similar opposition. Hardly had they stormed the forward bunkers, they were up against the fire from well-concealed positions in the built-up area behind. Then onwards it turned an arduous battle of flushing the enemy out from one position after the other. Krishnia, the Company Commander, went about it clinically, employing one platoon at a time in flanking moves, exercising utmost fire discipline. It was slow going; still they made it in fairly good time, and Sarajchak had been cleared by 2200 hours, just half an hour behind the C Company at Lalial. A body count in the morning gave the enemy dead on the objective as 15. Own losses were 11 killed and 27 wounded.

C Company, far too close to the Supwal Ditch for comfort of the enemy there, was by now being targeted intensely by their guns. The Pakistanis, stunned by the ferocity of the assault, soon gathered their wits and launched a blistering counter-attack about an hour before midnight. They closed in employing a ruse of imitating shouts and cries of other Indian troops; but it didn't get them far as the company rallied to take them on. Thomas Philipose, still on his feet, trumped his own exploit earlier by gathering his depleted platoon to lead a daring counter-charge. Battered badly, the enemy fell back in confusion and then fled, leaving three of their dead behind.

Even as C Company was battling it out at Lalial, the second phase of the battalion attack was well under way with A and B Companies going for the next two objectives, the twin features of 5r and 6r beyond Lalial and Sarajchak. As soon as the companies had executed the intricate manoeuvre of filtering the men through ranks of the lead companies holding the captured objectives, they struck out swiftly. Major JS Pathania with his B Company on the left went for an outflanking move to get at 5r from the southwest, completely surprising the enemy, to take the objective by 2300 hours.

However Major Mohinder Singh, moving on 6r from the right with his A Company, denied an outflanking option by the Supwal Ditch, had to go in for a blunt frontal assault. To compound matters, some of the enemy troops counter-attacking the C Company position at Lalial made a flanking entry to 6r, to intercede at the most dicey moment. It turned into a savage conflict wherein a resolute enemy had to be plucked out from bunker after bunker at the point of bayonets. One incident said it all; Sepoy Kotaiah who had thrust his bayonet into a Pak soldier's belly, had had his own thigh pierced by the same adversary. And his Platoon Commander, Naib Subedar Bhagiamani, shot dead another enemy soldier point blank as he made to grab Kotaiah. The fight ended by 2330 hours with 6r being taken. 20 of the enemy lay dead on 5r and 6r. Together, A and B Companies had lost 7 killed and 32 wounded.

The Grenadiers also captured their objective during the night and with the bridgehead formed, the tanks of 17 Poona Horse[1] – two troops – drove in early the next morning (16 December). The enemy artillery

1. The tanks of this celebrated armoured regiment were to play a pivotal role in beating back the enemy counter-attacks as the battle developed during the day. With barely one squadron strength of tanks available – the two troops inducted initially having been reinforced by two more later – to stop the enemy armour which outnumbered them almost ten to one, the Poona Horse men put up such a ferocious fight that they virtually wiped out two of Pakistan's famed cavalry regiments. Second Lieutenant Arun Khetarpal, a young officer commissioned only a few months earlier, became the Indian Army's ideal of ultimate courage under fire when he refused to abandon his burning tank when ordered to, with his legendary radio transmission, "My gun is still working sir". The lad, barely two months past his twenty-first birth day, was killed in action fighting to his last. He became the youngest soldier to be honoured with the nation's highest gallantry award, the Param Vir Chakra.

   Years later, in a touching gesture of outstanding chivalry, Brigadier Kwaja Mohammad Naser of the Pakistan Army, who, as a major during the war, commanded the squadron of 13 Lancers which was pitched against the Poona Horse tanks in the battle, was to praise the Indian youngster's valour in glowing terms. The Pakistani Brigadier insisted on being the host to Arun's father, Brigadier ML Khetarpal (an accomplished officer of the Madras Sappers), who was visiting his birth place in Pakistan with his family; so that he could tell the older man all about it, and feel at peace with himself for his role in the death of someone so young and brave, albeit in the line of his duty as a soldier. The gallant Pakistani officer's note, that accompanied some photographs he sent to his guest later, epitomized the nobility of the universal brotherhood of men in arms; and starkly revealed the tragedy of the fratricidal conflict that goes on between India and Pakistan, wherein good men are made to kill each other in wars which are not of their making. It read:

   "*To Brigadier* ML Khetarpal, father of Shaheed Second Lieutenant Arun Khetarpal, PVC, who stood like an insurmountable rock, between victory and failure of the counter-attack by the 'SPEARHEADS' 13 Lancers on 16 December 1971 in the battle of 'Bara Pind' as we call it, and battle of 'Basantar' as 17 Poona Horse remembers. Brigadier Khwaja Mohammad Naser, 13 Lancers; 02 March 2001, Lahore, Pakistan." (Source: Internet)

kept pounding the position with a vengeance; and past 1000 hours, with the shelling at its crescendo, a major counter-attack was in the offing; the enemy concentrating more than a regiment of tanks and a battalion of infantry to the north. VP Ghai, the Battalion Commander, reacted fast, moving troops from Sarajchak and 5r to Lalial and 6r which were under immediate threat. A furious battle soon took shape with the enemy assaulting in wave after wave. It became one desperate contest for the battalion with the attackers surging forward menacingly close.

Ghai, true to the finest traditions of the officer corps, led from the front, moving right under fire, relocating men and keeping them steadfast by personal example. The position held against overwhelming odds, until at last after two blood-curdling efforts the enemy called it a day. Their dead soldiers and smouldering tanks littered the battlefield. The battalion had paid heavily for the victory. Its brave commander, Ghai, had fallen prey to machinegun fire and shell burst; so had the medical officer, Captain Surendranath, who had made a gallant bid to attend to the fallen CO.

Late in the evening on the 16th the enemy counter-attacked again. The battalion now under the command of Major RP Sharma, Ghai's Second-in-Command, fought back as resolute as ever to throw the enemy back once again. But the Pakistanis were not done in yet. Early morning on 17 December they came in a big way, preceded by their aircraft strafing the position. The ground attack came at 0700 hours. They gave their best; but it wasn't good enough against the plucky warriors of the 'Shining Sixteenth'. Battle-weary, but hardened by more than thirty-six hours of intense combat, they fought like the devils. The attack was brutally rolled back with the enemy finding their enormously mounting casualties no more acceptable.

The battalion didn't come through it very lightly either. The new CO's (Sharma's) valiant command lasted barely a day – he fell like his predecessor, cut down in action while leading his men to greater glory. The rest of the officers weren't any less either with their fiery brand of leadership in the battle. The Adjutant, Major V Mahalingam, wounded but refusing to be evacuated and rallying the men against odds, set an inspiring pattern. Second Lieutenant Shivcharan Singh, the Intelligence Officer, young but full of courage, was killed in action. Another officer, Captain JP Singh, could be seen bodily evacuating the casualties himself fully exposed to fire.

The Pakistanis made their last desperate bid to overrun the bridgehead towards sunset on the 17th. Once again, despite the fatigue and mounting casualties, the battalion held on doggedly until the attack was repulsed. The battle died down after that, and the ceasefire was on by the next morning. That day, 18 December, the men of 11 Baluch, the Pakistani unit which had faced the Madras Battalion, carried away their dead from the area. 40 bodies were counted; merely a portion of the many the Pakistanis had had to count at Basantar. Repeated efforts by the bulk of their 8 Independent Armoured Brigade and 124 Infantry Brigade to overrun the Indian bridgehead had come to bear no fruit, and had cost them heavily.

'The Battle of Basantar' was over. It was a magnificent battle – the kind of stuff legends are made of. The casualty count of 16 Madras at the end of the war showed, 5 officers and 27 JCOs and Other Ranks killed, and 1 officer and 103 JCOs and Other Ranks wounded; a total of 136 casualties, among them, the unit's Commanding Officer, Second-in-Command, Adjutant, and three more officers. Lieutenant Colonel VP Ghai was awarded the Maha Vir Chakra posthumously. A second Maha Vir Chakra was awarded to Havildar Thomas Philipose of C Company for exceptional gallantry at Lalial. C Company's Commander, Major PV Sahadevan, was awarded a Vir Chakra; so was Naik A Sahadevan and the Regimental Medical Officer, Captain Surendranath, the latter two posthumously. The impressive tally of the gallantry awards won by the battalion during the 1971 War included two more Vir Chakras, 2 Sena Medals and 6 Mention-in-Dispatches.

17 Madras, operating off Muktsar under 116 Infantry Brigade of 14

Division (Command Reserve allotted to 11 Corps), captured two enemy outposts, Killi Sahu on 13 December and Churka on 17 December. Brief but sharp engagements, they won the unit five gallantry awards: a Vir Chakra to Naik Vasudevan Bhaskaran for his heroic initiative at Killi Sahu in silencing an enemy machinegun, a Sena Medal to Lieutenant Uday Shankar for his outstandingly courageous leadership in that battle, two more Sena Medals to Naib Subedar Kunhikrishnan and Sepoy Selvarajan Naidu for displaying exceptional bravery at Churka, and a Mention-in-Dispatches to Second Lieutenant Agarwal for his courageous initiative in the same engagement. One officer and three men being wounded were the only casualties the battalion suffered. The unit continued to be deployed on the banks of Sutlej after the ceasefire as part of the defences for a while.

The battalions engaged in Rajasthan were 9, 18 and 27 Madras. 9 Madras, commanded by Lieutenant Colonel DB White, which formed part of 330 Infantry Brigade under 11 Division, began the operations by joining the main offensive of the sector launched on 4 December on the Gadra City-Nayachor Axis. Temporarily placed under 31 Infantry Brigade in the initial phase, it took part in the capture of Gadra City before being assigned to 85 Infantry Brigade, which captured Khokhro Par subsequently. On 6 December the battalion went on to capture Mahendra Ro Par on the Gadra City-Umarkot Axis, before being reverted to 330 Brigade to join the main thrust on Nayachor. The division hit the enemy screen on the 12th. During the night 13/14 December a salient of prime tactical significance, Parbat Ali, was taken. Reconnaissance found Nayachor to be strongly held, and a divisional attack was planned to tackle it. This called for large scale preparations involving construction of vehicular tracks and laying of rail lines to facilitate forward concentration. The offensive was inevitably stalled, and the war ended with the enemy still holding Nayachor.

During the reconnaissance phase, a deep penetration patrol of 9 Madras had gone as far as Khat Singh. The battalion had advanced beyond Point 315, a strongly held enemy position, when the ceasefire came into effect. Captain R Gopakumar was awarded the Vir Chakra for the extraordinary initiative and boldness with which he conducted quite a few dangerous missions. The unit suffered 10 casualties during the operations; 2 killed and 8 wounded.

18 Madras, commanded by Lieutenant Colonel VS Parmar, made the Indian Army's deepest thrust in the western desert, as part of 31 Infantry Brigade of 11 Division, by advancing 285 kilometres on foot during the operations, and fought a fierce battle at Hingoro Tar in Sind, Pakistan. Initially they were involved in the capture of Gadra where 9 Madras was engaged too. In the exploitation phase of that operation they took a hamlet, Mahadan Ki Dhani, and brushing aside minor resistance moved up to Chachro in Sind, 80 kilometres short of the Pak defences at Umarkot, by 14 December. Ordered to form up in front of Umarkot, the battalion covered the distance in 48 hours without food or water, surviving on emergency rations, to contact the enemy on the afternoon of 16 December. Firming in beyond the village Hingoro Tar they probed forward, a platoon occupying one end of a sand dune held by the enemy. By then the battalion had outdistanced its artillery support, except for a light battery that fetched up by dusk on 16 December with its stock of ammunition almost exhausted.

The enemy, after subjecting the battalion to intense shelling during the night 16-17 December put in an attack on the 17th. Although the initial attack was beaten back, the battalion had to withdraw some distance under a second attack after about three hours of intense fighting, to a position where proper artillery cover was available. Captain SS Walker, the Mortar Officer of the battalion, whose leadership proved pivotal during the defence of Hingoro Tar and was killed in action, was awarded the Maha Vir Chakra posthumously. Two more of the fallen heroes, Subedar AP Sreedharan and Naik Mani, who both showed exceptional gallantry, were awarded the Vir Chakras posthumously. Four others, Major RG Shastry, Naik KM Haneefa, Naik N Sathyam and Sepoy Bhaskaran Nair, were awarded the Sena Medals. The battalion suffered 31 casualties: 1 officer, 1 JCO and 16 Other Ranks killed, and 3 officers,

2 JCOs and 8 Other Ranks wounded.

27 Madras, a battalion raised just six months prior to the operations (1 June 1971), joined action at Asutar in Jaisalmer Sector on 5 December, to reinforce 12 Infantry Division under attack at Longewala. Taking up position at Asutar they blunted the enemy thrust. After the situation stabilized they were moved to Kutch to contain an enemy intrusion. Although it was achieved, the CO of the battalion, Lieutenant Colonel AO Alexander, was killed along with six of his men, and another four men were wounded, when a reconnaissance patrol of theirs was ambushed across the international border.

19 Madras, commanded by Lieutenant Colonel AS Sidhu, the only battalion of the Regiment to be engaged in J&K, was initially deployed to defend the Ramgarh Ditch, but was inducted into Chamb-Jaurian Sector by 11 December. However since the situation in that sector had stabilized once the Pak attempts to cross the Munawar-Tawi had been thwarted, the battalion was moved back to its original location. They were then engaged in aggressive patrolling of the enemy defences in preparation for an offensive. Though the unit operated constantly under heavy artillery shelling and strafing at various locations during the operations, they were not directly engaged in any major battle. Consequently they suffered no casualties. Nevertheless they were winners of two gallantry awards; one Sena Medal to Naik Daniel Jacob for shooting down an enemy aircraft and one Mention-in-Dispatches to Captain TV Kannan for courage under fire while patrolling.

The Madras Regiment won the Battle Honour, BASANTAR RIVER and the Theatre Honours, PUNJAB 1971 and SINDH 1971, for the operations in the Western Theatre during 1971.

Seven regiments of the MEG, 1, 5, 7, 8, 9, 10 and 201, saw action on the Punjab Border; while two regiments, 6 and 14, were engaged in J&K, and one, 12, was engaged in Ladakh. On the Punjab Border, 1 (Lieutenant Colonel DSR Sahni), 8 (Lieutenant Colonel BM Seth) and 10 (Lieutenant Colonel K Kumaran) Engineer Regiments were in defensive role, and the remaining six regiments were part of one or the other offensive.

5 (Lieutenant Colonel OP Grower) and 9 (Lieutenant Colonel BT Pandit) Regiments advanced with 54 Infantry Division in its thrust towards Zafarwal, culminating in the Battle of Basantar, breaching minefields all the way.

The battle of Basantar turned out to be as much a glorious battle for the Madras Sappers, as it did for the Madras Regiment. Their contribution to facilitating the induction of tanks into the battle was immense. Major VR Chowdhary, commanding 405 Field Company of 9 Engineer Regiment, was killed in action during his gallant bid of supervising the breaching operations under intense shelling, while acting as the officer-in-charge of minefield clearance at Chakra across the Basantar. The officer's sacrifice didn't go in vain; his Sappers succeeded in breaching the minefields up to 1600 yards in depth with tank trawls – the first time the concept was tried in an operation – that ultimately made it possible for the tanks and anti-tank weapons to be moved across during the battle. He was awarded the Maha Vir Chakra posthumously. One of his JCOs, Naib Subedar Doraiswamy whose initiative in making a bypass for the tanks proved pivotal (when their passage was blocked by damaged ones), was awarded the Vir Chakra.

The battle of Basantar claimed the life of one more officer of the Madras Sappers. Captain Ravindranath Gupta had volunteered for a reconnaissance of the wide frontage of enemy minefield across the Basantar. His report was to prove of crucial significance when the tanks were inducted. Unfortunately this brave and resolute officer fell to enemy fire while working on improving the crossing on 17 Decmber, the day the battle was finally won. He was posthumously decorated with the Vir Chakra.

7 Engineer Regiment (Lieutenant Colonel VP Yadav) was part of the I Corps offensive in Shakargarh, supporting 72 Infantry Brigade and 2 Independent Armoured Brigade. In a daring bid they breached the minefield at Tugialpur in broad daylight. The advance had come to

a halt before the sappers could be provided a bridgehead, due to stiff enemy opposition and confusion about the location of the minefield. Undeterred, the Regiment got on with their job without waiting for the night. The Officer Commanding 61 Field Company, Major VK Bhaskar, set the pattern by walking right across the minefield to study its extent and type, absolutely aware that it was covered by fire and that he was making himself an easy moving target. Not too far from the officer was a bigger and more tempting moving target; a mine digger operated by Lance Naik Thyagarajan of 664 Plant Company. The officer was awarded a Vir Chakra and the NCO a Sena Medal.

201 Engineer Regiment (Lieutenant Colonel JP Thapliyal) with 36 Infantry Division faced its challenge when the division had to cross the river Ravi, a move not planned earlier. The site available to put up a bridge was that of a ferry, and a registered enemy target. A mile-long sandy approach posed more of a problem than the river itself. The Regiment made it to the water line by midnight 8/9 December. The enemy guns pounding the site claimed 1 sapper killed and 5 wounded; but they had erected a 1350-foot bridge-cum-causeway across the river before sunrise. The Division crossed over and advanced 20 miles within the next 36 hours to come up against Shakargarh.

6 Engineer Regiment (Lieutenant Colonel Thapper) supported 26 Infantry Division in its brilliant strike that cut off the Chicken's Neck Bulge in Jammu held by the enemy, and foiled his move on Akhnur. 14 Engineer Regiment (Lieutenant Colonel MS Kandal) was engaged in keeping the Srinagar and Awantipur airfields in Kashmir operational despite the havoc bombing caused, and the disposal of unexploded bombs.

In Ladakh, 12 Engineer Regiment (Lieutenant Colonel MM Kumar) supported the Ladakh Scouts in their dynamic foray along the Shyok Valley to capture Turtok and Chalunka.

The MEG won the Battle Honour, BASANTAR RIVER, and the Theatre Honours, JAMMU AND KASHMIR 1971 and PUNJAB 1971, for the operations on the Western Front.

Of 16 Cavalry, only one squadron deployed in the Ikhlaspur-Shakargarh area of the Sialkot Sector could see action in 1971. This was the only unit to contact Shakargarh. The personnel of the regiment won 2 Sena Medals and 6 Mention-in-despatches, besides a Commendation Card from the Chief of Army Staff.

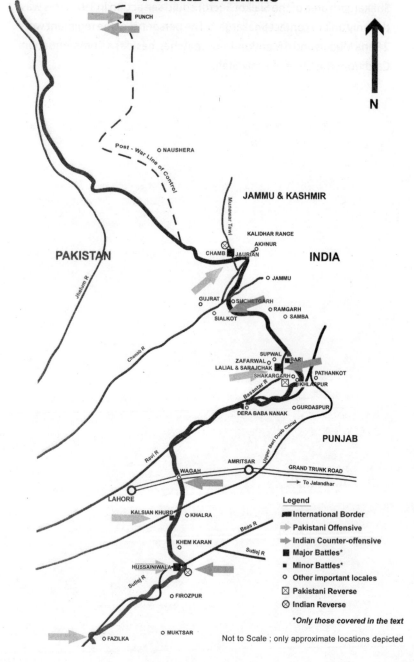

WESTERN FRONT 1971
PUNJAB & JAMMU

N

■ PUNCH

Post - War Line of Control

○ NAUSHERA

JAMMU & KASHMIR

KALIDHAR RANGE

AKHNUR

PAKISTAN

CHAMB ⊗ JAURIAN

Munawar Tawi

INDIA

○ JAMMU

Jhelum R

GUJRAT ○ ⊗ SUCHETGARH

○ SIALKOT

○ RAMGARH

○ SAMBA

Chenab R

SUPWAL

ZAFARWAL ○ ■ BARI

LALIAL & SARAJCHAK ○

SHAKARGARH ⊠ DIKHLASPUR

PATHANKOT ■

Basantar R

DERA BABA NANAK ○

○ GURDASPUR

PUNJAB

Ravi R

AMRITSAR ○

Upper Bari Doab Canal

WAGAH ○

GRAND TRUNK ROAD

→ To Jalandhar

○ LAHORE

KALSIAN KHURD ○ ○ KHALRA

Beas R

KHEM KARAN ○

Sutlej R

HUSSAINIWALA ■ ⊗

○ FIROZPUR

Sutlej R

○ FAZILKA

○ MUKTSAR

Legend

■ International Border
➡ Pakistani Offensive
➡ Indian Counter-offensive
■ Major Battles*
■ Minor Battles*
○ Other important locales
⊠ Pakistani Reverse
⊗ Indian Reverse

Only those covered in the text

Not to Scale ; only approximate locations depicted

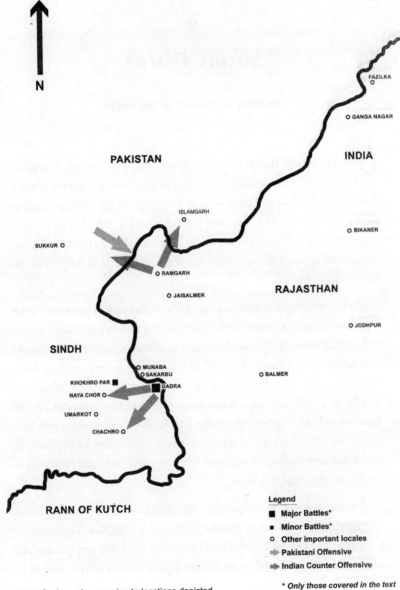

WESTERN FRONT 1971
RAJASTHAN SECTOR

N

PAKISTAN

INDIA

FAZILKA

GANGA NAGAR

ISLAMGARH

BIKANER

SUKKUR

RAMGARH

JAISALMER

RAJASTHAN

JODHPUR

SINDH

MUNABA
SAKARBU
KHOKHRO PAR
NAYA CHOR
GADRA
BALMER

UMARKOT

CHACHRO

RANN OF KUTCH

Legend
■ Major Battles*
▪ Minor Battles*
○ Other important locales
➡ Pakistani Offensive
➡ Indian Counter Offensive

Only those covered in the text

Not to Scale ; only approximate locations depicted

6

SIACHEN GLACIER

Battling on the roof of the world

Pakistanis have always been bad losers. Three successive defeats at the hands of the Indian armed forces in as many decades of their country's existence did little to alter their ego to try one-upmanship with India; and in 1984, less than a decade and a half after its historic humiliation in the paddy fields of Bengal, the Pakistani military was up to its tricks again, this time around in the uninhabitable heights of the Siachen Glacier.

75 kilometres long and varying in width from 2 to 8 kilometres, the Siachen Glacier lies lapped in the world's most forbidding mountainous region that make up the northwestern extremity of India. Forming part of the Karakoram Range beyond Ladakh in the Jammu and Kashmir State, it occupies some 10,000 square kilometres, at heights rising from 12,000 to 23,000 feet above sea level. After the first Indo-Pak War of 1947-48 the old kingdom of Jammu and Kashmir was divided into two along the ceasefire line, which left India in possession of the current J&K State comprising the southern Jammu, the central Kashmir, and the northern Ladakh regions.

The ceasefire line survived the 1965 War, since both sides returned the captured territories as per the Tashkent Accord. But it got altered to the current Line of Control (LoC) after the 1971 War since India had unilaterally declared the ceasefire, rendering neither party obliged to return the seized territory. However the starting and terminating points of the LoC remained unchanged. It terminates to the north at a point in the Karakoram Range, identified by the map reference NJ 980420, popularly referred as NJ 9842, the area beyond having been considered worthless militarily, being void of human habitation. The LoC from NJ 9842 was vaguely defined by the agreement to extend 'thence north to the glaciers' right up to China's southern boundary. The genesis of the Siachen conflict lay in the interpretation of that definition by India and Pakistan.

After the Sino-Indian War of 1962, the Chinese returned all territories they had occupied in the Northeast (practically the whole of what is Arunachal Pradesh today), but had held on to their gains in the Ladakh Sector, apparently for their need to secure the Aksai Chin Highway between Leh and the province of Zinjiang in Southern China. A year later they also managed a boundary settlement on the Karakoram with Pakistan, wherein the latter 'yielded' the Shaksgam Valley, an area of 4853 square kilometers, out of what was rightfully Indian Territory. The southern boundary of China was thus pushed closer to J&K. In less than two years work started on the Karakoram Highway between Pakistan and China, which was completed in 1978. Now there were two highways, one from Tibet to Zinjiang in China and the other from Northern Pakistan to Zinjiang, aligned close to the region, raising serious security concerns for India.

Pakistan began the mischief with a cartographic misrepresentation early in 1980s, displaying the LoC on its maps as a straight line proceeding northeastward from NJ 9842 to the Karakoram Pass. Surprisingly, in the 1970s itself, inadvertently or otherwise, some international publications of repute too have been showing the LoC wrongly aligned on their maps. Alongside, Pakistan had also been actively encouraging international mountaineering expeditions into the Karakoram from its territory. By 1978, alerted by the faulty international maps, and indications of Pakistan staking claims to the area by projecting the expeditions launched from its territory as proof, India too began to undertake mountaineering expeditions. It was the beginning of a mountaineering contest between the two militaries. Exchange of protest notes followed, each party complaining of the other intruding into its territory. Finally in August 1983, through one of the notes, Pakistan made its intention clear by asserting its own interpretation of the LoC, to be leading straight northeastward to the Karakoram Pass from NJ 9842.

The first Indian expedition led by the renowned army mountaineer, Colonel N 'Bull' Kumar[1], to Teram Kangri, brought indisputable evidence of the foreign expeditions entering the glacier from the Pakistan side. The army had also had evidence of an abortive attempt Pakistan made in September-October 1983 to occupy passes west of the glacier. Intelligence received in January 1984, of Pakistan's large-scale purchases of high altitude equipment, removed whatever doubt there might have been of its intentions. The Indian Army, obtaining the government's approval, occupied the Saltoro Range west of the glacier. This was essentially in keeping with the definition of the LoC extending 'thence north to the glaciers' from NJ 9842, since 'north' by the conventional logic of delineating a geographical boundary, meant northward along the nearest watershed[2], which in this case happened to be Saltoro.

The main pass in the Saltoro Range is Bilafond La, which Pakistan has been using to cross over. There was yet another negotiable pass, the Sia La. It was decided to deny these passes to the enemy as a precautionary measure. A small military presence of the kind, which was a cost-effective option, was considered sufficient to contain the Pak adventurism. The word 'Siachen' means mountain rose, which grew in abundance near the snout of the glacier. 'Pakistan has been getting into our rose garden by the gate of Bilafond La', said a simile among the army planners. 'Let

---

1. An Everest veteran and a legendary mountaineer who had lost some toes to frost bite, Colonel (later Brigadier) Kumar, was eventually to become a Fellow of the Royal Geographic Society.
2. Colonel Kumar's expedition, which climbed many of the major peaks on either side of the glacier, confirmed Saltoro as the highest watershed in the area, separating the two large glacier systems, the Baltoro to the west and the Siachen to the east.

us close the gate permanently'. And so it was closed.

Bilafond La was at an altitude of 18,000 feet, and Sia La another 2000 feet higher. The induction and sustenance of troops at such extremes of terrain and weather posed a logistics challenge no army in the world had ever had to face. But the senior commanders involved –Lieutenant General ML Chibber and Major General Shiv Sharma – contended that 'it would be easier to fight the elements than a determined enemy'. If the Pakistanis occupied the passes first, it would be a military impossibility to dislodge them, given the advantages such heights offered to the defender. It had to be done, and the army geared up to take the bull by the horn.

Troops were to be inducted in April 1984 as soon as the weather permitted, to pip the enemy at the post. A heli-borne operation was the only option, since the enemy air reconnaissance would have picked up any troop movement on foot. The transport helicopters India had at the time just couldn't reach such heights. The only machine that could do it, the Cheetah – indigenous model of the Alouette – could barely carry two men. Even then there was no infrastructure that would need to conduct an operation of such magnitude. It became a race against time to put in place the aviation fuel, technical support, landing and holding facilities and suchlike. 'Operation Meghdoot' was on.

The first troops to land, one officer and two men, jumped down from their hovering copters 3 kilometres short of Bilafond La on 13 April 1984. (To land the copter in soft snow without ascertaining the ground condition would have been suicidal.) Gritty and courageous, the three men, swiftly identified safe spots for copters to land, and reinforced them with some sacks of flour for the skids to touch down. The machines could now land. It took seventeen sorties for a platoon to be ferried across, as the weather held mercifully. A lance naik at the head of a small party soon made it to the pass and raised the Tricolour. Before the day was over the platoon had occupied the Bilafond La Pass. These men were now on their own with no artillery to support them, and except for the fragile radio link, cut off from the rest of the world until the next copter sortie arrived.

Frequently as it occurs at high altitude, the weather suddenly turned foul with a raging blizzard, and the second lift, which was to follow immediately carrying the next platoon to Sia La at a higher altitude, had to be put off. To compound matters, with the drop in temperature the radio contact with the platoon at Bilafond La was lost. It would be three days before the weather cleared and the platoon made contact again. It was safe; and working on the position. The second lift for Sia La was taken up on 17 April.

The Indian Air Force flew 32 sorties to Sia La that day, with hardly any technical support, creating a record in itself. The troops, put down 5 kilometres short, made the gruesome trek over the slopes the same day to occupy the pass. With the weather holding, some supplies could be ferried across to Bilafond La as well. The Pakistanis didn't take too long to find out what had happened. The same afternoon one of their copters flew over the passes. What they saw below couldn't have left them with any doubts – they had been thoroughly outsmarted.

The reaction of the Pakistan Army was as fast as any that could be expected of a force under the situation. In a week's time, the 'Burzil Force', a task force they had raised to occupy the passes under an operation codenamed 'Abadeel', had been spurred on to faster pace; and barely after a week of the Indian presence being sighted on the passes, forward elements of the force had appeared on the western slopes of the Bilafond La. Tough going as it would have been, the Burzil Force, made up of hardy men from their Special Services Group and the Northern Light Infantry, closed up on the passes and opened fire with small arms and machineguns on 25 April. The war of Siachen – in effect the contest for the domination of the Saltoro Range – to be fought ever since in the world's highest known battlefield, had just begun.

Taking the passes by assault was of course, a tactical impossibility. The Pakistan Army, stung by the public criticism back home (Benazir

Bhutto minced no words while ridiculing Zia-ul-Haq's military regime for its impotency at Siachen), went into overdrive to salvage its prestige; desperately trying to get a foothold anywhere on the Saltoro Ridge, only to be beaten back in every attempt.

Tactically it was adequate to hold the passes to deny access to the glacier to an intruder. However Pakistan's repeated efforts to occupy the ridges along the heights, which would have given them no tactical advantage but only scored political points, forced India's hand to counter the moves by occupying the heights themselves. (An easier option would have been to take the fight to the enemy by attacking him at chosen points; but approval for such a move was not forthcoming from the Government of India.) Soon what was perceived to be a small military presence of a company of infantry or so, turned into a major deployment of troops to the strength of a brigade. And that set in motion a logistics endeavour of unprecedented proportions.

Comparatively Pakistan was better placed to provide logistics support to her troops in the area, with a fairly elaborate network of roads and tracks on that side; whereas India had to support her troops almost exclusively by air. Beyond the Ladakh Range the supplies had to be first ferried over the Khardung La Pass to Shyok Valley along a road at a height of more than 18,000 feet – the highest of the kind in the world – which was open for only part of the year. A bridge where the road passed through a small glacier had to be reconstructed every summer. From the Shyok Valley the stores then had to be ferried across to the glacier, from where the helicopters, both medium and small, lifted the loads to where the troops actually held ground.

An infantry deployment of the magnitude, wherein the troops had to beat back persistent attacks on their posts, called for enormous artillery support, which meant more and more guns, spares and ammunition. While the army tried its best to improve the two roads to Ladakh over the Zojila and Baralacha La Passes to pump in as much supplies as possible during the summer months, the posts along the Saltoro had still had to be supplied by helicopters round the year. This meant a heavy demand for these machines which the army just didn't have. And no post could be kept short of essentials – shortage of ammunition could mean the loss of a post, which probably could never be retaken; if there was no kerosene for heating, men would freeze to death. The army's resources were being stretched to the limit.

By 1986 Pakistanis had become so feverish that they began mounting one suicidal attack after the other to gain a presence on the ridge somehow, flouting every tactical consideration. These brave but foolhardy attacks, against a well-entrenched enemy holding high ground, brought them colossal amount of casualties. Then the unbelievable happened. The Pakistani Special Services Group, in a spectacular feat of mountaineering in March-April 1987, established a post atop a vertical cliff 21,153 feet high. Pakistan's first foothold on the Saltoro Ridge, it overlooked the Bilafond La area, and artillery fire directed from the post could disrupt India's heli-borne activities at the pass.

The Pakistan Army and the media went to town blaring out the big news. They staked their national honour on the remote post by naming it 'Quaid', after Quaide-e-Azam, the founder of Pakistan. India had a 'thorn in its flesh', as the Northern Army Commander perceived. On 19 April the post opened fire, revealing its presence, to hit a helicopter evacuating casualties from Bilafond La, killing two soldiers and injuring one. Immediate reconnaissance found ropes slung for the climb, but more information was needed on what was atop before something could be done about it.

Helicopters dropped a patrol made up of an officer, a JCO and seven men on a nearby post where they were to get acclimatized, before taking up reconnaissance of Quaid. After the nightfall on 24 May, they climbed the ice wall on the northern face of the cliff and fixed ropes for an assault group to climb later. The feat, as outstanding as what the Pakistanis had accomplished, was all that was expected of the patrol

- explore and prepare the route to Quaid. But the daredevilry of the patrol leader wouldn't let him leave it at that. Having reached the ridge, the patrol crawled forward with fire support from a nearby post, which didn't amount to much for too long a range and poor visibility. The Pakistanis, alerted by the firing, opened machinegun fire on the patrol as it closed in, killing the patrol leader and four others. The four remaining members of the patrol made it back to own post by a super human effort, one of them only to die of his wounds. Few reconnaissance patrols had ever paid so heavily in lives, and achieved so much. The information it brought was priceless; and the ropes it fixed would now be used for an attack proper of the post.

The attack, by an all-volunteer force of 60 men under two officers, could be put in only after almost a month while the men got acclimatized and stores were stockpiled. Even as it got going on the evening of 23 June, it took the force five hours to cover a kilometre in the waist-deep snow, and then they found that the ropes the earlier patrol had fixed could no longer be located, with layers of snow all over. Left with not enough time before daylight, they made a tactical retreat, aided by a diversionary attack at another point to distract the enemy. Eventually however they had to risk exposure in the daylight before the ropes could be traced. They were there, and in tact.

Come night they launched the attack again. But as soon as the climb started the enemy opened up. The element of surprise had been lost. To compound matters the men found that the freezing temperature had rendered their weapons faulty. The attack had again had to be called off; the men spent another day in the open reorganizing.

During the following night (25-26 June), they made it to the top. Inching forward atop the cliff, six men under a JCO opened the fight with small arms and grenades. But the enemy reaction was swift and brutal with the defender's patent advantage. Some of the attackers were mowed down – one even rolled down the enemy's side of the mountain – and the others could make no headway. The assault had been blunted.

Nevertheless the force commander pressed forward another attack from a different direction, and this one in broad daylight (The attack went in around midday 26 June). Barely six men could form up as an assault group. The minuscule group closed in throwing grenades on what appeared to be the enemy command post. The Pakistanis rushed out to take them on. In the bloody hand-to-hand fight that ensued the Indians prevailed. Some of the Pakistanis were bayoneted; the others jumped down the mountain to perish. The ropes to the Pakistani side were promptly cut. 'Quaid' had been taken; 'the thorn in the flesh' removed.

If the Pakistanis had done the unbelievable, the Indians had done the impossible. It was an unparalleled feat in the annals of military history the world over, of troops having stormed and taken an enemy strongpoint at an altitude of over 21,000 feet. Out of the 60-strong force assembled for the mission, not more than a dozen or so could be put in to stage the actual assault. The final assault was led by Naib Subedar Bana Singh, who was later awarded Param Vir Chakra, the nation's highest gallantry award. And the captured post was renamed after him. 'Quaid', named after Pakistan's founder, would thenceforth be known as 'Bana' Post, named after one of India's bravest sons. And the legend of its capture would, for ever, remain a source of inspiration for all ranks of the Indian armed forces.

Better logistics support enabled the Pakistanis to maintain an aggressive forward presence constantly, despite their failure to dislodge the Indians from the ridge anywhere. With their posts so close and up front they could continually harass the Indian positions with artillery fire. It became imperative for India to go on the offensive instead of merely maintaining the defensive posture. Attacking the enemy forward posts wasn't an option available, since that would have escalated the conflict along the LoC. Eventually, the officers and men engaged at the heights themselves came up with a grand innovation – it called for the use of artillery on an offensive role.

With no civilian population around in the area, the guns could fire anywhere. The Bofors Howitzers and the 130 mm Soviet guns together packed a massive firepower, with devastating accuracy. And the heights occupied by Indians offered an excellent view of the glaciers, where Pakistanis had put up their supply dumps. All that was needed was for artillery observation posts to be located on these vantage points, and to provide them with some modern high-powered telescopes fitted with cameras that could give pictures with clarity. An effective fire plan could then be worked out. The gunners in small teams had to occupy these posts unobserved by the enemy whenever a shoot had to be undertaken, and pull out quietly as soon as it was over. The enemy would know what hit them, but not how.

The gunners went at it with gusto, and the effect was sheerly fantastic. Pak ammunition and fuel dumps burned like mad. Their vehicle convoys and pack mules were forced to choose the disastrous option of moving only after dark. Finally they had to pull back post after post. And often the Indian gunners went after their relocated posts. In frustration, the Pakistanis retaliated firing wildly with their guns at spots where they assumed the Indian OPs to be. This exposed their gun positions, which too were promptly engaged by Indians. The game was generally over for the Pakistanis; they could no more maintain an offensive posture. They just had to stay out of sight, and out of fight.

But Pakistan couldn't and wouldn't do that for too long. A nation borne out of mistrust, its regime after regime had traditionally come to stake its credibility and survival on how much each of them could fool its people with a single point agenda of hatred towards India; the poverty of its millions be damned. Its military leadership soon contrived a plan to isolate Siachen by cutting off its main line of communication. The Kargil heights were to be occupied to disrupt the Srinagar-Leh Road, followed by a thrust on the Shyok River. The plan however was shelved for whatever reasons. They would of course have a crack at it in little over a decade's time before the century ended. But then that's another story.

1986 to 1989 was the period of the hottest contest at the Saltoro. Pakistan made one last bid in early 1989. Air reconnaissance in April that year detected them to have occupied a post in the Chumik Glacier sector. A well-chosen post, it could only be identified by copters flying close. And the cliff was so vertical that there was no way the Indians could climb from their side. But then the Indian Army by now was seasoned in high-altitude combat, and had its techniques sharpened to perfection. The gunners went about it without much ado. They had a problem of the enemy support base being located too close to the cliff, where it was totally obscured and immune to shelling. Some OPs had to be put up at vantage points from where the base could be viewed properly; and the Bofors came in handy again. The trajectories and the angle of descent of shells had to be worked out; and then they were at the job. The supply base was hit so badly that the Pakistanis were soon asking for a meeting – and mercy – to pull out their post. And thus ended – and rather in disgrace – yet another Pakistani bid at the Saltoro.

The Indians had achieved indisputable supremacy at the Siachen. But that in no way ended this disastrously expensive conflict. With an adversary like Pakistan who could never be trusted to play the fair game, there was no way India could abandon the Saltoro to leave the glacier a no-man's-land; which should ideally be the choice for two neighbours like India and Pakistan, who both could use the money for far better things than sustaining a mutually destructive conflict for an expanse of wasteland where no human being can live. It is a hopeless and perverse situation, with the Pakistani military never getting tired of deceiving its own countrymen and the whole world by its ridiculously false propaganda of fighting the Indians at Siachen, when in reality their soldiers can not even see Siachen from where they are.

The Siachen Conflict which goes on and on to this day has no parallels in military history, or in any on-going contests anywhere. It is a war that is fought every day, from the corridors of power in the nation's capital to the snowy peaks of Saltoro where men struggle to keep alive. The glacier has nothing to offer but ice, mud and rocks. Every conceivable commodity that sustains human life has to be brought in from outside. And it is not a dozen-strong mountaineering expedition that is involved; 3000 fighting men hold the front line at Saltoro. At the heights of the likes of 20,000 feet they need everything more, whether it is food, clothing or shelter, just to live. Then to fight they need their arms, equipment and ammunition; all maintained and kept ready in operational fitness. Add to this that every bit of item to the glacier has to be brought in by helicopters, after being transported forward along a road system that is open for only six months a year; the army has a logistics war in hand that baffles imagination.

It is not as if the entire government machinery is backing the army to the hilt in this monstrous task. The apathy of the civilian establishment, whether bureaucratic or political, is both criminal and treasonable. Having engaged the army in an impossible war, they are content to drag their feet with peace time procedures of accounting and audit. It took a long time and a heck of a lot of persuasion for New Delhi to realize the all-important role of helicopters in high altitude warfare, and provide the army with the barely-essential number of these machines. The smaller Cheetah Helicopters are virtually the lifeline of the troops, since only they can land at such unimaginable heights, to evacuate casualties or deliver sensitive loads. Pushed to the limits of their endurance and capability, each landing they do – at helipads not larger than 10 feet by 10 feet – is the stuff for adventure movies.

The larger loads are air-dropped by the bigger transport copters or fixed-wing aircraft like the AN-32. Retrieving these stores which invariably gets scattered during a drop is a laborious process for men, who have to trace them, break them up into man-pack sizes and carry it to the posts, while each post itself is barely manned by ten or fifteen men, who have to guard and patrol the area as well as rest those who come off duty. The army came up with the ideal – and cheap – solution to the problem, by seeking snow scooters. The bureaucrats however chose to sit on the matter. Eventually one concerned Defence Minister had to order some 'babus' to go and stay in Siachen for a while before they could be shaken up to do something about this long pending demand of the army.

The provision of suitable clothing and equipment for the troops makes another sloppy story. It has been a constant fight for the field commanders to thwart the attempts to force the army to accept sub-standard stuff of indigenous make, procured through unscrupulous contractors. To fight on the glacier the troops require specialized clothing and mountaineering equipment which are absolutely reliable. They have to be invariably imported since the indigenous products cannot meet such high-quality specifications as yet. Even the Defence Research and Development Organization (DRDO), considered the specialists, couldn't come up with anything worthwhile. (Not surprising since their scientists didn't even want to visit the glacier for some field study.) It is a pity, since even the Ladakhi civilians shunned their products as not worth accepting, even as gifts.

The maintenance and repair of the equipment poses a challenge of its own, with acute shortage of spares. The EME men have often have to resort to the slapstick improvisation of getting the parts needed fabricated by the local ironsmiths of Ludhiana or Jagadhri, which of course gave way after a couple of weeks.

The systems the Indian Army has evolved to maintain its massive troop presence at the Saltoro round the year, and year after year, is probably the most remarkable piece of manpower management and mobilization attempted anywhere on the globe. To keep one soldier at his combat station on the Saltoro at any given time, twenty soldiers are needed behind in various states of readiness and activity. The soldiers posted to Siachen have to be first put through an induction training of ninety days. No soldier so inducted is kept at Saltoro for more than six months. This necessitates an infantry unit being turned over every nine months, with another unit in training, besides the reserve needed for ad hoc operations.

The complement of supporting arms and services needed are also far higher than in a normal operational area. A battalion which is normally provided with two forward observation officers from the artillery is provided with six of them at Siachen. Similarly the requirement of engineers and signalmen are also far higher. And on the medical front, a battalion which normally has one medical officer may have as many as six of them, and correspondingly higher number of other medical personnel. In fact one of the significant factors which keeps the men at Saltoro in high morale is their knowledge that medical help is always at hand. Unless the weather plays foul a casualty on the Saltoro is airlifted to a doctor within the hour, and will be on an operation table within the next. The entire story is that of uncompromising efficiency and commitment at all levels day by day, whether it is supplying the men with nutritious and hygienic food, garbage and excreta management or umpteen other services like the mail service to the troops, making the Indian military effort at Siachen a phenomenal one.

The saga of Siachen is that of the entire Indian Army. The prolonged engagement had had various battalions of every infantry regiment taking turns at the glacier; and the Madras Regiment has been no exception. The Madras Sappers were there right from the beginning itself when it all started in 1984, with 8 Engineer Regiment supporting 3 Infantry Division. 15 Engineer Regiment was inducted later the same year in support of 102 Infantry Brigade. A helipad they made turned out to be the world's highest, and they were the first to operate a snow vehicle in the glacier. A succession of Madras Sapper Units followed in the subsequent years, beginning with 203 Engineer Regiment. Providing close support to infantry for the legendary capture of the Bana Post was 17 Engineer Regiment. The fabricated Dexion Bridge was an improvisation 5 Engineer Regiment came up with to negotiate the crevasses. They were followed by 14 Engineer Regiment. The next in line, 2 Engineer Regiment, laid a 67-km long kerosene pipe line upward from the base camp. 12 and 4 Engineer Regiments were the first units to arrive in the new millennium.

In public perception in India and Pakistan, the more-than two-decade old Siachen conflict has almost come to be accepted as a regular feature of the subcontinental military activity, much as the case is with the more recent counter-terrorism operations in Kashmir, the two issues intertwined politically and militarily. Despite many rounds of negotiations between the two governments and a fragile ceasefire which has held for a couple of years now, a final solution is still to emerge. In an interview given to an Indian Magazine in November 2006, Aziz Ahmed Khan, Pakistan's High Commissioner to India, who was returning home after a 3-year plus stint which saw the peace process making some headway, vouches for his country's commitment to redeployment of troops to lower heights to ease the tension, but maintains that the current positions cannot be authenticated on the map. Even Pervez Musharraf's newly floated 4-point formula, which obviously has its merits, does not address this issue squarely. The mutual mistrust continues. As long as there is no political will and initiative to remove that, the Indian Army battles on.

It is an incredible story of unrelenting men and unforgiving mountains. More men die or are maimed fighting the elements, than the enemy. A man could die for sheerly the lack of intake of oxygen, by HAPO (High Altitude Pulmonary Oedema); one careless move, such as trying to warm his hands on a fire, could have him losing all his fingers to frostbite. An extract from the Regimental Diary of a battalion quoted in the book, *SIACHEN Conflict Without End,* a brilliant and the most comprehensive account of the Siachen War so far, written by one of India's most eminent strategic analysts, Lieutenant General VR Raghavan (who also happen to have been a Commanding General at Siachen), poignantly summarizes the travails of the Indian soldier at the glacier. It reads:

Siachen is not for the weak hearted...the men...needed time which was simply not there, to be acclimatised. It accounted for a sizeable number of cold injuries which took place later...The battalion took over operational responsibility on 1 March. Induction to certain posts was only by helicopters and it was always a battle between carrying the much needed supplies, mail or manpower. On 3 March Havildar Wankhede expired in his sleep to HAPO. Sepoy

Mohite suffered severe frostbite and lost all fingers of both hands. Siachen claimed its first victims within 48 hours of the battalion's arrival. On 12 March, one soldier fell 15,000 feet to his death. Every attempt to retrieve his body proved of little consequence.

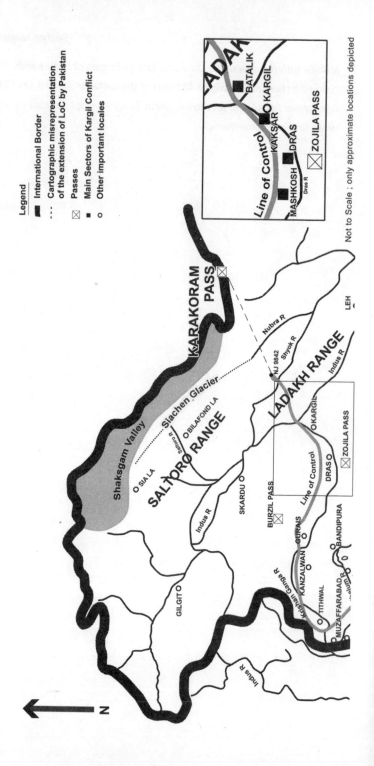

SIACHEN & KARGIL WARS

Legend

■ International Border

┈ Cartographic misrepresentation of the extension of LoC by Pakistan

⊠ Passes

■ Main Sectors of Kargil Conflict

o Other important locales

Not to Scale ; only approximate locations depicted

Inset map (top right): LADAKH, BATALIK, KARGIL, KAKSAR, DRAS, MASHKOSH, ZOJILA PASS, Line of Control, Dras R

Main map: KARAKORAM PASS, Shaksgam Valley, Siachen Glacier, BILAFOND LA, SIA LA, Saltoro R, SALTORO RANGE, LADAKH RANGE, NJ 9842, Nubra R, Shyok R, Indus R, LEH, Indus R, SKARDU, BURZIL PASS, GURAIS, Line of Control, DRAS, KARGIL, ZOJILA PASS, GILGIT, KANZALWAN, Kishan Ganga R, TITHWAL, MUZAFFARABAD, BANDIPURA, N

7

IPKF

The Sri Lankan fiasco

India, after her independence, fought five major wars; not counting Kargil which by comparison was smaller in magnitude, though intense in its ferocity. The first of these, the Kashmir War of 1947-48, still remains the Indian Army's best so far where professionalism mattered. It was an unexpected war fought with hardly any preparation. Yet the entire army, from the top brass to the rank and file, many of them steely veterans of the Second World War, went out there and did such a clinical job that Pakistan was left licking its wounds for the better part of the next two decades. Had the UN-sponsored ceasefire – meekly accepted by the Government of India with undue haste – not come to their rescue, they would have had no 'Azad Kashmir' to crow about either.

In 1962 when we took a drubbing from the Chinese in our second war, the bungling by the political set up was so much that no one could really comment whether the army was to be blamed at all. But on the third occasion, in 1965, when we clearly missed an excellent opportunity to score a decisive victory, the army could no more pass the buck. The Prime Minister had given a very clear green signal to let the enemy have it, and the army top brass alone stood to blame for whatever fumbling had taken place. In 1971, in our fourth and the most celebrated war so far, for once, mercifully, the army and the political leadership had acted with one mind, and we won hands down. (Every thing wasn't all that hunky-dory with the army's performance though, considering that our spectacular victory in the East partly owed to a dismal show by the

Pakistanis, and when faced by the same enemy in the West under a different operational environment, we could not fare equally well.)

The fifth and the longest war that we fought after the independence was in Sri Lanka, under the banner of IPKF, the Indian Peace Keeping Force, from 1987 to 89. No operation ever undertaken by the Indian forces, before or after independence, so much epitomized every thing that could go wrong with the political direction as well as the military execution, as did this ill-conceived affair which came unstuck. Together, an immature Prime Minister and an egoistic Army Chief engineered such an unholy mess, that the Indian Army, by the time it had extricated itself out of it, stood shamed by a guerilla force that it had itself armed and trained at some stage.

India's intervention in the Sri Lankan strife – between the government of the island nation and its Tamil inhabitants – resulted from her concern for the plight of the Tamils who were of Indian origin. While the concern in itself could not be faulted, the way the Government of India went about addressing it was rather bizarre. Firstly we violated the civilized norms of good neighbourliness when we helped the principal Tamil militant arm, LTTE, the Liberation Tigers of the Tamil Eelam, by providing it with weapons, training and money, in pursuit of rank political opportunism, while we should have been mounting a full-blooded diplomatic effort to resolve the issue. The air dropping of supplies on humanitarian grounds to the war-torn Tamil area of Jaffna in the island – Operation Poomalai – which we undertook later, further vitiated our relations with the Sri Lankan Government. Finally however an accord was signed between the Indian and Sri Lankan Governments in July 1987, and there lay the rub; the LTTE was not a signatory to this accord. The overbearing assumption on New Delhi's part, that the LTTE would tow the line in whatever mechanism India would champion, misfired. The LTTE supremo, Velu Pillai Prabhakaran, rejected the accord barely a week after it was signed.

Meanwhile Secunderabad-based 54 Infantry Division was inducted into the island to referee the peace process. The LTTE kept up the pretence of going along with the process by surrendering a few arms, to buy itself some time. An uneasy calm prevailed for a couple of months while the Indian troops, their role vaguely defined, remained mute spectators[1] to the occasional flare-ups between different Tamil militant groups or between the Tamils and the Sinhalese. New Delhi wasn't being particularly successful in getting Colombo to follow the terms of the accord either. The sentiments of the Tamil population, which had enthusiastically welcomed the Indian soldiers initially, were gradually turning bitter. Things came to a head with Thileepan, the LTTE political chief in Jaffna, going on fast unto death at the Nallur Kandaswamy Temple to press home the demands of the Tamils to redress their grievances. The IPKF opened fire on the protesting Tamils gathered outside its camp, killing a few of them.

The confrontation was building up. The die was cast with the IPKF gearing up for the showdown, and the Sri Lankan Government only too pleased to support its endeavour. (The Sri Lankans were eventually to revoke the amnesty and outlaw the LTTE.) The final straw was the arrest of 17 men of the LTTE cadre, some of their prominent leaders amongst them, early in October when a boat carrying them was intercepted by the Sri Lankan Navy. The LTTE demanded their release citing the terms of the peace accord. The Sri Lankans refused, and attempted to take them to Colombo for interrogation. India supported the Sri Lankan stand, and the IPKF guard was withdrawn. The militants swallowed the cyanide capsules they carried on their person, and 12 of them died.

The LTTE opened its account on 8 October, by ambushing an IPKF vehicle carrying five para commandos. All the five men were hacked to death and burned. They followed it up by opening fire on a CRPF patrol the next day and killing three. The IPKF reacted within a week.

---

1. Inaction and complacency invariably breeds indiscipline, and the army reportedly earned a bad name for itself due to the shopping spree – to satisfy the inherent Indian craze for imported electronic goods and such other stuff – all ranks were indulging in as if they were on a holiday.

1 Maratha Light Infantry, stationed at Jaffna Fort, moved out along with a Sri Lankan battalion and blew up the printing presses of two LTTE newspapers. They also captured the TV centre and arrested some one hundred civilians, besides rounding up another five hundred. The operation was mounted to deprive the LTTE of its communication and propaganda set-up; unfortunately it also gave away the IPKF game plan of going for Jaffna first.

The 1300-square kilometre area of Jaffna was home to half the Tamil population of the island, and formed LTTE's main stronghold. The IPKF plan, codenamed Operation Pawan, envisaged taking it in a 3-pronged offensive in a matter of 72 hours. 54 Division went into the operation, supplemented by one of the brigades from 36 Infantry Division which was by then being inducted. Three brigades – almost all of them having only two battalions each, which too were mostly under-strength[2] – advanced, one on each of the three axes from their locations on almost an identical distance of about 20 kilometres from Jaffna. 1 MLI was already in Jaffna (fort), and one more battalion was being moved up to join the formation. A regiment of light artillery and some four tanks had also been made available. Some artillery cover was to be made available by the Sri Lankan Army too during the advance.

Things went awry right from the very beginning. The LTTE was no conventional enemy, and its methods were absolutely unorthodox. And their level of motivation and training had been grossly underestimated by the Indian planners. It turned out to be, as was later admitted by the last IPKF Commander himself, one of the most committed and highly motivated guerilla forces in the world. They didn't take on the IPKF in any kind of proper field battle. Instead they relied on delaying actions by skillful use of snipers, explosives and mine warfare. Their remote controlled mines played havoc with the advancing columns; and the heavily populated built-up area, that Jaffna was, gave them the ideal

---

2. For no sustainable reason, the strength of the units had not been brought up to adequate levels even after they had been deployed in the operational area for more than two months.

setting to fight an advancing enemy to a stand still. Lack of intelligence and anticipation, poor planning – the army still had the 1937 maps – and overconfidence saw the IFKF outwitted, and the advance faltered.

Rattled by the outcome, the IPKF went into overdrive, mounting a hastily plotted heli-borne operation to capture the LTTE Tactical Headquarters, reported to be located in a house near the Jaffna University. A company of para commandos was to land first and secure a football field in the university complex, followed by a company of 13 Sikh Light Infantry[3], which would then be transported by helicopters there to carry out the assault. The para commandos landed into an inferno of ground fire as the buildings overlooking the field was strongly held by LTTE. Two of the copters were damaged and six men killed. The advance platoon of 13 SLI landed on a different spot, but into a holocaust worse than the earlier one, and another three copters were damaged. The platoon, caught up in the murderous fire and its casualties mounting, never received the message that the remainder of the company would not be coming in. With five copters down and enemy resistance so stiff, further heli-lifts had been called off. The platoon battled on against odds, until finally with the ammunition exhausted, its gallant commander chose to end the show in a blaze of glory. He led a bayonet charge, brave but suicidal – only one man survived to tell the story. The para commandos managed to cling on to their toehold, and link up with the rest of the battalion advancing up the railway track supported by tanks.

The main advance resumed on 21 October along the three axes. More troops were being inducted by now until there were two brigades on each axis. An armoured regiment and two mechanized infantry

---

3. The saga of 13 SLI exemplified the callous handling of the units by the higher-ups during the Sri Lankan operations. This unit was brought to Jaffna in August, then was returned to Gwalior on 7 October; only to be air-lifted to Bangalore, and then to Palaly air base in Sri Lanka the very next day. One company was earmarked for the heli-borne operation as soon as it arrived, and the advance platoon took off immediately. The factor of troop fatigue was given the short drift.

units were also moved in. The Air Force supplemented the clout with more aircraft including MiG-25, the Jaguar and the Mi-25 Helicopter Gunships, besides the Mi-18 Copters equipped with rocket launchers and machineguns. Yet the going was tough. The LTTE extracted a heavy toll of casualties through ambushes and explosive devices. By the 26th all three advancing columns had converged to a common point, and the combing of the area began the next day. The battle for Jaffna was over.

The taking of Jaffna, which was estimated to be accomplished in 72 hours, had demanded 15 days. The IPKF admitted a casualty toll of 262 killed including 15 officers and 14 JCOs, and 927 wounded; while claiming to have inflicted some 700 to 800 casualties on the LTTE. It has to be taken with a pinch of salt, since only about 100 weapons were captured, tending to suggest that a fair amount of the casualties could have been civilians. None of the top militant leaders were killed or captured either. The loss of equipment admitted by the IPKF amounted to less than ten armoured vehicles, besides five helicopters and some vehicles damaged. While the counter claims by the LTTE put the human casualties on IPKF side generally at the same or even a lesser number than what had been admitted, they claimed to have destroyed some 15 armoured vehicles. More significantly, they accused the IPKF of having killed 900 civilians and injured 451, besides indulging in 144 cases of rape.

After about a month, on 21 November, with the insurgency continuing, India declared a unilateral ceasefire. The LTTE rejected it, and the fighting continued. India, preparing for a long haul, pumped in reinforcements. 4 Infantry Division was moved into Vavuniya and 57 Infantry Division[4] was moved into Batticoloa, while 36 Division completed its concentration at Trincomalee. 340 and 55 Independent

4.   This insurgency-hardened division serving in Northeast India should have been the ideal choice for the first formation to be inducted into an operation of the kind that took place in Sri Lanka. However expediency seems to have had overcome sound reasoning in the conduct of the operations.

Brigade Groups were also inducted additionally, besides plenty of special equipment. The Tamil-dominated Eastern and Northern Provinces of Sri Lanka were now saturated with Indian troops. Troops on stand-by were also concentrated at Madras[5]. An ad hoc Headquarters on a par with that of a corps under a Lieutenant General, designated the Deputy Overall Force Commander, was also set up in the city ('Deputy', so as not to upset the command hierarchy wherein the GOC-in-C Southern Command was to be considered the OFC, Overall Force Commander, making it comfortable for the Air and Naval Commanders who were senior to the incumbent to take their orders).

Counter-guerilla warfare over a long period taxes the energy and morale of any army. The Sri Lankan campaign dragged on for another year and a half, with the IPKF making no significant gains. Operation after operation launched only added to own casualties. In one instance (Operation Virat, May-June 1988), an attack mounted by a 15000-man force of the IPKF with armour and para support, on an LTTE prepared position, merely succeeded in killing a small number of guerillas. The IPKF did come close to nabbing Prabhakaran once, but he escaped while some members of his cadre staged a gallant rearguard action in which twelve of them perished. The holding of general elections boycotted by LTTE and under threat of sabotage, but successfully overseen by the IPKF, was probably the only discernible achievement India could claim.

With the public pressure mounting in India against the prolonged military engagement in Sri Lanka, the IPKF was called back home by March 1989. There were no rousing receptions for the returning soldiers. They had gone out there as heroes and saviours, but had come back shame-faced from a failed mission. The Sri Lankans had used India

---

5. Interestingly, the city of Madras, where the Indian Army had its beginnings, was figuring in a military operation of significance almost after a period of two centuries. Little did the soldiers concentrated in an open ground in the southern half of the city realize that more than two hundred years earlier, their predecessors under a stocky Englishman called Stringer Lawrence had made a stand at St. Thomas Mount, the hillock that now overlooked their camp, to defend the city from the invading French.

for their dirty work, and India had let her soldiers become pawns in the miserable game. Even by the conservative official estimate, over a thousand of them were killed – a veteran officer asserted in a TV talk show that the toll was far more, in the range of 6000 – and many more wounded. Casualties aside, the army's morale took a terrible beating. That they haven't been able to beat a guerilla force – however motivated it might have been – in two years of battling, was a humiliating thought that would have rankled the troops' mental make-up more than anything else. (And to add insult to injury, the Indian Army, for the first time in its history, was accused of large-scale rape!) On the other side of the coin, it was an elating achievement for their opponents. That they had withstood the might of the Indian Army for two years and survived in one piece, in itself was enough for the LTTE cadres to rejoice. To have fought the fourth largest professional army in the world to a standstill, is no mean morale booster for any guerilla force, as is evident from the zeal with which they continue to engage the Sri Lankan Army to date.

The information available on the action at units' level – in most cases even at the formation level – during the operation is very very sketchy. We know that at least seven battalions of the Madras Regiment – the 2nd, 5th, 7th, 11th, 12th, 19th, and the 25th – were in Sri Lanka. Of these, the 2nd and the 19th were in Batticoloa, the 5th was in Kankesanturai, the 7th was in Velvettithurai, the 11th was at the Palaly Airfield, the 12th was in Jaffna and the 25th was in Trincomalee. The casualties of the regiment, the figures of which are not yet available, were considerable. Many of its officers and men have also been decorated for gallantry during the operations.

Three Regiments of the MEG, 3, 4 and 8, served with the IPKF in Sri Lanka. 8 Engineer Regiment was one of the first units to be airlifted to Jaffna Peninsula with 54 Infantry Division at the beginning of the operations in July 1987. Two officers and one JCO of the unit lost their lives in the de-mining operations that followed. 60 Field Company of 3 Engineer Regiment formed part of 41 Infantry Brigade under 4 Infantry Division, which attempted to relieve the besieged Sri Lankan Army garrison at Jaffna.

Captain BNN Rao of 3 Engineer Regiment, who showed exceptional courage in operations to clear areas of booby traps and improvised explosive devices (wounded himself, he carried an injured NCO to safety half a kilometer away), was awarded the Vir Chakra. Second Lieutenant AS Bedi of 417 Independent Field Company chased some fleeing insurgents in a boat across a lagoon. In the fire fight that followed he killed one insurgent and injured three, but with the opposition garnering support, the young officer was shot down with two of his men while passing through a narrow channel. He was awarded the Vir Chakra.

Sri Lanka has often been portrayed as India's Vietnam. Be that as it may, it certainly offered valuable lessons to the country's political and military bosses on how not to go wrong in future. It would be another decade before the moment would come by, on the heights of Kargil, to test how far had they benefited from the lessons.

8

KARGIL

'Their's not to reason why'

The Kargil conflict, India's first televised war, more than anything else, reinstated the Indian Army to its rightful status in the public minds of being the finest fighting force in Asia, after the by-then fading images from the bad dream that was Sri Lanka. But that doesn't mean that whatever happened that made this war necessary was an inspiring commentary on the way the security of the country's borders was being handled. It was very definitely an instance of our entire intelligence gathering mechanism, civilian as well as military, miserably failing to do their job. No wonder the Pakistanis managed to have a few thousand of their soldiers, masqueraded as 'jihadi' militants, intrude into our territory right under our army's nose.

The northern segment of the 740 kilometre-long LoC, where Kargil falls, runs along the mountain ridges and peaks of the Ladakh Range as high as 16,000 to 20,000 feet. Traditionally, a mountainous border is defended by an army by holding the dominating heights, with the gaps in between thinly held or patrolled regularly. While that generally had been the pattern followed by the Indian Army in Kargil, there had always been the tendency to lower the guard during the winter months, under the assumption that the enemy was not likely to try anything with the passes blocked by snowfall. Benefitting from this assumption and braving the heavy odds of operating in inclement weather, the Pakistanis delivered a master stroke when they occupied the strategic skyline of Kargil during the months that preceded the summer of 1999. They could, from their positions, effectively disrupt the traffic on the Srinagar-Kargil-Leh Highway, the Indian Army's vital link for logistics support of its troops at Siachen. The once-shelved Pakistani plan of an offensive in Kargil – that could shake off the Indian hold on Siachen – was on to a splendid start. The Indian intelligence agencies, having failed to detect the massive build up and infiltration, had been caught napping.

121 Independent Infantry Brigade of the Indian Army, deployed in the area, failed to keep up regular and vigorous patrolling of the gaps, which could have prevented the intrusions. Neither did the next higher formation, 3 Infantry Division, prove any more vigilant in the matter. As it happened, even after the intrusions were detected by mid May, the brigade headquarters either dismissed them as insignificant militant movements, or was too busy passing the buck. And inconceivable as it might sound, the brigadier concerned, with some three thousand men under his command, assigned to guard the border, would later complain of absence of orders from top, to shoot down a few miscreants trying to intrude. Worse, his indecorous 'revelations' to the media of having been corresponding directly with the Army Chief – as if no formation commanders existed in between – marred the reputation of the entire service; not surprisingly, resulting in his ignominious exit. The net consequence of whatever failure was that, once again the nation was left to depend solely on the grit and courage of her young officers and men to fend off a disaster; which they did, as always in the past, gloriously well. More than 400 of them paid the price with their lives.

In responding to the aggression at the strategic level, the Army Headquarters, unlike in 1965 and 1971, did not have the luxury of opening alternate fronts, or even that of crossing the LoC. The government policy in dealing with the situation – which pinned a lot of hope on a diplomatic resolution of the crisis – was one of no escalation at any cost, which put a severe restraint on the army to keep the fight localized; in other words to go for it hammer and tongs. What followed – Operation Vijay – was a magnificent feat of arms unparalleled in the history of warfare. The Indian infantrymen, in a breathtaking display of guts and glory, scaled the murderous heights and virtually plucked a stunned enemy out of their formidable vantage points in a series of do-or-die operations. On 17 June, about a month after the infiltrations were noticed, the Indian troops snatched its first victory when they took Tololing. Pak reverses followed one after the other. Point 5140 (Dras) fell on 20 June, Point 5203 (Batalik) the following day, on 29 June Three Pimples (Dras) fell, followed by Jubar Complex (Batalik) on 2 July, Tiger Hill (Dras) fell on 4 July, and Point 4875 (Mashkoh) on 7 July.

Pakistan had by now been reduced to the pitiful state of the quintessential school bully who picks up a fight with someone, only to get himself hammered silly and then glances all round pleading for someone to step in and save his skin. In the event, it was President Bill Clinton of the United States who came to the rescue, with a beleaguered Premier of Pakistan knocking at his door. Consequently, a ceasefire brokered by the United States came into force by the middle of July, and the battered remnants of the Pakistani army was permitted to withdraw to their side of the LoC. The operations formally ended on 26 July.

The Kargil Operations, in many ways, brought out all that is best about the Indian armed forces. The army was eminently supported in its ground manoeuvres by the air force. Notwithstanding the loss of some aircraft in the beginning – and an officer being taken prisoner and loss of another – they maintained consistent close-support air strikes. In a remarkable show of their flying skills, the pilots were able to effectively engage targets right close to the LoC while under the severe restriction not to cross it. The navy too, with its aggressive posture in the Arabian Sea, kept the enemy on tenterhooks. Within the army itself, it turned out to be as much glorious a feat by every one of the arms and services, as it was by the infantry. The artillery, like at Siachen, took on an offensive role, bringing down its massive firepower. Nothing demoralized enemy as did the havoc the guns caused on their positions. And there were the forward observation officers leading an assault on occasions when a company commander fell.

Being a localized engagement involving only one formation (15 Corps under the Northern Command), there were no South Indian infantry units available or engaged in the Kargil War. Interestingly, 16 Cavalry chipped in on a dismounted role, two squadrons providing firm base for attacks on Tololing and Tiger Hill while one squadron held the Zojila Pass; the farthest an armoured regiment was employed in the sector. There were of course the Madras Engineers, who lived up to their reputation, and the scores of South Indians in the ranks of the artillery and signal units, besides many from the various services, who all did their bit splendidly.

2 Engineer Regiment of the MEG, commanded by Colonel Krishnaswamy, was the only Sapper unit covering the entire sector, which extended to a frontage of almost 250 kilometres from Mashkoh in the west to Batalik in the east. The enemy having had heavily mined the approaches to their hilltop positions, the sappers had the extremely risky job of clearing them before the infantry could advance, besides an array of challenging tasks like laying of tracks and helipads, all of which had to be carried out fast paced. And often the Sappers had to move at the head of the assaulting infantry to do the bunker-blasting, the highly hazardous task of blowing up the enemy bunkers by placing shaped charges against them.

For the Madras Sappers, it was once again professionalism and courage all the way. Captain Rupesh Pradhan[1], who was severely wounded in one of the mine clearing missions, was awarded the Vir Chakra. Another young officer, Lieutenant Amit Kaul, fell to enemy fire while engaged in track building. One of the NCOs, Lance Naik Jayavelu,

---

1. Rupesh Pradhan, who lost the use of both his hands, was later to demonstrate the never-say-die spirit characteristic of a soldier, with his resilience. After spending two years in the hospital, and having recovered only partial use of the hands, he continues to serve in the army, and as a major, now commands a company. Refusing to play the role of the victim in need of sympathy, he gets on with his life as normal as the other man could. He drives, uses a key board and does almost everything else. And if that isn't enough, he has already cleared his B.Tech and is preparing for the M.Tech exam. He aspires to join the IIT.

was killed in action while bunker-blasting during an assault by 4 Jat at Kaksor. He was posthumously decorated with the Sena Medal. The Regiment was decorated with two more Sena Medals, 5 COAS Commendation Cards, and the GOC-in-C Northern Command Unit Citation for 'Kargil', for its participation in Operation Vijay. The MEG was awarded the Battle Honour, KARGIL.

The Kargil War will go down in history as a sterling testimony to the Indian Soldier's raw courage. It will also be remembered as a paradigm of treachery by one neighbouring nation towards another anywhere in the world. Two pieces of intercepted tele-conversation just prior to the war, between Lieutenant General Mohammad Aziz Khan, the then Chief of General Staff of the Pakistan Army, and his Chief, General Pervez Musharraf who was visiting China, unambiguously exposed their bogus claim that the intruders were 'jihadi' militants and not Pakistani soldiers. The infamous controversy whether their Prime Minister was aware of it or not is of little relevance to India. That the Pakistan military was contriving this diabolic subterfuge, even as the Prime Ministers of the two countries were engaged in peace efforts that produced the Lahore Declaration, is one ugly fact which Pakistan has no way of talking its way out of.

The double-dealing by the Pakistani military brass in the affair didn't end with deceiving India, a neighbour whose destruction they are sworn to anyway. They put one over on their own people as well. Initially they pretended that it was all 'jihadi' stuff, going to the extent of not even accepting the dead bodies of their soldiers. But when finally the game was up, with the mounting evidence of Pakistani soldiers killed – nearly 300 of their dead bodies were identified by the end of the operations – or captured by the Indian Army, they changed tack, falling back on their favourite charade of painting a glorious 'victory', as they always did after so many defeats in the past. As it turned out, there weren't many takers for it even in Pakistan – the people of that country had too long been taken for a ride by their generals.

The best of armies may lose battles or even a war for a variety of reasons. But no army worth its salt should have its soldiers found wanting in chivalry and sense of honour, whatever the circumstances. Elements of the Pakistan Army proved themselves rather the unworthy descendants of the proud force that was the pre-independence Indian Army, when they indulged in barbarism of a kind unheard of in the civilized world while dealing with Indian Prisoners of War during the Kargil Operations. The mutilated dead bodies of Lieutenant Saurabh Kalia and five jawans of an Indian patrol, handed over a month after their capture by the Pakistani troops during the build-up to the operations, bore telltale signs of the soldiers having been tortured to death in captivity, an atrocity which shocked the nation. (And the fact that those valiant six didn't break despite being subjected to the worst kind of atrocities – bones broken, eyes gorged out and even limbs chopped off – spoke volumes on the courage and dedication of the ordinary Indian soldier.) Squadron Leader Ajay Ahuja of the Indian Air Force, who was taken prisoner on 24 May when his MiG-21 was shot down, was murdered in cold blood. Such rank depravity may very well be the beginning of the end – the disintegration of a once professional army injected by the venom of religious intolerance and fanaticism.

In stark contrast was the conduct of the Indian Army which endeared itself to the entire nation, not only by its valour, but by upholding the human values in the finest of military traditions. The televised images of the Pakistani dead being buried with due respect by the Indian soldiers brought home the human face of the Indian Army to millions of its countrymen. Nothing exemplifies what moulds the attitudes and outlook of the soldiers of the two armies, as do two books which have since been published on Kargil, one each by the rival chiefs who held the posts during the war. *Kargil, From Surprise to Victory,* by General VP Malik, gives us an honest, down-to-mother-earth account with barely a word of self praise, which no one could have complained of had he indulged in, given the magnificent show the army he commanded put up. Then comes the much hyped account by the army chief turned President of

Pakistan, General Pervez Musharraf, *In the Line of Fire*, a pack of lies his own countrymen has come to scoff at. That just about sums it up – it is not that an ordinary Pakistani soldier is any less in his professional traits than his Indian counterpart; it's just that Indian generals think like soldiers, while the Pakistani ones think like politicians.

Thanks to the media, with the Kargil War, the selfless dedication of the Indian soldier has come to be imprinted on the public minds as never before. On 8 July 1999, when the victorious soldiers of 18 Grenadiers hoisted the National Flag on Tiger Hill, the highest feature and the most formidable objective of the war, the entire nation proudly rejoiced with them. The Indian soldier had announced his invincibility loud and clear. Pakistan got the message; so did the rest of the world; but the political leadership of India remains stone deaf. Within the year of Kargil victory, we had the disgraceful spectacle of the country's External Affairs Minister escorting a bunch of under-trial terrorists to be handed over to the hijackers of an Indian Airlines aircraft, who were holding 167 passengers and crew hostage. Another two years thence the Indian Parliament itself was attacked. The terrorist scourge continues; be it at the streets of Srinagar, the markets of New Delhi, the trains of Mumbai, or down south at Bangalore at an institute of education. And one impotent government after another keeps outdoing its predecessor in the shrillness of its lame rhetoric, that the nation's security will not be compromised. It's already compromised, and no fat chance that things will change as long as we remain sitting ducks. We can talk till the cows come home, or take the fight to the enemy *now*, and win this war.

At Point 5140, Captain Vikram Batra, a young officer who was to make the supreme sacrifice in a subsequent action, had proverbially radioed '*Yeh dil maange more*' (the heart wants more). The brave hearts of his likes would always want more; but would the noxious hearts of our politicians want anything at all beyond the winning of next election!

9

COUNTER-INSURGENCY OPERATIONS

The war without an end

Insurgency has been independent India's biggest curse where national integration is concerned. Given the vastness of the land and the remoteness of some of the border states, it wasn't very surprising that differences should arise between them and the Union, due to the various irritants related to socio-cultural frictions, economic disparities and the like. And there were always negative elements that form part of every society, power-seekers and bigots, to exploit the situation to meet their selfish ends, their sinister designs invariably aided and abetted by the country's unfriendly neighbours. While the government is compelled to resort to use of military power whenever things get out of hand and the police and the para military forces can no more handle the situation (which happens far too often and in most cases in our country), it calls for the armed forces to perform in a manner that isn't in conformity with their training and inclination. Whereas in a war a soldier's role – to kill the enemy who is invariably a foreign national – is cut out for him, the counter-insurgency operations place restrictions on him which are tantamount to reducing his role to that of an armed police man. He is at a constant disadvantage, since the 'enemy' is never clearly identifiable from the rest of the citizenry which cannot be harmed. And even when identified, an insurgent, being an Indian citizen, is entitled to his rights and privileges which have to be respected. Such cumbersome activity, besides sapping the morale of the troops to the grave detriment of their combat potential, erodes the respectability of the armed forces among the civilian population.

Traditionally, Northeastern India has been the most insurgency-prone region of the country. The movements there, which began with the Naga and Mizo unrest that took roots in the nineteen fifties and sixties, have gone on to include the Manipuri and Bodo movements as well. While both Nagaland and Mizoram have shunned the insurgency and have joined the mainstream of Indian politics with regular general elections, some irritants still continue to impede a final solution in Nagaland. The Bodo and Manipuri troubles are still to show signs of an early settlement.

Insurgency did raise its ugly head, for a comparatively brief period though, in the prosperous state of Punjab too in the 1980s. Notwithstanding the two operations, 'Blue star' and 'Black Thunder', when the army was used to flush out the militants who took refuge in the Golden Temple at Amritsar, the Punjab Insurgency has been the only one so far to have been successfully put down by a police force. There is of course the ongoing Naxalite trouble in Andhra Pradesh and the neighbouring states, which is so far being handled by the police; but they have still not been able to see the last of the 'People's War Group'.

The last insurgency to have taken shape in India, and the most trying so far, has been the one in Kashmir, which began in early 1990s. A decade and a half later, this proxy war sponsored by Pakistan still keeps bleeding the country white. There is also an element of rabid cynicism that characterizes a Kashmir militant, a trait not often shared by his counterparts elsewhere in the country. For instance, in all fairness, it should be stated in praise of the Mizo and Naga militants, that throughout their insurgency, they have been maintaining a certain sense of honour and code of conduct. Even at the peak of hostilities, by and large, they had not been known to harm the civilian population, or for that matter, even the army ambulances. They fought the gentlemen's fight, against armed soldiers.

The military option could never be the final answer to any insurgency. As a matter of fact, it could well be possible to find a peaceful solution to all

Northeast insurgency – and most others as well – if only the government can put an end to the political exploitation, and make sure the economic benefits offered reaches the genuinely poor who, unfortunately form a huge chunk of the population in these areas even after more than half a century of independence. While the developmental measures should intrinsically form the part of any package to settle the Kashmir militancy as well, the situation would continue to defy a solution as long as Islamic fundamentalism rules the roost across the border. And the Indian Army will have to continue fighting this senseless war, which the common people, Indians, Pakistanis and Kashmiris, do not seem to be interested in anymore.

Like most infantry regiments of the Indian Army over the years, the Madras Regiment too has borne its share of the burden of fighting insurgency with equanimity, with battalion after battalion doing their tenure in different areas. 2 Madras, which was inducted into Nagaland in early 1963, was the first battalion to get involved. 28 Madras earned accolades in June 1981 for the operations in Phomching in Mon district, and later in June 1983 for apprehending a self-styled captain, Wungmattem Thangkhul. In early 1980s 16 Madras served in Mizoram. Quite a few officers and men of the Madras Regiment have been decorated for the CI operations in Nagaland. 433, 61 and 46 Field Companies of the Madras Sappers contributed enormously in improving the road communications in the early years of insurgency in Nagaland.

26 Madras was engaged in Operation Blue Star during the Punjab insurgency (5/6 June 1984). This suicidal mission, in which troops had to flush out diehard militants from their fortified hideouts within the Golden Temple Complex at Amritsar, cost the unit heavily in lives. Lieutenant Ram Prakash Roperia of the unit, who fell fighting the militants, was awarded the Ashoka Chakra – the highest gallantry award for an operation not against enemy – posthumously. 7 more personnel of the unit were decorated – 3 with Kirti Chakras and 4 with Shaurya Chakras – for this operation, 4 of them posthumously.

The details of the units which had been, or are being, engaged in Kashmir are not readily available. We do know that four Rashtriya Rifles units of the Madras Regiment are deployed in Kashmir. The record of the Madras troops, infantry, engineers, as well as others, wherever they have served in CI operations so far, remains one of cool courage and steadfast discipline under trying conditions, men often contributing cheerfully to the overall fraternization drive of the army to win over the populace, a measure which has often paid greater dividends than armed confrontation.

10

UNDER THE UN FLAG

The warriors of peace

India has been one of the chief contributors of troops for the United Nations peace keeping missions, ever since the world body began getting involved in trouble spots across the globe, whether it was Korea, Palestine or Africa. The toughest of these missions, and one where the UN troops had to assume a clear combative role, was in Congo in early 1960s. This West-Central African state, falling just south of the equator, comprises mainly tropical forests spreading over an area of almost two and a half million square miles, notorious for its hot and humid climate. A power struggle broke out in Congo soon after the country obtained its independence from Belgium in June 1960. The authority of Prime Minister Patrice Lumumba was challenged by the secessionist Katangese leader Moise Tshombe, and the UN troops moved in to help the government save the country from secession, following the murder of the former.

13 Field Company of the Madras Sappers, commanded by Major Adarsh Rattan, formed part of the first Indian Contingent – an independent brigade group – that landed in Congo early in 1961. As soon as they arrived a platoon was rushed to Kabalo to extend an airstrip, with only a derelict road-roller by way of equipment. The Company then moved on to Albertville in June to conduct patrolling, and in August was assigned the task of flushing out foreign mercenaries in the area under an operation launched for that purpose, codenamed 'Rumpunch'. They did a remarkable job apprehending 13 of these villains of European

descent – '*les affreux*', meaning 'the frightful ones' as they were called – who, armed to the teeth and with their rough demeanour, were proving the scourge of the land.

In September the Company joined 'Operation Marthor', launched to seize the communication networks and airfields, and found itself in an infantry role defending the airfield at Albertville with a troop of armour for support. The Sappers were soon involved in one fire fight after the other. First they had to foil an attempt by a Katangese plane to force land. Then two of their platoons, under Lieutenant Man Mohan Singh, fought it out with three jeep loads of armed gendarmerie trying to break through, destroying their jeeps and capturing a number of them. As the enemy harassment increased, Man Mohan took the fight to them by taking a sortie out with a platoon and two armoured cars. Clearing some of the enemy strong points the group shot up quite a few of their vehicles and equipment. The officer was mentioned in-despatches for this action.

The enemy attempted a retaliatory raid and managed to lob a grenade into another officer's tent. The officer was away, but his batman wasn't. A steel hard Sapper by the name of Kulandappan, he stormed out in a classic bayonet charge and finished off the leading attacker with such fury, that the rest of the Katangese needed no further persuasion to run for their dear lives.

An uneasy truce was called by the end of September. After being engaged on internal security duties until February the following year, the Company embarked for home on being replaced by another field company.

A second Indian contingent, another independent brigade, joined in May the following year. 4 Madras (WLI), commanded by Lieutenant Colonel DS Randhawa, formed part of this brigade, the other two battalions of which were 4 RAJ RIF and 2/5 GR. The armoured element of the Indian force was made up of 5 Independent Armoured Squadron of 63 Cavalry. (Both the brigade groups, incidentally, were commanded by officers of the Madras Regiment, the first one by Brigadier – later Major General – KAS Raja, and the second one by Brigadier – later Lieutenant General – RS Noronha, the hero of the Sita Ridge in Burma during World War II. The GOC Katanga Forces was also an Indian, Major General Dewan Prem Chand.)

The trouble began with the Katangese under their self-styled president, Tshombe, attempting to celebrate their independence in July 1962. They challenged the UN ban on the celebrations by provocative demonstrations, wherein women were used in large numbers to insult the troops by vulgar means of spitting, strip-tease and pelting stones. Nevertheless an uneasy calm prevailed with the troops refusing to be provoked to react. Towards the end of December however the Katangese began acting in open hostility by firing on UN positions and camps in their capital town of Elizabethville. The UN resolved to evict the hostile gendarmerie from the main highway that ran from the capital to the mining town of Jadotville, about 90 kilometres southwest and beyond.

The brigade advance commenced on 31 December with 4 RAJ RIF in the lead. The RAJ RIF men pushed the enemy across the first obstacle, the river Lufira, by a flanking attack on their position on the first day itself. 4 Madras then took over the advance, assigned to capture the Gendarmerie Cantonment of Karavia and the town of Jadotville. The advancing column spearheaded by the armoured cars of 63 Cavalry, with 4 Madras following in troop transport, set off in the wee hours of New Years Day 1963, and hit the Lufira by night fall under torrential rain, to find as had been generally anticipated, that the rail and road bridges across the 200-foot wide river had been blown.

However the Katangese hadn't been quite professional with the demolition, and men could still cross over in single file by balancing on the steel girders of the rail bridge lying twisted and half submerged in the swirling water below; a precarious affair though with the river crawling with man-eating crocodiles. To add to their woes the enemy opened up with automatics as the crossing began. Nevertheless, A Company led by a brave JCO of its No. 3 Platoon, Jemadar Ganapathy, made it through in the semi-darkness, and B Company soon followed. By then it was too dark and further crossing was called off for the night with two companies across. Sepoy Kadamalai Kunchaiah, who exhibited nerves of steel helping his comrades to get across (he plunged himself into the river twice to rescue others who had slipped and fell), was later to be awarded a Sena Medal.

During the night two European mercenaries of the Katangese camp, too confident that the UN troops couldn't have crossed over, drove in in their machinegun-mounted Land Rover to fire across the river; only to be surprised by a Madras patrol some 200 yards from the river. Outwitted in a brief struggle by two young sepoys, Kochappan Pillai and Prabhakaran, the two were taken prisoner, their daft attempt to pose off as soldiers of the Tunisian Contingent getting them nowhere. Shortly the Katangese propelled an explosive laden rail wagon across to the bridge site which blew up with great force, but causing no harm other than minor injuries to two men.

Meanwhile a resourceful Pioneer JCO, Jemadar Ganeshan, was at it throughout the night reconnoitering for and improvising a ferry. Locating an old raft downstream, he had his team working through the night and by daybreak he had a ferry afloat. The heavy mortars and ammunition went first and then the jeeps, one by one. By then the bridgehead was being subjected to heavy mortar fire by the enemy. The Commando Platoon moved out swiftly and in a brilliant right flanking manoeuvre, closed in on the mortar position; and the enemy fled, wary of a bayonet charge by the platoon. The platoon bagged yet another mercenary prisoner. The Platoon Commander, Lieutenant MM Walia, and an NCO, Naik Issac who snatched and neutralized a machinegun, were to be awarded Sena Medals.

As the mortars were being neutralized, another platoon, under Second Lieutenant VN Madan, probed ahead along the rail line to cut off the retreating enemy. They ran into an enemy position about five miles from the bridgehead, but the young officer made a skilful approach with the platoon, and though wounded on both legs, made a gallant charge to overrun the enemy. He was later awarded the Vir Chakra.

Even while the patrol actions were progressing, Major HM Siddalingaiah's D Company forged ahead leading the battalion advance towards Jadotville. The town fell the following day with the collapse of the Katangese resistance. The operations were virtually over with that, although the rebel leader, Moise Tshombe, surrendered only on 20 January. With the UN troops entering Kalwezi, the last Katangese town, the next day, the civil war was brought to an end. 4 Madras returned home by the end of March. 16 of its personnel had been wounded during the UN mission. Apart from one Vir Chakra and four Sena Medals (of which one went to Major Samikhan of B Company), the gallantry awards won by the unit's officers and men included 10 Mention-in-Dispatches and 4 COAS Commendation Cards. The Commanding Officer of the battalion was honoured with a Vishist Sena Medal.

In the 1990s and later into the 21st Century the MEG took part in umpteen UN peace keeping missions abroad, mostly carrying out sapper tasks and helping civil administrations with reconstruction and essential services, as also often performing on an infantry and police role.

A task force sent to Cambodia in 1990, as part of the sapper contingent of the United Nations Transitional Authority Cambodia (UNTAC), trained some 2500 Cambodians to handle mines and explosives. In 1993, 412 Independent Field Company sent to Mozambique provided engineering services to that country torn by civil war since its independence from Portugal eight years earlier. The same year a Trawl Troop of 38 Assault Engineer Regiment was grouped with 1 Bihar, to carry out infantry tasks like convoy protection and road opening in Somalia. They were also assigned to rebuild the police force of that country. Later as the situation there became more volatile, they took on the task of guarding important installations.

A small detachment of 4 Engineer Regiment went to Rwanda in 1994 as part of the United Nations Assistance Mission for Rwanda (UNAMIR), and carried out major sapper as well as infantry support tasks, earning appreciation from the African Humanitarian Action Mission. 417 Independent Field Company which went to Angola in 1995, as part of the United Nations Angola Verification Mission (UNAVEM III), was to be personally commended by the UN Secretary General for its dedication and ingenuity.

A detachment of 7 Engineer Regiment which went to Lebanon in 1998, as part of the United Nations Interim Force in Lebanon (UNIFIL), earned laurels rendering assistance and guidance in sapper tasks. A field company of the same Regiment, which went to Sierra Leone in 2000, joined a rescue force that went to free Indian troops taken hostage. They also provided great humanitarian relief to the local populace. A field company of 10 Engineer Regiment went to Ethiopia in March 2002, as part of the United Nations Mission in Ethiopia and Eritrea (UNMEE), and performed laudably on multiple roles. The company was replaced by another one in September that year.

With their motto 'Sarvatra' – which means 'everywhere' – the Madras Sappers, with their Bombay and Bengal brethren, continue to present the best human face of the Indian Army overseas, as much as they do within the country. What Major General GC Tausignant of Canada, the Commander of the United Nations Assistance Mission for Rwanda, had to say while paying tribute to the Indian Contingent, probably summed up all that's laudable about the Sappers:

"You brought to UNAMIR, to the United Nations, to Rwanda a sense of pride. You came in and you demonstrated what is it to be a good soldier and you brought respectability to the mission. You brought also a sense of professionalism in everything that we have to do for the Rwandese. I say this without any reservation, you are probably one of the best soldiers in the world at this time."

11

Arms, Uniforms and the Legacy

Matchlocks to Automatics, Red Coats to Olive Greens and Mercenaries to Soldiers

Professional soldiering in India has come a long way since the European trained soldiers of the Carnatic took on a Mughal Army across the Adyar on an October morning more than two hundred and fifty years ago. An Indian Army soldier today, in his smart combat gear and boots, carrying a semi automatic rifle, and under sacred oath to defend the nation, hardly bears a resemblance to the scantily clad freebooter with his matchlock or spear who set out to make a living out of warfare so far back in time. The story of this grand transformation wouldn't be complete without a peep into the kind of weaponry the 'Madras Sepoy' fought with and their evolvement over the years, as well as the type of uniforms he wore that added splendour to his progression. And who those men were, who made up the old Madras Army and where they came from, isn't just a corollary, but the main story itself; so are the origins of some of the battalions of the Madras Regiment today, which even date back earlier than the British raising the sepoy army at Madras.

The only firearms used by the sepoys before 1758 were matchlocks carried by some of them, the rest making do with spears, swords or whatever they could find. The matchlocks were guns in which power was ignited by a match. In 1758, the flintlock muskets, which were discharged by the spark from a flint, were issued to everyone. Nicknamed 'Brown Bess', they were clumsy weapons of 14-bore calibre, weighing little over 11 lbs with a maximum range of 200 yards, and not very accurate even at 100 yards. The percussion fired smooth bore muskets superseded the flintlocks from 1845 onwards. These capped muskets had a backsight graduated up to 150 yards, and weighed almost the same as the Brown Bess, but with powder weight reduced. In 1872, the muzzle loading Enfield Rifle came into general use. It had a 0.577 bore which was 3-grooved. These were replaced five years later by the breech loading Snider Rifle of the same bore, which could fire six to eight rounds a minute. During 1891-93, Snider Rifles were replaced by Martini-Henry Rifles of 0.577 / 0.450 bore. Lee Metford Magazine Rifles of 0.303 bore, which were introduced in 1902, replaced the Martini-Henry ones. With a horizontal sliding shutter it could allow one round up the chamber, and keep the rest pressed down in the magazine. Lee Metford later gave way to the long Lee Enfield Rifle, and in 1912 the latter was superseded by the bolt action Short Magazine Lee Enfield Rifle, sighted up to 2000 yards, with better rifling. This type of rifle (0.303) was to remain the mainstay weapon till many years after World War II.

The era of the automatics began in 1904, with each battalion being issued two (later four) bolt-fed Maxim Machineguns, which had a rate of fire of 600 rounds a minute, and was water cooled by means of a jacket enclosing the barrel. In 1921 gas-operated and air-cooled Lewis MGs came to replace the Maxims, and the number of machine guns per unit also began to be increased. In 1926 the grenades (rifle and hand) were introduced. Between 1930 and 1946 infantry armament was further supplemented by the 2 and 3-inch mortars. The Bren MG replaced the Lewis, and special MG units were equipped with Vickers MGs. The 0.45 mm Tommy Gun and the 9 mm Sten were introduced in early 1940s. With all this, a rifle section of 1944 could fire off 200 rounds a minute, and a platoon with 2-inch mortars had more firepower than a whole battalion 40 years ago.

In the early days, the European officers and the Indian commandants traditionally carried swords and lighter firearms like fusils (light muskets), which were also given to light infantry for better mobility. Later the officers were issued the Enfield pattern revolvers, when they were introduced in 1881. They were subsequently superseded by Webley Mark III Revolvers of 0.45 mm calibre. Both officers and men had to carry the bayonets (17-inch long for a flintlock musket), and ammunition pouches – that were heavier for men – slung on either side by means of cross shoulder straps. The Havildars at one stage carried halberds, which were wooden shafts about six feet long with a billhook for cutting and thrusting, and a cross piece of steel turned down at one end into a hook for pushing and tearing down defensive works. Until 1786 the Indian officers carried a spear cum battleaxe called spontoon.

With the modernization of the infantry armament after the 1962 debacle, 0.303 rifles were replaced by 7.62 mm self loading (SLR) rifles. LMGs of the same calibre were also issued, and so were 9 mm carbines and pistols. 7.62 mm rifles have since been replaced by 5.56 mm ones. The firepower of the present day infantry battalion is further boosted by antitank weapons like the rocket launchers and the jeep-mounted RCL (Recoilless) guns. To meet the modern combat requirement of the infantry having to be as mobile as the tanks, one battalion each from each of the infantry regiments – the 1st Battalion, in case of the Madras Regiment – has since been mechanized; equipped with ICVs, the Infantry Combat Vehicles, which are armoured and have armaments mounted on them. These mechanized units have been integrated into a separate arm, the Mechanized Infantry, and along with the Armoured Corps, have been brought under the Directorate General, Mechanized Forces.

The earliest dress of the Madras Sepoy was a scarlet coat cut away from the chest on both sides, with drawers fringed with blue reaching to a few inches above the knee. The headdress consisted of a blue turban in the form of a round hat, with iron plates on all four sides and an iron rim with a rosette of linen in front. A blue cummerbund was worn round the waist. The facings of the coat were different for different regiments. They went barefoot in the beginning, and were not issued sandals until 1811. The officers (Indian) wore a similar dress, but with drawers reaching down to the ankle, lighter turbans, tinsel epaulets and sandals. The Pioneers wore blue coat in the beginning, but later changed over to red. French grey or blue coats were worn by the Cavalry and the Artillery too at some stage or the other. Over the years many changes took place, making the uniform more comfortable. The cummerbund was done away with, the short drawers were replaced by pantaloons, the heavy basket type turbans were replaced by cloth pugris, the cumbersome knapsacks (in which the men carried the rice for their meal) were replaced by haversacks, and trousers and boots introduced.

Finally in 1883 the entire uniform was substituted, as the red coats vanished with the army going khaki. The new dress was a Zouave jacket and knickerbockers of serge, with khaki gaiters, blouse and a turban having a band in the colour of the regimental facings and a khaki fringe. Brass numerals showing the number of the regiment were to be worn on the shoulder straps. The battle dress of belted blouse and trousers was introduced in 1939. Later after the XIV Army's choice of the olive green for the Burmese campaign during World War II, OG became the standard uniform of the army, although khaki is still worn by the troops in desert formations. Terry-cotton replaced drill as the uniform material, and camouflage jackets came to be worn as the battle dress from 1980s. The old leather-soled 'ammunition boots' have been replaced by rubber-soled 'Boots DMS' (Directly Moulded Sole); and steel helmets, canvas field service caps or berets form the headgear, according to the area of service and the operational situation.

The first ever 'sepoys' are believed to have been recruited by the French in the 1720s, from Malabar on the West Coast where they had formed a settlement at Mahe, and were engaged in hostilities with the British in their nearby settlement of Tellicherry. The French were to later use these men on the East Coast against the British at Madras. However when the British began forming the sepoy levies, their main recruiting ground was the Carnatic. The recruits were both Hindus and Muslims (more of the latter initially) from the Tamil heartland. Later the Telungus also began to be recruited. Once the British dominance was established over Mysore and the West Coast in the 19th Century, recruitment began from these areas as well. In the hectic campaigning days of the Madras Army it was not uncommon for it to enlist men – though in negligible numbers – from other parts of the country as well, like Rajputs, Marathas and Brahmins, to replace casualties and suchlike. The later day 'Madras' units of the Indian Army were to swell their ranks with men from all over the South. The Madras Army always had a secular composition, and so have its descendants, 16 Cavalry, the Madras Regiment, the Madras Sappers and units of the other arms of the Indian Army with South Indians troops.

The politico-military events of the 19th Century had resulted in the 'State Forces' of Travancore, Cochin and Mysore being retained in some form or the other, independent of the Madras Army. These forces, often quite as trained as the Madras Army, were to contribute to the British war efforts during World War II, and after independence, were to augment the Madras Regiment by four battalions. The history of these forces thus forms an inseparable part of the Regiment's legacy.

Venad (later Travancore) started emerging a prominent military power under its 18th Century ruler, Marthanda Varma (1729-1758), who organized the state into a strong entity, by putting down internal dissent and expanding its boundaries by the annexation of several neighbouring kingdoms. He defeated the Dutch at Colachel[1] in 1741, and took into his service one of their officers taken prisoner, M. Eustace Benedict de Lannoy, to whom goes the credit of training the Travancore Army on modern lines. It had a highly competent force of 50,000 men by the time Lannoy, who became its commander, died in 1777. (Of these, five battalions of infantry and one of artillery, organized into a separate 'Carnatic Brigade', were commanded by European officers, and the rest by Indians.) The number was reduced to 8000 under a treaty with the East India Company in 1805, and in 1809, following

---

1. In this first ever decisive victory of a native army of India over the Europeans, the invading Dutch were routed with a large number of them getting annihilated, and 24 being taken prisoner. The Madras Regiment maintains a memorial of the battle at Colachel.

Velu Thampi's unsuccessful revolt, they too were disbanded. 700 men of the 1st Nair Battalion were retained, who were reorganized into the 1st Battalion, HH The Rani's Troops, in 1818. Although a 'Nair Brigade' was raised in the following year by adding one more battalion, they were kept only in a police role until the withdrawal of the Company's troops in 1836. In 1901 they were taken off all police work and made purely military, commanded by a British officer. In 1934, with Travancore joining the Indian State Forces Scheme, the brigade and the Maharaja's Bodyguard were merged to form the Travancore State Force, and were trained by officers and NCOs of the Indian Army. They had four battalions of infantry, one company of artillery (for ceremonials only), and the Bodyguard as the cavalry element. Two of the battalions, the 1st and the 2nd, served in Burma, the Middle East and Egypt, guarding installations and fuel supply during World War II. On disbandment of the State Forces in 1951, these two, with additional men chosen from the remaining units, were merged with the Madras Regiment as the 9th and 16th Battalions respectively.

Like Travancore, Cochin also had an army, predominantly of Nairs (estimated 15,000-strong as early as 1694). The army was disbanded after the abortive revolt of 1808, retaining only a small force for ceremonial purposes, which was later expanded into a battalion called 'Nair Brigade'. With Cochin joining the Indian State Forces Scheme in 1934, the 1st Cochin Infantry was formed and trained on modern lines. A garrison company of the battalion served outside the state in Central India during World War II. The Travancore and Cochin states were integrated as one in 1949, and the Cochin Infantry became part of the integrated force. In 1951, on disbandment of the force, Cochin Infantry became the 17th Battalion, the Madras Regiment.

The history of the Mysore Army as a capable fighting force began in 1766, when Haider Ali organized them into cohesive fighting units with French and German assistance. Following the success in various campaigns, he was able to augment the strength of his army with captives enlisted as soldiers. After the fall of Seringapatam in 1799 most of the army was disbanded, retaining only a few regiments of cavalry (the Mysore Horse), and some battalions of infantry under the name 'Mysore Local Force' for police work. In 1831 they were restricted to seven regiments of the Horse with 300 troopers each, and four battalions of infantry with a total of 2000 men in their ranks. In 1892 the cavalry was reorganized into two regiments, the Imperial Services Lancers stationed at Bangalore and the Mysore Horse at Mysore. In 1895 the infantry was brought down to three battalions; one each stationed at Bangalore, Mysore and Shimoga, and later renamed the Mysore Infantry. The 1st Battalion saw action in Malaya during World War II, and was among those taken prisoner when Singapore fell. Following the disbandment in 1951, the 18th Battalion of the Madras Regiment was formed from the Mysore State Force.

That then, is the story of the great Madras Army and its descendants. God and soldier, the adage goes, are remembered only in times of crisis. In the current socio-political environment, when it has become fashionable to sensationalize the `atrocities by the security forces' during counter-insurgency operations, with hardly any awareness of the conditions in which the troops operate, it might be worthwhile for the armchair intellectuals to ponder the fact that time and again, whenever a natural calamity or a communal strife hits the country, the armed forces are the only agency the people of this country come to rely on to deliver the goods. The record of the Madras Engineers alone, of missions in aid to the civil authorities, would take pages to chronicle. An addendum to this book lists the principal non-combat missions of the MEG.

Sports is yet another area in which the soldiers, sailors and airmen from the South on the whole have been consistently making their mark, both at national and international levels. But then again, in a country like ours with a sporting culture so obsessed with the hype and hoo-ha of cricket that Mammon has come to outstrip the game itself, VJ Peter who represented India in three successive Olympics for hockey, or Anil Kumar who broke the National Record of Milkha Singh for 200-metre dash before he wore the country's colours at the Sydney Olympics in

2000, won't figure as celebrities. With their well-known penchant for boxing, the Madras Sappers have had six of their pugilists making it to Olympics so far; a record by any standard.

Most soldiers of the old Madras Army, Indian and European, who were killed in action in great numbers, have passed into oblivion. The names of a few among the Europeans appear at the memorials or the tombstones at the St. Mary's Church, Fort St. George, Chennai. Many Europeans who died after 1763 were buried at the St. Mary's Cemetery – beside the Stanley Viaduct opposite Madras Central – which opened in that year, and was being used for burials until 1952. The tombstones of many who died prior to 1763 were also shifted to this cemetery from an earlier one which was sited where the High Court complex came up in the city later.

As for the Indians, there are hardly any memorials for those who died prior to World War I. There are war memorials built by the Commonwealth – originally 'Imperial' – War Graves Commission, like the one in Neuve-Chapelle in France, for the Indian soldiers who fell fighting for the empire in World War I. Then there are the war cemeteries maintained the world over by the Commission after World War II, for the soldiers of the countries in the Commonwealth who fell in the war. The famous one in Kohima, Nagaland, sited on the battleground itself, incorporating a Cremation Memorial for the Hindu and Sikh soldiers, commemorates the Madras soldiers too.

The graves at the Madras War Cemetery at Nandampakkam in Chennai contain the remains of about 860 soldiers of the Commonwealth, who were originally buried at different places in the south and east of India, brought together in 1952 for proper care. There is also a memorial erected within the cemetery, to commemorate over 1000 Commonwealth soldiers who died in World War I and were buried at various places in India. 49 graves in the cemetery and 103 names on the memorial are of the soldiers from undivided India. The Commission also maintains a smaller cemetery of its own within the St. Mary's Cemetery, containing more than a 100 graves, of which 25 are of the soldiers from undivided India. Some 25 casualties of World War I are also buried at the St. Mary's, scattered outside the War Cemetery.

The best known monument for the Madras soldier we have – apart from the ones maintained by the Madras Regiment and the Madras Engineer Group – is the War Memorial opposite the Island Grounds in Chennai, dedicated *'To the memory of all those from the Madras Presidency, who lost their lives in the service of the Nation',* which commemorates the South Indian soldiers who fell, not only in the two World Wars, but in the four major wars India fought after independence, in 1947-48, 1962, 1965 and 1971. Few of the passers-by would recognize it as anything more than a traffic island on the approach to the state secretariat a stone throw away.

The men who are commemorated therein had lived and died by a legacy as proud as any the subcontinent has ever known. They were the descendants of a rare breed of adventurers who made history happen. They didn't know it then, but they had set in motion the process that was to result in the creation of a unified India, which would one day be a sovereign state capable of defending itself. They were no visionaries; but they were men of courage who fought the good fight. No matter how and why, they did the people of the land a good turn, one that ultimately would see them free citizens of an independent nation. In their own way, they had contributed in taking this ancient land forward to find its rightful place among the nations of the world, from a state of anarchy that had torn it apart.

They, and the thousands of their comrades in arms who quietly faded, or are fading, into the sunset of their lives with proud memories of their days in arms, carved a tradition with their blood and guts; a tradition of valour, patriotism and unflinching sacrifice; the best guarantee that India will survive.

Afterword

The Final Inspection

The Soldier stood and faced his God,
Which must always come to pass.
He hoped his shoes were shining,
Just as brightly as his brass.

"Step forward now, you Soldier,
How shall I deal with you?
Have you always turned the other cheek?
To My Church have you been true?"
The Soldier squared his shoulders and said,

"No, my Lord, I ain't.
Because those of us who carry guns,
Can't always be saints.
I've had to work most Sundays,
And at times my talk was tough.
And sometimes I've been violent,
Because the world is awfully rough.

But I never took a dollar,
That wasn't mine to keep...
Though I worked a lot of overtime,
When the bills got just too steep.
And I never passed a cry for help,
Though at times I shook with fear.

And sometimes, God, forgive me,
I've wept unmanly tears.

I know I don't deserve a place,
Among the people here.
They never wanted me around,
Except to calm their fears.
If you've a place for me here, Lord,
It needn't be so grand.
I never expected or had too much,
But if you don't, I'll understand."

There was silence all around the throne,
Where the saints had often trod.
As the Soldier waited quietly,
For the judgment of his God.

"Step forward now, you Soldier,
You've borne your burdens well.
Walk peacefully on the streets of Heaven ,
You've done your time in Hell."

~Author Unknown~

ADDENDUM

Madras Sappers in non-combat missions

Traditionally the Corps of Engineers is one arm of the army whose services to the country goes well beyond the realm of national security. In the history of the infrastructural development of India during the 19th Century, the contribution of the military engineers has been immense. They ushered in a new era to the country, of services such as railways, survey, telegraphy, engineering education, irrigation canals and roads. The East Coast Canal on the Coromandel Coast, the Periyar system and the early marine works at Madras were some of their achievements in the South, apart from rail routes like Madras-Salem-Coimbatore and Madras-Bangalore-Bellary-Raichur conceived by the 'Consulting Engineers' provided by the army. (The association of military consultants with the railways continued till 1930.)

The Madras Sappers' contribution to the Border Roads Organization, ever since its inception in February 1960 following the threat perceptions on the Sino-Indian Border, has been significant, in manpower and expertise. The BRO has grown to become one of the greatest road builders in the world, making even the remotest border areas easily accessible. A large number of officers and men on deputation from the Madras Sappers serve with them at any given time.

In the early years of 20th Century, the Madras Sappers contributed significantly to the development of Bangalore City. Some of the landmarks of the city like the BRV Theatre on Cubbon Road and The Oriental Building on St. Marks Road were constructed by them. The Ulsoor Lake, one of the most beautiful sights in the city (used for waterman ship training by the Sappers), owes its current environment-friendly existence to the initiative and commitment of the Madras Engineers, who painstakingly cleared the entire water body of hyacinth which was choking it to death.

In times of natural calamities, the services of the military engineers in aid to the civil authorities have always proved to be of great benefit to the people at large. 16 Army Troop of the Madras Engineers were in the forefront of rescue and relief operation at Quetta during the earthquake of 1935. 203 Engineer Regiment was airlifted to Mauritius to restore normalcy after the island was devastated by a cyclone in 1975. In July 1978 a task force of the Madras Sappers, rushed to Kudremukh, saved the Lakhya dam there from an imminent collapse due to unusually heavy rainfall, by constructing a revetment that involved the placing of one lakh sandbags. In 1980, 9 Engineer Regiment undertook the strange task of flushing out thousands of gallons of crude from pipeline in Assam, when terrorist threat had brought the oil operations to a halt, and the static oil in the line would have damaged the pipes. The Uttar Pradesh floods of 1982 saw 14 Engineer Regiment engaged in extensive relief and rescue. In July 1988, when the Bangalore-Quilon Island Express derailed from the Munrothuruthu Bridge near Quilon and plunged into the Ashtamudi Lake, a detachment from MEG Centre rushed to the scene and retrieved all the coaches along with the dead bodies of the passengers who were trapped.

In April 1990 when the Bodo militants demolished the bridge over the river Minas, severing NH-31, the lifeline of Assam and the Northeast, 10 Engineer Regiment constructed a 160-foot Double Triple Bailey Bridge in 48 hours, with WWII vintage Bailey equipment foraged from railway and PWD yards near by. 7 Engineer Regiment laboured day and night with rescue during the Latur earthquake of 1993. During December 1994, a task force from the Madras Engineer Group and Centre constructed a 125-metre Class 70 Kruppman Bridge over the river Vennar in Tamil Nadu in little over 24 hours, to facilitate a bypass to cater for the heavy traffic anticipated during the 8th World Tamil

Conference that was to be held at Thanjavur during the following month, which was expected to be attended by 15-20 lakh Tamils from all over the globe. 7 Engineer Regiment, during 1998, undertook the task of creating high grounds in the Kaziranga National Park on the banks of the Brahmaputra, for animals to take refuge when the river was in flood and submerged vast stretches of the park. 9 Engineer Regiment was in the thick of rescue and relief operations when a cyclone hit Orissa in 1999. The devastating earthquake that rocked Gujarat on the Republic Day of 2001 found 12 and 13 Engineer Regiments being rushed in for rescue and relief. And when the tsunami hit South and Southeast Asia in December 2004, the Madras Sappers were out there providing the much-needed succour to thousands of victims, not only in India but in Sri Lanka and Maldives as well.

BIBLIOGRAPHY

Ali, Sheik, B., *Tipu Sultan A Study in Diplomacy and Confrontation.* Geetha Book House, Mysore, 1982.

Anon: (Compiled under the direction and authority of the Engineer-in-Chief, Army Headquarters, New Delhi) *History of the Corps of Engineers.* Palit & Palit Publishers, New Delhi, 1980

Betham, R.M., *Marathas and Dekhani Musalmans.* Superintendent of Government Printing, India, Calcutta, 1908, Reprint: Asian Educational Services, New Delhi, 1996.

Collins, Larry; and Lapierre, Dominique, *Freedom at Midnight.* Vikas Publishing House Pvt Ltd, New Delhi, 1976.

Daniel, Lt. Col., J.R., *The Black Pom-Poms History of the Madras Regiment 1941 – 1983.* The Madras Regimental Centre, Wellington, 1986.

Dalrymple, William, *White Mughals.* Penguin Books India, New Delhi, 2002.

Dodwell, H.H., M.A., *The Cambridge History of India The Indian Empire.* S. Chand & Co., Delhi, 1958.

Duff, James Grant, *History of the Mahrattas.* First Published, 1826, Indian Reprint: Exchange Press, Bombay, 1863.

Farwell, Byron, *Armies of the Raj From the Mutiny to Independence 1858 – 1947.* Penguin Group, London, 1990.

Gommans, J.L. Jos; and Kolff, H.A. Dirk, *Warfare and Weaponry in South Asia 1000 – 1800.* Oxford University Press, New Delhi, 2001.

Gopalakrishnan, Dr. S. (Ed), *The South Indian Rebellions (Before and*

After 1800). Palaniappa Brothers, Chennai, 2007

Harvey, Robert, *The Life and Death of a British Emperor.* Hodder and Stoughton, London, 1998.

Hill, S.C., *Yusuf Khan The Rebel Commandant.* William Clowes and Sons Limited, London and Beccles, 1914, Reprint: Asian Educational Services, New Delhi, 1998.

Jacob, Lt. Gen., J.F.R., *Surrender at Dacca Birth of a Nation.* Manohar Publishers & Distributors, New Delhi, 1997.

Keene, H.G., C.I.E., *History of India.* Researchco Publications, Delhi, 1972.

Kirmani, Mir Hussain Ali Khan, *History of Tipu Sultan Being a Continuation of the Neshani Hyduri.* First Published, 1864, Reprint: Asian Educational Services, New Delhi, 1997.

Lawford, James (Ed), *The Cavalry.* Roxby Limited, Indianapolis, 1976.

Llewellyn-Jones, Rosie, *A Very Ingenious Man Claude Martin in Early Colonial India.* Oxford University Press, New Delhi, 1992.

Logan, William, M.C.S., *Malabar.* The Government Press, Madras, 1887.

Love, Henry Davison, *Vestiges of Old Madras 1640 – 1800.* John Murray, London, 1913, Reprint: Asian Educational Services, New Delhi, 1996.

MacMunn, Lt. Gen., Sir George, *The Armies of India.* Crecy Books, Bristol, 1984.

Mahadevan, Madhavi S. (Ed), *THE MADRAS SAPPERS An Enduring Legacy.* Madras Engineer Group & Centre, Bangalore, 2002

Majumdar, R.C; and Chopra, P.N., *Main Currents of Indian History.* Sterling Publishers Pvt Ltd, New Delhi, 1987.

Malik, Gen., V.P., *KARGIL From Surprise to Victory.* HarperCollins

Publishers India, New Delhi, 2006.

Menezes, Lt. Gen., S.L., *Fidelity and Honour THE INDIAN ARMY From the Seventeenth to Twenty-first Century*. Oxford University Press, New Delhi, 1999.

Mollo, Boris, *The Indian Army*. Blandford Press, Dorset, 1981.

Pate, H.R., I.C.S., *Madras District Gazetteers TINNEVELLY*. Government of Madras, 1917.

Phythian-Adams, Lt. Col., E.G., OBE, *The Madras Regiment 1758 – 1958*. The Madras Regimental Centre, Wellington, 1958, Reprint: Ave Maria Commercial Printers, Coonoor, 1981.

Powell-Price, J.C., C.I.E., M.A. (Cantab), F.R. Hist.S., *A History of India*. Thomas Nelson and Sons Ltd, London, 1955.

Raghavan, Lt. Gen., V.R., *SIACHEN Conflict Without End*. Penguin Books India, New Delhi, 2002.

Ramaswamy, Dr., A., M.A., M.Litt., Ph.d (London)., *Tamilnadu District Gazetteers, Ramanathapuram*. Government of Tamilnadu, 1972.

Reid, Col., D.M., *The Story of Fort St. George*. Diocesan Press, Madras, 1945, Reprint: Asian Educational Services, New Delhi, 1999.

Sastri, Nilakanta, K.A., *A History of South India From Prehistoric Times to the Fall of Vijayanagar*. Oxford University Press, New Delhi, 1975.

Smith, Vincent, A., C.I.E, *The Oxford History of India*. Oxford University Press, New Delhi, 1998.

Sodhi, Brig., H.S., *TOP BRASS A Critical Appraisal of the Indian Military Leadership*. Trishul Publications, Noida, 1993.

Sreedhara Menon, A., *A Survey of Kerala History*. S. Viswanathan (Printers & Publishers) Pvt. Ltd., Chennai, 2003.

Sri Sathyan, B.N., B.A. (Hons), *Mysore State Gazetteer, Coorg District*. The Director of Publications, Bangalore, 1965.

Subrahmanian, N., *Social and Cultural History of Tamilnad (A.D.1336 – A.D.1984)*. Ennes Publications, Udumalpet, TN, 1999.

Subrahmanyam, Sanjay, *Penumbral Visions – Making Polities in Early Modern India*. Oxford University Press, New Delhi, 2001.

Velu Pillai, T.K., Sadasyatilaka, *The Travancore State Manual Vol.II History*. The Government of Travancore, Trivandrum, 1940.

Warren, W.H., and Barlow, N. (Ed), *The Church in the Fort A history of St. Mary's*. St. Mary's Church, Fort St. George, Chennai, 2002.

Wheeler, J, Talboys, *Madras in the Olden Time being a History of the Presidency*. Higginbotham and Co., Madras, 1861, Reprint: Asian Educational Services, New Delhi, 1993.

Wild, Antony, *The East India Company Trade and Conquest from 1600*. HarperCollins Illustrated, London and HarperCollins Publishers India Ltd, New Delhi, 1999.

Wilks, Mark., *Historical Sketches of South India History of Mysore*. First Published 1810, Reprint: Asian Educational Services, New Delhi, 1989.

INDEX